Morgan Three-wheeler

THE COMPLETE STORY

Other titles in the Crowood AutoClassic Series

Morgan
Three-wheeler

THE COMPLETE STORY

Peter Miller

THE CROWOOD PRESS

First published in 2004 by
The Crowood Press Ltd
Ramsbury, Marlborough
Wiltshire SN8 2HR

www.crowood.com

British Library Cataloguing-in-Publication Data
A catalogue record for this book is available from the British Library.

ISBN 1 86126 626 X

Designed and edited by Focus Publishing,
11a St Botolph's Road,
Sevenoaks,
Kent TN13 3AJ

Printed and bound in Great Britain by CPI Bath

Contents

'HFS' – Henry Frederick Stanley Morgan – Creator of the world's finest three-wheelers.

Preface

H.F.S. Morgan's Runabout offered a unique solution to the problem of economic transport when first offered to the public in November 1910. The machine represented mechanical innovation of the highest order. More importantly it offered a level of performance and driving enjoyment rivalled by few machines of any price. The Runabout was right from the start and few alterations to its design were required for it to remain in production and be competitive long after its rivals had been consigned to history. Indeed, features of the design are still apparent in the latest Morgans, still built in Malvern by the same family.

My fascination with Morgans began long before I purchased my 1930 Family and I have now owned it for over thirty-five years. I therefore welcomed the opportunity presented by this book to delve more deeply into the history of the cars and the company. This would not have been possible without the assistance of numerous Morgan enthusiasts whose knowledge is much greater than mine. Foremost I would like to express my thanks to Charles Morgan, who kindly allowed access to the Morgan Motor Company archives and agreed to my use of company photographs and illustrations. Also to Mark Aston, who arranged

HFS Morgan accompanied by his wife, Ruth, on the ACU Six-Days' Trial, August 1921.

my visits to the company.

The Morgan Three-Wheeler Club comprises an unsurpassed repository of information and photographic records on the three-wheeler, and I have been fortunate to call upon the willing assistance of the club and of individual members. In particular I would like to express my thanks to the club librarians, Pete Jones and Chris Shorrock, club archivist Jake Alderson, and the following members, Chris Booth, Nev Lear, Tony Morton, Bill Wallbank and Martyn Webb. I have also benefited from the many historical and technical articles in the club's *Bulletin* and a general note of appreciation is appropriate to the various authors of the articles. Additional photographs were provided by Ted Walker of Ferret Photographics. I have listed at the end of the book the various catalogues, periodicals and books to which I have referred.

Chris Booth and Nev Lear willingly accepted the unenviable task of checking the historical accuracy of my text. Thanks are due also to Donald Curren for additional checks and comments upon style and layout. Also to my wife, Janet, for checking the drafts and for her understanding during my writing of the book.

Mike Bamber, Oliver Brooke and Jim Rolf kindly agreed to their Morgans being photographed for the colour section.

A note concerning the layout of the book is appropriate. It has been arranged in parts, which are largely self-contained. In the first part I have described the history of Morgan by reference to the commercial background and sporting activities, which influenced the development of the company and its cars. I have not attempted to cover the sporting activities in depth; these are outside the scope of the book and fully covered elsewhere. The second part covers the technical features of the car and describes the proprietary engines fitted during the production period. The third part describes in greater detail the various Morgan models. I have accepted that some duplication with earlier sections is unavoidable in order to make these chapters self-contained. The final part attempts, in as concise a manner as possible, to bring up to date the ongoing Morgan Three-Wheeler story.

THE HISTORY AND DEVELOPENT OF THE MORGAN THREE-WHEELER

1 The Birth of a Marque

A visitor to the Malvern Hills during the early part of the twentieth century might well have contemplated the inadequacy of most of the available motorcars when faced with the narrow roads and steep hills of the area. If of a mechanical bent, he might well have conjured in his mind's eye his ideal machine. It would surely have been of light construction and with a powerful engine to provide the ample power-to-weight ratio necessary for good hill-climbing capability. It is quite likely he would have contemplated the three-wheeler layout as the best option, as such machines were quite common and of light weight. It is most unlikely that he would have envisaged a machine of such elegance of design and engineering innovation as the Morgan. It is certain he would not have envisaged the background of the machine's inventor, Henry Frederick Stanley Morgan.

H.F.S. Morgan was born into a prosperous ecclesiastical family on 11 August 1881 at Moreton Jefferies Court, the manor house of Moreton Jefferies, a village to the south-east of Stoke Lacy and twelve miles to the west of Malvern. He was known as 'Harry' to his family, but later he would be known and more widely recognized by his initials, H.F.S. His family derived from the London area, but by the time of his birth it had been established in Malvern for ten years.

HFS's great-grandfather had been vicar of Trethern and his two sons, George and Henry, in turn also entered the church. Henry, HFS's grandfather, had been rector at St Mary Magdalen, Blackheath before appointment as chaplain to the Nunhead cemetery. Henry George, HFS's father, was born at Nunhead, the only son of Henry's second marriage. He was educated as a day pupil at Dulwich College.

In July 1871, his grandfather, when aged seventy-three, purchased the living of Stoke Lacy, a village in the diocese of Hereford, in order to retire from the city bustle to the more gentle life of a country parson. The purchase provided Henry and his family with the perpetual right of patronage and presentation to the rectory and parish church. In addition to the imposing rectory with its extensive gardens, stables, coach houses and other outbuildings, the family acquired some nineteen acres. With the purchase Henry Morgan became rector of Stoke Lacy. After a few years HFS's father, Henry George Morgan, began working alongside his father as curate to the parish. Upon Henry Morgan's death, aged eighty-eight, in 1886, Henry George (HG) in turn became rector.

Whilst living in south London, HG had met Florence Williams, the daughter of wealthy London merchants, whom he married in 1875 when both of them were twenty-three years old. Henry Frederick Stanley, who was born six years later, was the couple's first child. Harry had three younger sisters, Freida, Ethel and Dorothy. A second son, born three years after Harry, was to die just short of his third birthday.

Schooling

The family expectation was that Harry would follow his father into the church and his early

Above *Stoke Lacy Rectory.*

A photograph of the young Harry Morgan. Harry found pleasure in all forms of transport and the model yacht must have proved a popular toy.

schooling was to this end. He was educated at home until the age of ten, when he was sent to the Stone House School in Broadstairs. A frail boy, he was frequently ill with many of the common juvenile illnesses and confined to bed for long periods. As a consequence he was to suffer mixed academic fortunes. His interests were with mechanical things and he displayed an inventive nature. He was encouraged in this by one of the schoolmasters, Mr Wallis, and his letters to his parents often contained drawings of boats, trains and bicycles. By the time he left Stone House he was skilled in mathematics and drawing and had developed an abiding interest in engineering. It had been intended that his preparatory schooling should equip him to follow his father to Eton and the church. Happily, as it turned out in the light of subsequent history, his academic qualifications were not acceptable for Eton and he had developed a preference for engineering. Whether disappointed or not, his father would

in future give his son every assistance in choosing a profession.

Harry was enrolled in 1894 at Marlborough College in Wiltshire. The college had been founded to provide schooling for the sons of clergymen and retained strong ecclesiastical links. It provided a good classical education but did not appreciate his mechanical leanings. On one occasion Harry was hauled before the headmaster to be reprimanded. 'It is all very well for you to have an inventive genius but it is an intolerable nuisance at school.' The education was not to Harry's liking and he was not alone in detesting the school food, which was insufficient to provide proper nourishment and frequently maggot-ridden. Matters came to a head when the boys were served a particularly maggot-ridden ham and Harry was delegated by his fellow pupils to complain to the head about the quality of the food. His impertinence earned him a severe reprimand but did nothing to improve

Prebendary George Morgan

Henry George Morgan, who was known within the family as George and by the abbreviation HG in circles where his son was to become HFS, served the parish of Stoke Lacy for sixty years. He was not, however, an archetypal country clergyman. When it became clear that his son's interests lay in engineering rather than the church, he determined to assist him fully in his chosen career. This must have been a hard decision to take, as Victorian society considered it improper for a clergyman's son to enter trade. However, as well as being a devoted father, who placed the interests and aspirations of his children first, he shared their enthusiasms and was captivated by the developments of the age. It is interesting to conjecture as to whether through Harry he was able to experience the career he would have wished for himself had his circumstances been different. Like many clergymen he was interested in art and enjoyed drawing and painting. He took up photography and became quite accomplished at a time when amateur photography was in its infancy. He was also quick to embrace the innovations of the day and, for example, installed electricity and water into the rectory and church.

HG was a wealthy man and he was able to enjoy a comfortable lifestyle. Much of his wealth derived from inheritances through his wife's family. However, he took a keen interest in the stock market and by investment was able further to enhance the family's wealth. This was to have an important bearing on the Morgan Motor Company. It ensured that ample funds were available to establish his son in business without recourse to external investors and to maintain the company as a family business. This proved of great importance when decisions became necessary over the future direction of the company. Furthermore, through his guidance and financial acumen the Morgan Motor Company became not only a successful motor manufacturing company but also a highly profitable investment company. The wealth thus created would prove useful as a buffer to allow the company to survive during periods of economic depression.

HG was a man of imposing stature and of extrovert personality. He proved an excellent chairman and spokesman for the company, both in person and in print. He was a regular correspondent to the letter pages of the various motoring journals and would write, often under assumed names, on issues aimed at promoting the company. If his letters did not elicit the hoped-for discussion, then he considered it entirely proper to respond to himself under a second, assumed, name!

It is as much due to George Morgan's expert guidance and financial management as his son's engineering talents that the Morgan Company was able to survive and prosper.

George Morgan provided the financial backing to establish the Morgan Motor Company and the sound business sense to ensure success during the early years of the company. He is often glimpsed in the background of early photographs; an imposing figure, in formal dress, with white hair and moustache.

the food. Shortly afterwards his parents withdrew him from Marlborough.

The future career of the young Harry was still uncertain and, for a while, enrolment at an art school was considered. George Morgan was a keen amateur artist and early photographer and would clearly have been delighted had his son taken up this option. He did, however, make it clear to Harry that he was free to choose for himself between art and engineering. To encourage an interest in art and, possibly more importantly, to help him regain his health after the period of malnutrition at Marlborough, the family took Harry on a trip to Italy. It was immediately apparent that Harry's interests remained in engineering rather than in the arts and, upon his return from Italy, he was enrolled at the Crystal Palace Engineering College.

This was a particularly happy time for Harry. The college was the perfect environment, as it provided him with a sound engineering foundation and the opportunity to experiment and explore his engineering ideas. He studied engineering and design, and became proficient at engineering drawing.

He enrolled in the college's School of Practical Engineering in September 1899 and completed his studies two years later in August 1901. During this period he was able to develop his talents for innovation and to construct objects of his own design; more importantly these were encouraged and received due praise rather than derision. In hindsight, perhaps his most meritorious achievement in this respect was to construct a bicycle of his own design, which he used in student races and to set a new college cycling speed record. Possibly this taste for speed and the thrill of being 'fastest' helped shape his future thinking and provided the inspiration and design philosophy behind the Morgan car!

Now that an engineering career had been agreed for Harry, his father acted with his characteristic enthusiasm and drive to ensure his son received all the necessary assistance and the best training available. He was able to arrange an apprenticeship with the Great Western Railway under the direct tutelage of William Dean, chief engineer of the Swindon Works. Men like William Dean would only take on one or two pupils and the appointments were highly prized. The training was comprehensive, covering all aspects of locomotive manufacture and engineering. It was during this period that HFS became increasingly interested in motoring.

First Motoring Experiences on Two, Three and Four Wheels

HFS had had his first personal experience of a motor vehicle in 1899 when he hired a Minerva motorcycle from Mr Marriot, the first motor trader in Hereford. His view of this particular machine is not recorded, although he subsequently expressed a dislike of motorcycles. His first experience of a motorcar, which occurred in the same year, must have proved even less satisfactory, as the brakes of the hired $3\frac{1}{2}$ hp Benz were inadequate to cope with the steep 1-in-6 descent into Hereford. The £28 repair bill was paid by a tolerant father and no doubt a lesson was learnt on the importance of adequate braking as well as good performance in hilly districts.

The first motor vehicle purchased by HFS was an Eagle Tandem. This was a three-wheeler with a single rear wheel and an 8hp de Dion engine. The passenger sat between the front wheels, whilst the driver was perched on high in a bucket seat ahead of the rear wheel. The engineering of the machine derived from the cycle industry and must have been studied with considerable interest by the young engineer. It demonstrated that with a bought-in engine there would be very little additional expenditure to construct a similar machine. In 1902, after eighteen months of ownership, HFS replaced the Eagle with a 7hp model Star, known as 'The Little Star', which was purchased on his twenty-first birthday with the help of a legacy from his godfather. The Star was a four-wheeler with a twin-cylinder

MORGAN SPORTS CAR RENTAL

DIRECT FROM THE MORGAN MOTOR COMPANY LTD

FOR ALL YOUR SPECIAL OCCASIONS

Weddings

Birthdays

Anniversaries

Romantic Weekends

MORGAN MOTOR COMPANY

DRIVEN AT HEART

WEDDING CARS

Add that finishing touch to your special day. Just imagine driving off as man and wife with a breeze in your hair and the sun on your face...

The Morgan will create as much of a stir as the bride and groom, and it will always have a smile for the photos!

The Morgan can be trimmed with ribbon or your flowers as required, and a chauffeur service is available with the four seater option.

GIFT VOUCHERS & SURPRISES

Hire vouchers are a popular gift option, and allow the recipient to arrange their Morgan experience at a time to suit them (within 12 months of purchase).

Vouchers can be personalised and mailed to you in a plain envelope so your secret is safe until you are ready to reveal the surprise!

We can also arrange 'surprise' collections here at the factory. Just let us know your requirements and we'll do the rest.

MORGAN SPORTS CAR RENTAL TARIFF

Please find below the most popular options for Morgan car hire. However, we endeavour to meet individual requirements whenever we can, and welcome all enquiries.

1st January 2007

DAILY CAR HIRE £100

Available Monday to Thursday 9am – 4pm

24 HOUR HIRE £165

Available Monday to Thursday 8.30am – 8.30am

WEEKEND HIRE £375

Collect Friday before 1.00pm return Monday 8.30am

WEEKLY HIRE (7 days) £675

Collect 8.30am return 8.30am 7 days later

(All prices quoted include VAT and Personal Accident Insurance)

Terms and conditions of Morgan Car Hire:

Driving Licence: Drivers (2 permitted per hire) must hold a full and current driving licence, which must be produced on collection of the vehicle, and should have more than 3 years driving experience. Drivers should have no more than 3 penalty points on their licence - drivers with more than this should contact the Morgan Motor Company before booking.

Age Restrictions: Drivers must be aged between 25 and 70 years inclusive.

Accidental Damage: A £500 deposit is held during the hire period (usually as a pre-authorisation on a credit card)

Fuel: The vehicle will be supplied with a full tank of fuel, and should be returned at the same level.

Mileage: No restrictions apply, the open road awaits! (However, our insurance only permits travel within the UK).

PLEASE NOTE: Models are subject to change and may differ from those pictured.

MORGAN MOTOR COMPANY

DRIVEN AT HEART

MORGAN SPORTS CAR RENTAL

For further details, or to make a booking please contact:
Sarah Jane Stubbs
The Morgan Motor Car Company Ltd
Pickersleigh Road
Malvern, Worcs, WR14 2LL

Tel: 01684 573 104
Fax: 01684 892 295

E-mail: sarah.stubbs@morgan-motor.co.uk

HFS with his first car, an Eagle Tandem. The Eagle was responsible for HFS receiving his first summons for exceeding the heady speed of 12mph (19km/h)!

engine and chain drive to the rear wheels. With minor modifications it provided good service over many years. The Eagle and Star machines were used to travel home from Swindon and must have provided HFS with ample opportunity to assess the relative merits of the more reliable four-wheeled car against the lightweight, and more zestful, trike.

First Steps in the Motor Trade and the First Runabout

In January 1904, a new Highways Act raised the speed limit for vehicles under 1½ tons from 12mph to 20mph (19–32km/h) and, as a result, the general public in Britain started to become more aware of the motor car. The following year, aged twenty-three, HFS left the GWR to return to the Malvern area with an ambition to establish his own business. A dwelling, named Chestnut Villa, was purchased in Worcester Road, Malvern Link, two miles northeast of Malvern. The property came with an adjacent plot of land with some small build-

ings. In a short space of time plans were drawn up and planning permission obtained for a larger workshop. This was quickly constructed and consisted of a single-storey brick building with high-ridged roof. Running over the full forty-foot frontage of the building onto Worcester Road was a sign, gold painted on a dark red background, declaring 'Morgan & Co. Garage and Motor Works'. HFS opened the garage in partnership with his long time friend Leslie Bacon. They jointly operated the garage and the associated business ventures through to the launch and early days of the three-wheeler.

The garage was fortunate to acquire the agencies for Darracq, Wolseley and Siddeley cars, and upon opening was able to offer a 12hp Darracq and a 6hp Wolseley for immediate delivery. In addition, a number of good quality second-hand cars was available for sale. A full range of repair services was offered 'by competent workmen using first class machinery', and petrol and tyres were stocked. With some justification Morgan & Co was able to

claim to be one of the largest and best-equipped garages in the West of England.

From the start, Morgan & Co had offered chauffeur-driven hire cars. However, once the garage business was firmly established the partners agreed upon a more ambitious proposal, namely a public bus service. A 22hp Daimler coach and, later, a 10hp Wolseley were acquired and services run in the vicinity of Malvern and to the local towns. Unfortunately the genteel inhabitants of Malvern and the surrounding areas were staunchly conservative in attitude and not yet ready for the motor vehicle, which was viewed with suspicion and disapproval. Whilst motorized transport might be appropriate in London and the large cities, it was not considered an acceptable alternative to the horse for rural communities. Furthermore, it was not considered proper that a clergyman's son should be involved in such trade. Letters of complaint were soon received. HFS's response was to display the letters in the garage window. This provided certain amusement and had the effect of stopping the letters, but did not get passengers onto the buses and the service folded.

The Worcester Road Garage.

HFS was a talented and inventive engineer and must have studied the various machines of the day, noting their good points and their weaknesses and working out how he could do better. In 1908 he decided to explore his ideas and build a machine of his own design. He had intended to build a motorcycle and acquired a suitable twin cylinder 7hp Peugeot engine. Ever since building a bicycle at the Crystal Palace Engineering College, he had remained a keen pedal cyclist but had never enthused about motorcycles. It is not surprising, therefore, that the idea of a motorcycle was soon dropped in favour of a tricycle. HFS could design the tricycle, but he lacked the engineering facilities to turn his ideas into a functioning machine. Fortunately he was friendly with the Stephenson-Peach brothers, great-grandsons of the railway pioneer George Stephenson, who shared his interest in mechanical matters. Their father, William Stephenson-Peach, who was engineering master at Malvern College, agreed to assist HFS with the design and also allowed him access to the engineering facilities at Malvern College and Repton School, near Derby, where Stephenson-Peach had previously worked. Without this assistance it is unlikely the machine would ever have been built, as HFS's commitments to the garage and car hire business would not have allowed time for its completion. Work entrusted to others included the bevel box and front sliding axles, which were cast and machined by J Smith and Co. of Derby, and the chassis, which was assembled by a local metal worker, Thomas Jones. The machine took twelve months of HFS's spare time to complete.

HFS began testing the new three-wheeler as soon as it was completed. He wrote of his experiences in the *Light Car* magazine of December 1949:

> I drove the machine, which I called the Morgan Runabout, in 1909. It was most successful, due to its rigid frame, independent front-wheel suspension and light weight; the power-to-weight ratio was about 90bhp per ton, and it was, therefore,

more than capable of holding its own with any car on the road at that time.

The tricycle was registered for road use with the local registration number CJ743 in June 1910. The same registration number would be widely used on works cars for several years.

HFS would later admit that he had built his first machine for his own personal transport and enjoyment rather than with any thoughts of commercial manufacture. However, this first Morgan Runabout was a truly remarkable machine and created great interest and favourable comment wherever it was seen. It was a totally functional design, yet possessed a simplicity and elegance unmatched by any other vehicle on the road. Before long his friends were requesting similar cars and suggesting that he should make the model available to the public. Thus encouraged he decided to make a few and sought the backing of his father to purchase the necessary machine tools and to enlarge the garage. George Morgan was as enthusiastic as his son and soon the Morgan Motor Company was in being.

William Stephenson-Peach driving the prototype Morgan Runabout, which he helped HFS to construct.

2 The First Morgans

The public at large first became aware of the Morgan Runabout when HFS displayed two machines and a chassis in the annex at the first International Motor Cycle Show, which was held at Olympia, London, in November 1910. The machines were well received. The review in *Motor Cycling* stated:

> A most attractive runabout suitable for carrying one person is exhibited on this stand. It is called the Morgan Runabout and is fitted with a 4hp 85mm by 85mm JAP engine. A very luxurious model is also exhibited and this is driven by an 8hp twin-cylinder air-cooled JAP engine. The bodywork is entirely enclosed, and gives to the machine a most attractive appearance. A chassis is also shown, and this makes clear the features of the patented frame and front axle, which are well worth inspecting.

The *Motor Cycle* was equally laudatory:

> A three-wheeled runabout which should on no account be missed by visitors to the show is the Morgan in the annex. It is very lightly constructed throughout, and some very clever notions have been adopted in its design. It is low and rakish looking; so low, in fact, that it might with its present sized wheels prove unsuitable for use in districts where the roads are very rough.

Such misgivings could easily be proved groundless and the performance potential of the lightweight machine with its large engine must have been apparent. However, HFS was to learn that design novelty and innovation, whilst attracting attention, do not necessarily attract buyers. Most exhibitors reported excellent business and several firms were able to announce full order books for 1911. HFS, on the other hand, was disappointed to receive no more than a handful of orders for the single-seater, although he became aware that there would be much greater demand for a two-seater model.

Two visitors to the Morgan stand at Olympia had been particularly impressed by the machines on display and immediately appreciated their potential; both of them would play an important role in the future history of the firm. The first of these, W. Gordon McMinnies, was an Oxford graduate and keen motorcyclist who had won the first motor cycle race held at Brooklands in 1908 and competed in the Isle of Man TT races in 1909 and 1910. He was employed on the editorial staff of *Motor Cycling* and wrote on cyclecar matters under the pen name 'Platinum'. He quickly became an enthusiastic supporter of the Morgan and did much to promote the machines in *Motor Cycling* and the *Cyclecar* magazines. He would also in the future provide Morgan with valuable publicity as a result of a famous racing victory.

The other person to be impressed with the Morgans on display at Olympia was Richard Burbidge, managing director of Harrods. At this time the Knightsbridge store was still getting established and was looking for vehicles to market. He contacted HFS after the show, with the result that Harrods became the first agency for Morgan Runabouts. The involvement with Harrods resulted in the number of machines on order increasing to about thirty and the

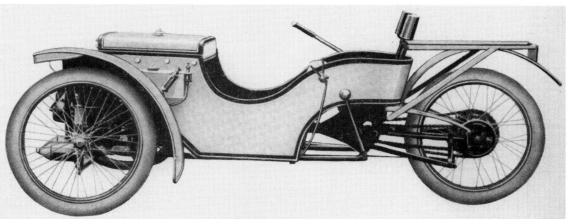

Above and top *The public was first shown the Morgan Runabout at the Motor Cycle Show held at Olympia in November 1910. The single-cylinder 4hp car (top) was extremely spartan, with only the minimum of bodywork and with all its mechanism exposed. The twin-cylinder 8hp car (bottom) was more fully bodied and fitted with front mudguards. It was aptly summarized by the reporter from the Car magazine as a 'car for one person'.*

The first Morgan advertisement, which appeared at the time of the 1910 Olympia Show.

— The —

MORGAN RUNABOUT

THE	THE
COMFORT	**CHEAPNESS**
AND	AND
SAFETY	**SIMPLICITY**
OF A	OF A
Motor Car.	Motorcycle.

Trials can be arranged. Apply

Morgan & Co., Malvern.

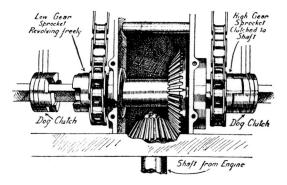

The change gear mechanism accounted for much of the early success of the Runabouts; it was simple but very effective and robust. Separate sprockets for the high and low gear ratios rotate freely about a transverse drive shaft in the neutral position. Sliding dog clutches, keyed to the square ends of the shaft, are moved by a simple lever and linkage to lock either one sprocket or the other to the shaft to obtain drive.

deposits provided working capital. This was the encouragement that HFS needed to persuade him to continue with car manufacture. However, the financial risk associated with the venture was unacceptable to his business partner Leslie Bacon and the two parted company.

The Importance of Competition Success

Construction of motorized vehicles of various different types was being carried out in small factories and workshops around the country about the time of the launch of the Morgan Runabout. The objective was to build small, lightweight, single- or two-seater machines using available motorcycle engines and components to provide economical personal transport. Many of the machines, like the Morgan Runabout, were produced by enthusiastic engineers and were soundly designed and constructed. Others were the product of get-rich-quick merchants who adopted expediency, in preference to engineering principles, in order to achieve their aim to be first to the marketplace. The machines, both the good and the bad, invariably appeared to be of spidery construc-

---

H.F.S Morgan's Patents Covering the Design of the Three-Wheeler

The first patent covering the design of the Morgan three-wheeler was taken out in 1910. Number 20,986, it was titled 'Improvements in the Design and Construction of Tri-cars or Other Light Automobile Vehicles'. The submission was prepared by Stanley, Popplewell & Co. of Chancery Lane, London. The drawings were the work of John Black, who was articled to Mr Stanley and was later to become better known as Sir John Black, chairman of the Standard Motor Company.

The patent provides a detailed description of the design and ends with specific claims. These comprised:

- a frame consisting of a large central tube attached to the gearbox at the rear and to 'transversely extending members' at the front
- in addition, the large tube used to contain the driving shaft, and two parallel longitudinal tubes
- in addition, the mounting of the engine on the forward extending tubes and the use of engine mounting plates
- in addition, the use of the two parallel longitudinal tubes as silencer extensions; and,
- the general design and arrangement of the frame

Interestingly, the sliding pillar front suspension, which was to become such a famous feature of the Morgan, was illustrated in the drawings and covered in the detailed description, but was not specifically mentioned under claims. HFS would certainly have appreciated the benefits of independent front suspension and the worth of his design. Perhaps he was concerned that earlier sliding pillar designs by pioneering manufacturers, such as Stephens and Decauville, or more recently by Sizaire et Naudin, meant that his design could not be patented. Rather than have his application turned down or delayed, he therefore relied upon the catch-all fifth claim and did not mention the suspension specifically.

There were six additional patents taken out in respect of the three-wheeler. The first of these, patent No. 19,467 of 1914, was concerned with the modification of the earlier design to produce a four-wheeler.

The third patent, No. 134,390 filed in 1918, was concerned with the design of demountable wheels for light cars and motor cycles; a design relying upon the use of tapered dogs on the wheel drum or sprocket, locating with corresponding grooves on the wheel hub.

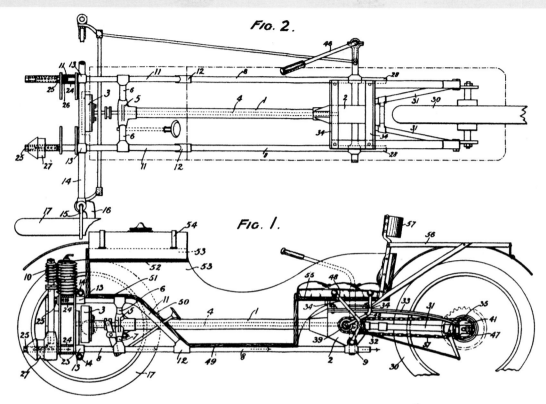

FIG. 2.

FIG. 1.

The drawings prepared by John Black for the patent submission of 1910.

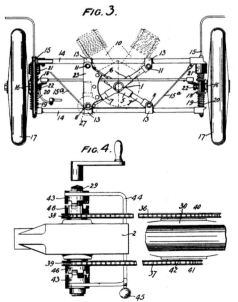

FIG. 3.

FIG. 4.

The fourth patent, No. 135,789 filed in 1918, described a method of chain adjustment based upon a short, moveable, arm attached to the end of each fork leg.

The fifth patent, No. 289,272 filed in 1927, was for the design of a tapered track-rod end with spring loading to provide steering damping.

The sixth patent, No. 343,058, filed in 1929, covered the design changes to the rear section of the frame for the M-type chassis, in which the bevel box was bolted to a flange at the end of the large diameter chassis tube; modifications which would be carried over to the three-speeder model introduced in 1932.

The final patent, No. 410,395, filed in 1933, was in respect of the introduction of the Z-section, rather than tubular, frame required for the installation of a 4-cylinder Ford engine.

tion and, being of innovative design, to be weird and wonderful in the eye of the beholder. With current motoring awareness it is easy to judge the machines, but the public of the day had neither the experience nor knowledge to distinguish between the sound designs and the lemons. The only way a prospective purchaser could assess the various machines was by how well they performed in the various reliability trials and sporting events of the day. Thus the obtaining of awards in sporting events became vital to any manufacturer wishing to achieve sales success.

HFS entered his first competition event a month after the Runabout was first shown to the public at Olympia. The event was the first London–Exeter Trial, organized by the Motor Cycle Club and held on 26 and 27 December 1910. Heavy rain preceded the event and the poorly surfaced and pot-holed roads were inches deep in mud. HFS drove his tiller-steered 8hp JAP-powered single-seater and his only concessions to the appalling conditions were the use of coil ignition, with covers over the sparking plugs, and a metal shield to

HFS entered the Exeter Trial on Boxing Day 1910 and was successful in winning a gold medal on his first competitive outing with the Runabout.

The Cyclecar

It is an acceptable generalization to say that the car industry of the late nineteenth century grew from the already established cycle industry. By the early years of the following century the industry had established its own identity and cars were more soundly engineered and robust. They were also extremely expensive and, like the cycles when first introduced, were largely toys for the rich. Motorcycles represented a more affordable if less sociable form of transport and were taken up by less wealthy enthusiasts keen to experience motorized transport. It was during the latter part of the first decade of the century that several enthusiasts, HFS amongst them, conceived the idea of combining cycle construction methods and powerful motorcycle engines to construct cheap, lightweight cars of excellent performance. It was quickly appreciated that this new type of vehicle could be a practical form of transport and also great fun. The machines, a cross between the motorcycle, or motorcycle and sidecar, and the motorcar, soon became known as cyclecars.

Cyclecars could be constructed by anyone with modest workshop facilities and basic engineering abilities, and very soon a wide range of machines was being offered for sale to the public. Construction techniques varied widely. Chassis frames were usually constructed with steel tubing and brazed lugs, although thin-section pressed-steel or, occasionally, wood were often called into use. Suspension usually relied on cart springs, as used generally by the car industry, and quarter-elliptic springing was preferred, as it provided cost and weight savings. Coil springs and wood were also popular, whilst some manufacturers considered suspension an expensive frivolity having no place on an economy vehicle. Steering was usually un-geared and often based upon the wire and bobbin arrangements used to move a ship's rudder. The first machines often relied upon belts for transmission, but these proved troublesome and chains soon became more popular. A conventional gearbox was the exception rather than the norm and various arrangements of chains and dogs, variable pulleys, or friction drive were utilized.

The cyclecar industry, born in the years prior to the Great War, would boom in the early post-war years due to public demand for motorized transport. However, the popularity of the cyclecar would ultimately lead to its downfall, as established car manufacturers, fearful of losing their market, began offering lightweight cars of conventional design. Cyclecar manufacturers were forced to improve their product and only the very best, Morgan amongst them, survived.

It did not take long for the sporting potential of the cyclecar to be appreciated. The Auto-Cycle Union (the motorcycle branch of the R.A.C.) applied to the Federation Internationale des Clubs Motocyclistes in Paris and received approval for the following cyclecar classifications.

Group 1: Large Class (International Class G)
Maximum weight 772lb (350kg) (just under 7cwt)
Maximum engine capacity 1100cc

Group 2: Small Class (International Class H)
Maximum weight 660lb (299kg) (just under 6cwt)
Maximum engine capacity 750cc

The Cyclecar Club was established on 30 October 1912 and held its first race meeting at Brooklands the following year. On 1 April 1919 the name was changed to the Junior Car Club and with a change of name came changes of definition. Light cars up to 1500cc were accepted and cyclecars were defined as up to 1100cc and with an unladen weight of 9cwt (457kg).

The following brief descriptions of a few of the better, more successful, cyclecars illustrates the diversity of the engineering designs and the nature of the competition faced by HFS as he attempted to establish his business.

AC Sociable – The Tradesman's Carrier

The AC Sociable was one of the most popular cyclecars of the era. It was derived from the Autocarrier, which was first produced in 1904 as a tradesmen's box-tricycle and was once a common sight on the streets of London. The power unit was an air-cooled single-cylinder engine of 5.6hp located at the rear of the machine under the driver's seat. Transmission was by chain to an epicyclic gear unit contained within the single rear wheel. Operation could not be simpler; a foot pedal engaged the low gear for pulling away and a hand lever engaged top gear. Steering was by tiller. The goods compartment consisted of a box positioned above the front axle. The production of a passenger version was started towards the end of 1907. Now known as AC, an abbreviation of Autocarrier, the

Continued overleaf

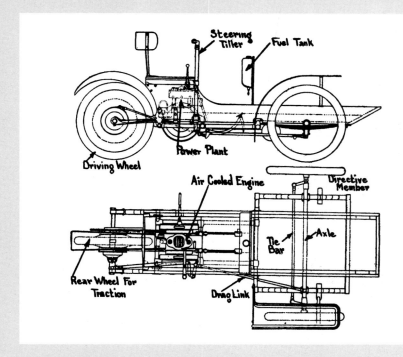

The illustrations show the general mechanical arrangement of the AC. The engine was a single-cylinder air-cooled side-valve unit. The rear wheel hub incorporated a two-speed epicyclic gear, clutch and brake drum.

Continued from previous page

first machines left the driver seated above the engine and replaced the commercial box with a seat for the passenger. The AC Sociable, introduced in 1910, sat the driver alongside the passenger in front of the engine. The price of the basic machine was £85. AC, like Morgan, appreciated the benefit of competition success and competed in all the major trials. A works team of three machines was in existence from 1909. Recognizing the changing market, AC produced a conventional light car in 1913. Production of the Sociable was discontinued at the start of the Great War and did not recommence with the cessation of hostilities.

GWK – The Light Car With Friction Drive.

Messrs Grice, Wood and Keiller succumbed to the attractions of friction drive for their GWK. By arranging for a friction disc to slide on a shaft across the face of a 'driver' disc rotated by the engine, they obtained gear ratios according to its radial position across the driver. Gear changing was simple and the ratios were infinitely variable over the range. It did not matter that the system would prove incapable of transmitting much power, as the engines of the day produced very little!

The prototype GWK was constructed in 1910/11 using a Coventry-Climax boat engine and proved successful. In late 1911 a company was formed and a factory set up in Datchet for the manufacture of an improved version. The first models used a 2-cylinder Coventry-Simplex engine but, with aspirations for the light car market, a 4-cylinder version was developed in 1915. With the intervention of the war this would not be offered to the public until 1919. Production of GWKs finally ceased in 1931.

The GWK was a better quality product than most other cyclecars and the asking price of £150, although

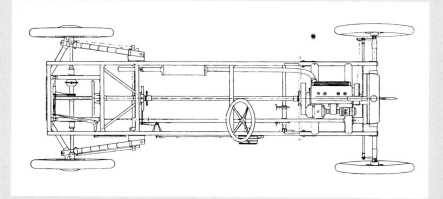

The chassis of the GWK was of conventional construction and appearance. The novelty was represented by the gearing mechanism. A friction disc, sliding along splines forming part of the rear axle, was driven by a driver disc attached to the end of the prop shaft.

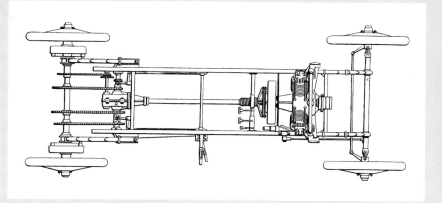

The illustration is of the later GN chassis fitted with three speeds and reverse. The chassis was of simple channel steel construction and quarter-elliptic springing was used front and rear. Dog clutches and chain drive allowed rapid change of gear.

much higher than that of the Morgan Runabout, represented good value for money. GWK appreciated the benefit of reliability trials to demonstrate the car and its friction drive to the public. The prototype car, driven by Wood, completed the tough Scottish Six-Day Trial and two gold medals were won in the London–Edinburgh Reliability Run. With a top speed of almost 55mph (88km/h) the cars also proved successful at the Brooklands track. A GWK was the main rival to HFS in the competition for the hour record trophy presented by the *Cyclecar* magazine in 1912.

GN – Chains, Dogs and a Sporty Performance

Ronald Godfrey and Archibald Frazer Nash, who had first met as engineering students in 1905, had separately built a number of experimental machines before combining to build the machine that would become the first GN. It was described in the *Motor Cycle* magazine in December 1910, a few weeks after the launch of the Morgan Runabout. The first GNs, which were built in the stable block of Frazer Nash's family house, had wooden chassis, and cable and bobbin steering. JAP or Peugeot V-twin engines were used, fitted with the crankshaft at right angles to the frame, and drive was by chain to a gear change unit in front of the rear axle. Final drive was by belt or chain to the rear wheels.

By 1912, Godfrey and Fraser Nash had developed their own engine based upon the Peugeot unit. This was placed across the chassis and fitted with a single-plate clutch and shaft drive to a bevel box under the driver's seat. This drove a cross shaft fitted with sliding dog-clutches and chain sprockets. The chain sprockets, which ran loose until engaged by the sliding dogs, provided chain drive to the rear axle. The mechanism was identical to that of the Morgan and the first GNs were also two-speeders. However, as the cross-shaft was the full width of the chassis, there was space to include more gears and it was a simple matter to add an additional gear or an intermediate pair of spur gears to provide a reverse. As with the Morgan, the change of gear ratios required no more than a change of sprockets.

From the start, Godfrey and Frazer Nash placed the emphasis on sporty performance. With its simple yet robust construction and light weight the GN proved to be the most formidable sporting four-wheeled cyclecar of its day. However, both Godfrey and Fraser Nash left the company in 1922 and the company folded in May of the following year.

protect the carburettor. He achieved a penalty-free journey and was awarded a gold medal. Journalists from the motorcycling press, having enthused about the Runabout at Olympia, were again lavish in their praise. They noted that the Runabout could more than hold its own with the motorcyclists and, contrary to general opinion, mud from the front wheels was not thrown onto the cylinder.

HFS recognized immediately that competition was not only an enjoyable pastime and a good means of product testing, but provided valuable publicity for sales promotion. The success in the Exeter Trial was widely advertised. Soon he was competing regularly in a wide variety of events and had an increasing number of competition successes to publicize.

The coil and accumulator ignition, fitted for the London–Exeter Trial, was still fitted to the 8hp single-seater for the Auto-Cycle Union quarterly trials in May 1911. HFS gained a certificate but was penalized for failure to use a magneto as demanded by the regulations. As a consequence of this, magnetos became standardized on the Morgan.

Misjudging the severity of a bend at Salt-burn Bank on the London–Edinburgh Trial in June 1911 resulted in a collision with a wall. Despite bending the chassis back several inches and putting the wheels out of line, HFS was able to make roadside adjustments and to continue largely unaffected. Not only did this fully demonstrate the soundness of his design, but he was also successful in winning a gold medal.

The design of a two-seater Runabout was commenced during mid-1911 and the long awaited machine was finally launched in August of that year. Mechanically it was very little changed from the single-seater, but was an altogether more attractive machine. Not only was there space for a companion, but the styling had been greatly improved by fitting a coal-scuttle bonnet. Also, for the first time, the tiller was replaced by a conventional steering wheel.

The first competitive appearance of the new two-seater was a disappointment. Entered in

The Morgan Runabout.

Not an EXPERIMENT, but a well-tried Machine

Some Successes to Date.

London to Exeter and back (M.C.C. Trial, Christmas, 1910) ... ... **Gold Medal.**

Quarterly Trial. A.C.U., January, 1911,
Non-stop Certificate.

Quarterly Trials. A.C.U., May, 1911 ... **Certificate.**

London to Edinburgh and back (M.C.C., 1911)
Special Gold Medal.

Inter-club Run (Norwich Club) June, 1911. **Non-stop.**

Inter-club Championship A.C.U. (Oxford Club) September, 1911 ... **Non-stop and Gold Medal.**

Quarterly Trials. A.C.U., October, 1911, Non-stop,
First-class Certificate.

One Machine only was entered for each of these events.

Morgan & Co., Malvern.

One or Two-seaters ... **85 Guineas.**

Above *Competition successes were widely reported in the motoring press and publicized by Morgan & Co. The advertisement dates from January 1912.*

The two-seater prototype with HFS at the tiller. The machine had the minimum of bodywork necessary for testing. The passenger is William Copeland, who was to marry HFS's sister Ethel.

the Auto-Cycle Union's Six Days' Trial in August 1911, HFS was forced to retire on the second day with a broken propshaft. The failure was probably due to the extra load imposed by the two-seater and HFS capitalized on the problem by noting: 'We have gained experience, which has enabled us to detect faults and make improvements'.

An Enthusiastic Road Test and Expanding Demand

Motor Cycling magazine lost no time in requesting the loan of a two-seater for a lengthy test on the road by 'Platinum' (W. G. McMinnies). HFS agreed and met up with McMinnies at Banbury following a 160-mile (255km) non-stop run in the ACU club championship trials. He then drove McMinnies to Moreton-in-Marsh, in order to instruct him in the art of driving a three-wheeler, before passing over the Runabout. The road test resulted in a most favourable article in the magazine for 26 September. The author wrote:

> After a trial of the 8hp twin Morgan runabout, both as a single and double-seater, extending over 300 miles, I must admit that it is one of the sportiest and speediest little vehicles that I have ever driven. Indeed barring a T.T. motor-bicycle and a 75hp Bianchi car, I have never been on anything that gave me more pleasure on the road.

He then compared the Morgan against the motorcycles of the day and praised its performance, comfort, weather protection and luggage carrying capacity. Comparing it with the motorcycle combination he went on:

> Let anyone try the Morgan, and I'll warrant that he will forsake the unmechanical side-car for ever.

Mention was made in the *Motor Cycling* article of testing the new machine as both a single- and a double-seater. This is understandable, as the seat could best be described as comfortable for one but cramped for two. The unladen weight

of the machine was only 3cwt (150kg) and it was well able to cope with the extra passenger.

The sociable nature of the two-seater must have been appreciated by HFS, as he was now able to take a companion on the long-distance trials and more often than not the companion was his future wife, Ruth.

By the end of 1911, HFS and other drivers of the Morgan Runabout had achieved numerous competition successes. The little car could claim the first ascents of famous hills, such as Porlock Hill in Somerset and Honister Pass in Devon, to add to its list of laurels. These successes were widely reported in the press and featured prominently in the company's advertisements. The public could by now have small doubt that the little Morgan was as robust as it was ingenious; a truly practical vehicle at an affordable price. The availability of the two-seater removed the remaining obstacle to sales and soon a steady trickle of customers began placing orders. The number of orders further increased following the very laudatory road test report by 'Platinum' in *Motor Cycling*.

Harrods were sole concessionaires and contracted the whole of the output of Messrs Morgan and Co. at this time. Towards the end of the year they circulated a letter to over four hundred prospective purchasers who had made enquiries of themselves or the works. In this they noted that they had arranged for a slightly increased output from the works of seven Morgans per month.

Twelve months after its first announcement, the Morgan Runabout was back on display at Olympia for the 1911 Motor Cycle Show. This time HFS already had an almost full order book and was confident of the commercial viability of his Runabouts. Moreover, he also displayed several two-seaters. *Motor Cycling* described the exhibits as racy monocars or two-seater tourists and noted: 'These little Runabouts have wheel steering and are extremely comfortable, and will climb any hill. Two models are on view – a natty little single-seater and a smart looking two-seater.' The ability to restart the engine by a handle when

The natty little single-seater and the smart looking two-seater cars displayed at the 1911 Olympia Show. The tall, upright, hood gave the two-seater a much less sporting appearance and provided little protection from driving rain. Luggage could be carried on the grid above the rear wheel.

the driver was seated was noted as being of great consideration should the engine be stopped at any time. The machines again created considerable interest and this time HFS was overwhelmed by orders from both the public and the trade.

The orders placed at the show were so great that HFS thought his resources would be inadequate to cope with the demand. Accordingly he approached several larger firms with pro-

posals for the manufacture of the Runabouts but, fortunately for the future of the company, was turned down. Thus, forced at an early stage to operate independently, he would in future ensure the independence of the Morgan Company; a policy maintained to this day by his son and grandson. Following the 1911 Olympia show, HFS would cease being a garage owner and part-time car builder and, instead, become a full-time car manufacturer.

3　The Morgan Motor Company

The year 1912 was to be a momentous year for HFS and the Morgan Company, and for the cyclecar movement as a whole. It was the year that HFS changed from a garage owner, who also made tricycles, to a committed car manufacturer. It was also the year he married. It was the year that cyclecars began to prove themselves in speed events as well as in reliability trials and, as previously, Morgans were in the forefront. It was also the year that the cyclecar found full public acceptance and found its own voice in a magazine devoted specifically to the interests of the cyclecarist.

The demand for the Morgan Runabout had grown steadily since the announcement of the two-seater and, following the 1911 Olympia Show, had increased far beyond the capacity of the Morgan Garage. This was largely due to the enthusiasm of the Harrods store in marketing the cars. The circular they had sent to prospective customers at the end of 1911 had born fruit and, on 12 January a further order was placed for fifty Runabouts. Obtaining this number of orders was satisfying for the store, but Richard Burbridge appreciated the problems this

presented for Morgan; he was, moreover, concerned that production delays could damage the store's reputation. HFS had made attempts to increase production but, within the constraints of the garage business, this was not possible. It was clear that if he was to satisfy demand then a total commitment to car manufacture was required.

The original garage business had operated under the name of Morgan & Co. In early 1912, the name was changed to the Morgan Motor Company to reflect the revised business objectives. On 1 April 1912 the Morgan Motor Company was registered as a limited company, with a nominal share capital of £100,000 and HFS and his father as shareholders. H.F.S. Morgan was appointed managing director and was responsible for manufacture. His father, H.G. Morgan, was appointed chairman and would look after the management and financial affairs of the company.

Planning permission was obtained in July 1912 to build new workshops on the land behind HFS's home, Chestnut Villa, and the original garage building in Worcester Road.

The new letterhead, dating from 1912, clearly identified the interests of the Morgan Motor Company Ltd.

Above *The chassis assembly area in the Worcester Road factory in 1912. HFS, in cap, is standing in the centre.*

1912 Standard Morgan.

The new factory was, in effect, merely an extension of the original garage.

The works were equipped with some machine tools, but most parts were bought in and the Morgan factory was little more than an assembly plant. Mechanical components came largely from Birmingham manufacturers. The factory assembled and brazed together the tubular chassis, using lugs and bought-in bevel boxes. Next the sliding-pillar front suspension and quarter-elliptic rear suspension were added, together with the brakes and steering linkages. Finally, the wheels and engines were added to complete the rolling chassis. These were then stored awaiting the wooden body frames supplied by William Clare, who had works nearby in Worcester Road. Edmund Langley, who had recently opened a sheet-metal workshop in Redland Road adjacent to the Morgan site, was contracted to make the metal panels to fit the wooden frames. The same firm also constructed the fuel tanks. Engines for the first cars were side-valve V-twins supplied by J.A. Prestwich of Tottenham. The cars were then transferred to wooden sheds, located in what had been the garage yard, for final assembly and painting. The transfer of partially completed cars from building to building, which began in these early days of the company history, would become a traditional feature of Morgan manufacture.

Morgans never had what would now be called a design department during the period of three-wheeler production. The usual procedure in the design of bodies, for example, would be for HFS to sketch out his ideas in chalk on a black-painted wall of the factory. His works manager, Alfie Hales, his pattern-maker and the other workmen were then expected immediately to interpret the sketch in order to produce a prototype of the new body design for approval by Mr Morgan. Adjustments would then be made until the lines of the body were pleasing to the eye.

In June 1912 HFS married Hilda Ruth Day, whom he had met in 1907 at a dance in the Grand Hotel in Malvern. Ruth was the younger daughter of the Reverend Archibald Day, vicar of St Matthias Church, Malvern Link, and HFS's junior by about six years. They set up house in Chestnut Villa next to the Morgan works. In the years to come Ruth would be HFS's regular companion in trials and in races, whenever a passenger was allowed.

Above *Ruth Morgan, née Day. Despite being an enthusiastic driver of Morgans and owner of a number of sporting cars, Ruth never drove a Morgan in competition.*

Both HFS and Ruth wore all-white motoring clothes to set out for their honeymoon in Wales. Their transport was a white painted two-seater Runabout carrying the works registration number CJ743.

First Racing and Record Successes

The first appearance of a Morgan in a speed event occurred, with some style, in March 1912 at the British Motor Cycle Racing Club meeting at Brooklands. Harry Martin, who was an experienced motorcycle racer and constructed his own motorcycles, entered a two-seater Morgan in the first international cyclecar race held at the circuit. The machine was powered by a JAP ohv twin engine of 986cc (90 × 77.5mm) and fitted with a streamlined body. Martin led from the start and completed the first standing start lap at 53mph (85km/h) and the second flying lap at a little under 60mph (96km/h). He completed the race in 8 minutes and 32 seconds, with a margin of more than two and a half minutes over the second-placed Sabella-JAP. As a result of this trouncing of the opposition, all future cyclecar races at Brooklands would be run as handicaps. The race was widely reported and within days of the race Morgan received more than a hundred new orders.

To promote the new breed of cars, *Motor Cycling* magazine offered a prestigious silver trophy to be presented to the person holding the one-hour distance record for a cyclecar by the end of 1912. Most attempts on the hour record took place at the banked Brooklands circuit, which had been constructed in 1907 to provide the British motor industry with a facility for sustained high-speed running and testing. The circuit was equipped with

The Pick of the Bunch.

The First Cycle-car Race held, and run off at Brooklands, 27th March, resulted in a great triumph for the

MORGAN RUNABOUT, driven by Mr. Harry Martin.

SEVEN STARTED ——— RESULT

MORGAN 1ST. at an average speed of **57** m.p.h.

Successful on Road and Track.

MORGAN MOTOR CO., MALVERN.

Above *The advertisement placed following Harry Martin's success in the first cyclecar race held at Brooklands.*

Harry Martin's ohv JAP-powered racer was the first Morgan to compete in a race at Brooklands. Despite appearance to the contrary, the machine carried a 'riding mechanic' to comply with the race regulations; the unfortunate passenger knelt out of sight on the floor to reduce wind resistance.

HFS in the machine he used for the one-hour record attempt. The smile on the front of the body had been painted over by the time of the record run.

officially recognized timekeeping equipment and offered engineering support facilities. The hour record was hotly contested by several drivers and manufacturers. By the middle of the year the main contender was J. Talfourd Wood, driving a GWK of his own manufacture. The rear-engined friction-drive machine was a sporting rival to the Morgan and a major competitor in the market place. By the August of 1912, Talfourd Wood had raised the hour record to almost 50 miles (80km). HFS entered the fray in a one-hour race run concurrently for both sidecars and cyclecars at a meeting of the BMCRC held on Saturday 9 November. He led the race from the start, winning by almost four laps, and covered 55 miles 329 yards (88.305km) in the hour. In the process he also took the 50-miles (80km) world record in 54 minutes and 39 seconds, plus the flying kilometre and mile records. Not to be out-done, Wood responded the following Tuesday and retrieved the record by covering more than 56 miles 76 yards (89.669km) within the hour. HFS's reply was to return to the track on

HFS is seen at the start of his record breaking hour run. The photograph was used to proclaim the achievement on the front cover of the Cyclecar. Ruth and his father, wearing a top hat, accompanied HFS to Brooklands to provide encouragement before the start of the record attempt. HFS was a modest man and became very tense before an event, concerned that deficiencies in his driving performance might reflect badly on the car.

"Nearly 60 miles in one hour"

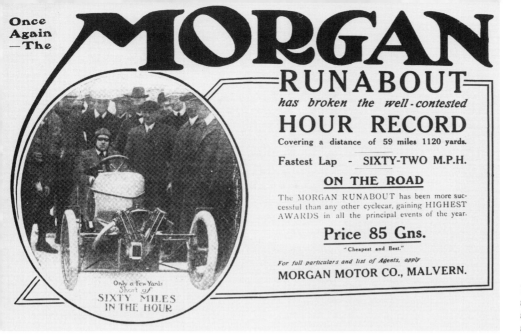

The advertisement recording Morgan's success in taking the cyclecar hour record.

23 November, in order to retrieve the record by covering 59 miles 1120 yards (95.418km) within the hour, fractionally short of the magic average of a mile a minute. This placed the record beyond contention for 1912 and the Cyclecar (formerly Motor Cycling) Trophy was Morgan's.

The attainment of the Hour Record was well timed to provide maximum publicity at the 1912 Motorcycle Show. The Morgan stand featured a victor's laurel wreath and notices proclaiming the achievement.

During the year, HFS had concentrated his efforts on increasing the rate of production of the Runabouts in an attempt to satisfy demand. He had successfully raised output to about twelve cars per week but orders continued to exceed supply. The 1912 models had been unchanged from the previous year and comprised the single-seater and the two-seater, which was available with three body options. The standard body retained the low-cut sides of the prototype. The Sporting and De Luxe bodies were high sided, with the De Luxe offering the luxury, implied by its name, of a door on the passenger side. The single seater was dropped by the time of the show.

Mention has already been made of the magazine, the *Cyclecar*, in relation to the hour record. The magazine was the brainchild of W. G. McMinnies, who was already an enthusiast for cyclecars by the time the Morgan was launched at the 1910 Olympia show, having first seen a French Bédélia cyclecar in Paris. He worked as a journalist for *Motor Cycling* and, under the pen name 'Platinum', would often write articles about the new machines. He suggested to Arthur Armstrong of Temple Press, the publishers of *Motor Cycling*, that there was a market for a magazine dedicated to cyclecars. Armstrong was initially reluctant, but finally relented, and the first issue of the *Cyclecar*, with McMinnies as editor, was issued, price 1d, to coincide with the Motor Cycle Show. The initial print run of 100,000 was quickly sold out and the magazine was soon established. McMinnies would do much to promote HFS's speedy tricycles through both competition and the pages of the magazine. In December 1912 he bought his own Morgan, a sparsely bodied single-seater with JAP air-cooled engine, which was christened 'Jabberwock' after the fierce creature in the Lewis Carroll poem. The intention had been to use the car for reporting on trials and within the week he had covered more than 500 miles. The car was subsequently used in hill climbs and for circuit racing at Brooklands.

Recognition at Home and Abroad

The end of 1912 saw Morgan established as a cyclecar maker and already operating profitably. New agencies had also been established. Harrods and a second famous store, Whiteleys, were both now offering Runabouts for sale in London. Outside London, established garages such as R. James in Sheffield and T.A. King of Hereford, amongst others, were appointed. With full order books the company could look forward to the coming year with confidence.

In January 1913, an announcement was made that a Cyclecar Grand Prix would be held in conjunction with the French Grand Prix at Amiens, France on 13 July. The race regulations were typical of French motor racing events of the period, being full of petty restrictions and providing no clear definition of a cyclecar to confirm eligibility to compete. Indeed, it was by no means certain whether a Morgan entry would be accepted, as three-wheelers were not recognized as cyclecars in France. In the event, three-wheelers were included. Gordon McMinnies was an enthusiastic supporter of the event and ensured it received considerable coverage in the *Cyclecar*, both in the run-up and in the reporting of the race.

Possibly with the Cyclecar Grand Prix in mind, HFS began looking at alternative engine options for his Runabout. Prior to 1913 all the production models had been fitted with JAP air-cooled engines, but these were prone to overheating with resultant failure of the

The special Runabout offered for sale by Harrods and displayed in their Knightsbridge store. The luxurious two-seater bodywork was made in London to the special order of the store.

exhaust valve. To overcome this problem HFS was keen to investigate water-cooling. However, power, as well as reliability, was required if he was to remain competitive and he now had a wider choice of engines from new manufacturers attracted by the success of the cyclecar movement. An 8hp Blumfield engine was tested on the Liverpool AC Trial in February 1913, but proved equally prone to overheating when climbing the Bwlch-y-Groes pass.

Preliminary announcement of two new Morgan models was made at the beginning of June 1913. Morgan drivers had considered themselves disadvantaged in trials when compared to their competitors, whose machines were equipped with four or more gears. To redress the balance a new trials Morgan was produced, with a two-speed gearbox fitted at the front of the torque tube, which when combined with the two-speed transmission gave four ratios.

The other new machine was designed with the Cyclecar Grand Prix in mind. Alterations to standard practice involved lengthening the chassis by 11in (280mm) to allow the driver and passenger to be moved from a position above to one directly in front of the bevel box. Larger-diameter side tubes were used to stiffen the lengthened chassis. The new seating position resulted in lowering the centre of

Vernon Busby achieved a 750cc class win in the BMCRC High Speed Reliability Trial at Brooklands on 29 March 1913, using a Sporting model fitted with a 670cc Blumfield engine. HFS later gave the machine to his sister Dorothy and her name was painted over the competition number. Dorothy was a regular entrant in reliability trials and gained many first class awards.

HFS driving a Sporting model in the Bristol Open Trial of April 1913.

HFS, accompanied by sister Dorothy, carried out preliminary testing of the prototype Grand Prix car on the London–Edinburgh Trial held in May. Pending delivery of the special water-cooled engine, an air-cooled sv JAP engine and torpedo fuel tank were fitted.

gravity and significantly improved both the stability of the cars and the cornering speeds.

The car was tested with an air-cooled side-valve JAP engine in the London–Edinburgh Trial in May, before speed testing was carried out with an overhead-valve water-cooled engine at the Shelsley Walsh hillclimb and Porthcawl sand races.

The Morgan entries for the Grand Prix comprised works Grand Prix models for HFS and for Rex Mundy, together with a similar machine, entered by the newly formed Cycle-car Club, for McMinnies. The Mundy machine was powered by a water-cooled V-twin Green-Precision engine, whereas both HFS and McMinnies favoured the ohv water-cooled JAP engine. The Mundy machine was of striking appearance, as the water jackets, which were attached to the cylinders by the Green patent India-rubber joint, were of high-ly polished copper. A fourth entry was made for N.F. Holder with a side-valve Blumfield powered machine, but he non-started due to remaining in England to compete in the

BMCRC 6-hour scratch race to be held three days later at Brooklands. Ruth had hoped to accompany her husband in the race, but the race regulations did not allow lady passengers and Ruth's brother, Geoffrey Day, partnered HFS. McMinnies was partnered by Frank Thomas, the honorary secretary of the Cycle-car Club.

The starting grid for the race comprised eleven machines in the sidecar class, which included the Morgans, plus a further twenty-six machines in the cyclecar class.

The initial stages of the race proved disap-pointing for the Morgan drivers. Three miles out and still on his first lap, HFS was forced to retire with a broken piston. Mundy fared little better. He completed the first lap but on tak-ing a corner at about 35mph (56km/h), his offside front wheel appeared to double up under the strain. It was on the point of total collapse at the second bend and Mundy was forced to retire. McMinnies suffered mixed fortune. He was in the second group of three to be flagged away and, lapping at approxi-mately 50mph (80km/h), was soon leading the race. His first problem was a misfire necessitat-ing a change of plugs. This was quickly com-pleted and he was able to maintain his position at the head of the race, although he had lost the lead on time. A puncture on the third lap took

twelve minutes to repair and dropped him back to fifteenth; the position looked hopeless. However, from that point on McMinnies enjoyed a steady and, in his words, 'horribly boring' race as he lapped 'without excitement or trepidation'. He steadily increased speed and, one by one, began to overhaul the leaders until by the tenth lap he was in third position. The second placed man, Boneville, dropped out when his Bédélia caught fire on the eleventh lap. The suspense heightened when McMinnies stopped for fuel, rather than risk running out, before the twelfth and final lap. He completed the race covering the 162.9 miles (260.6km) in 3hr 53min 9sec at an average of 41.9mph (67km/h). Because of the staggered start, McMinnies was unaware he had won and some time lapsed before he learnt that he was fastest in both the sidecar and cyclecar classes, beating second-placed man Bourbeau in his Bédélia by some 45sec. The French authorities denied McMinnies the overall winner's laurels, owing to classifying the Morgan in the sidecar class, and first place was awarded to the Bédélia. The merits of the Morgan were, however, recognized by the French public and the newly appointed French agents Darmont et Badelogue were soon inundated with orders. Within days HFS was offering for sale replicas of the race-winning machine.

It would be pleasing to record that N.F. Holder's decision to compete at Brooklands rather than in the Grand Prix at Amiens had

A line-up of Runabouts awaiting collection in Worcester Road during 1913.

born fruit. Sadly this was not the case, as he suffered problems due to engine overheating, when a fractured fuel pipe caused fuel starvation, and the loss of the bottom gear chain. He was finally forced to retire after 206 miles (330km) due to clutch failure.

The Scottish Six-Days Trial held later in the month following the Grand Prix was a very different event, yet proved to be equally demanding. Twelve cyclecars were entered, including the Morgans of HFS and an amateur driver, J. Blackburn. Both Morgans had the benefit of four-speeds. The course comprised steep climbs and descents, severe hairpin bends and rocky surfaces, which tested the stamina of machine and driver alike. HFS was unfortunate to suffer the fracture of a wheel-bearing cone on the final day and was forced to retire. Blackburn, despite suffering engine problems and losing time, completed the event and was rewarded with a silver medal.

McMinnies did not compete in the Scottish Six-Days Trial, but followed the course in his Grand Prix winning machine in order to report for the *Cyclecar*. The hard going over the terrible surfaces eventually proved too much for the car and the steering fractured whilst travelling along the main Falkirk to Edinburgh road. The car careered off the road at some 35 to 40mph (55–65km/h) and struck a telegraph post. Both McMinnies and his passenger, Johnny Gibson, were thrown from the car and had lucky escapes, although Gibson suffered a cracked rib and minor leg injuries. The car was extensively damaged and its remains were loaded onto a passing laundry cart to be taken back to Falkirk station en route to the Morgan works. Fortunately the engine of the car was undamaged and McMinnies poor 'Jabberwock de Picardy' was rebuilt as an extremely potent single-seater.

HFS was accompanied by Ruth on the ACU Six-Days Trial in August 1913. Conditions were severe and justified the expressions of concern. HFS was amongst three of the original eight starters to reach the finish. He gained a gold award and a great deal of valuable publicity.

The New Pickersleigh Road Factory

By the end of 1913 the Morgan Motor Company had almost seventy employees and intended shortly to employ a further thirty. However, the factory, based on the extended garage at Chestnut Villa in Worcester Road, was at the limit of its capacity. Larger premises became a priority if the demand created by the sporting successes was to be satisfied and if an ever-lengthening waiting list was to be avoided. A suitable site for a new factory was identified on land belonging to Lord Beauchamp, at the opposite end of Pickersleigh Road from Chestnut Villa. Negotiations were completed in November 1913 for the purchase of a 2-acre plot with a frontage of 240 feet along what would become Pickersleigh Avenue. The site remains the Morgan factory to this day.

The Morgan models for 1914, displayed at the Motor Cycle Show in November 1913, comprised the Grand Prix model based upon the racing machines, a new commercial variant, and the Standard, Sporting and De Luxe models carried over from previous years. Improvements to the Standard and Sporting models included a strengthened chassis and a rear body extension replacing the rear mudguard, to which was fitted a luggage carrier. The Grand Prix models were available with

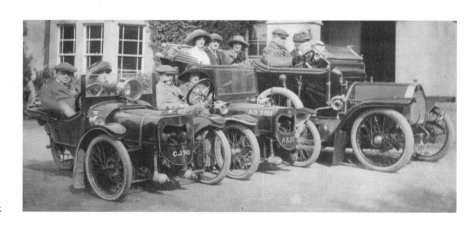

The line-up of Morgan family cars at Stoke Lacy includes HFS with Ruth in the late 1912 trials car.

either the JAP side-valve, 85mm × 85mm, engine or the JAP overhead valve, 90mm × 77.5mm, engine. A wider-bodied version of the side-valve machine was available for those intending to use the machine mainly for touring. No such provision was made in the case of the overhead valve machine, which was intended only as a racer. A commercial Carrier, which comprised a simple box attachment on the Standard model, was displayed in the livery of the Sheffield agents, James and Co. In all, ten vehicles were exhibited, including an air-cooled three-wheeler chassis to show the general arrangement. The show proved a resounding success for the company and orders poured in. More than seven hundred orders, including over one hundred and fifty from overseas customers, were placed before the company, concerned about over-commitment pending completion of the new factory, decided to close the order book. By this time the company had appointed more than fifty agents.

Many of the trials of the period were proving to be tests to destruction. In order better to

The Morgan factory with a line-up of the runabouts to be displayed at the Olympia show in November 1913. Chestnut Villa is to the right of the photograph.

assess the all round merit of cyclecars, the Cyclecar Club organized a General Efficiency Trial in March 1914, in which points were awarded for performance, braking, economy, and so on. HFS, accompanied by Ruth, entered a Standard model with water-cooled JAP engine and finished second, despite lapping Brooklands at only a modest 36mph (58km/h).

The severity of the 1913 Scottish Six-Days Trial was as nothing to the problems faced by competitors in the ACU Six-Days Trial held during July 1914. The tight time-schedule and poor terrain proved hazardous to both man and machine, many of the tests proving impossible for all of the contestants. HFS became so disgusted by the morning of the fourth day that he drove home rather than compete when his number was called. McMinnies drove Jabberwock, with disregard for life and limb, to gain a gold award, whilst W. James obtained a bronze. The *Cyclecar* referred to the trial as 'A Perfect Farce' and the event was widely criticized for its severity. However, George Morgan wrote a letter supporting occasional tests to destruction as being as important as speed events in demonstrating the worth of a machine. He noted that 'a certain firm' would be strengthening steering components as a result of the trial.

Morgan: the Economical Choice

The *Motor Cycle* review of the 1913 Olympia Show summed up the Morgan Runabout: 'Besides being one of the most thoroughly proven exhibits, it has the advantage of being very moderate in price.' Certainly by the end of 1913 it was established as amongst the most sporting and reliable of the new cyclecars. Competition success created interest, but sales success depended upon the Runabout offering excellent value for money. Its price, relative to the competition, may be judged from a review of the cyclecars and light cars for 1914, which was published in the *Light Car and Cyclecar* in November 1913. The list comprised thirteen three-wheelers, one hundred and five four-wheelers and five monocars, from approximately ninety manufacturers. Of the four-wheelers thirteen were chain driven, twenty-one were belt driven, nine were friction driven with final drive chain and sixty-two were shaft driven. The Morgan Runabout appears four times in the list of three-wheelers at £89 5s for the Standard Model, £91 for the De Luxe Model, £105 for the Grand Prix Model with water-cooled side-valve engine and £115 for the Grand Prix Model with water-cooled ohv engine. The cheapest three-wheeler was the long established AC Sociable, with single-cylinder air-cooled side-valve engine at £78 15s. The most expensive of the three-wheelers was the German Phanomobile at £167, but this boasted a reverse gear and full equipment, including hood, windscreen and lights.

The single-cylinder chain driven LAD was the cheapest of the four-wheelers and, at £75, cost less than the AC. Generally chain- or belt-driven machines cost in the range £100 to £140. Friction-driven machines cost an additional £10, with the GWK, a major sales and competition rival to the Morgan, priced at £150. The shaft-driven four-wheelers cost between £110 and £200. However, many of these should more correctly be considered to be light cars, as machines such as the early 'bullnose' Morris Oxford at £180 are included.

Motorcycles were an alternative option and machines could be purchased for £50 to £60 depending upon specification. A sidecar could be fitted for less than £10 and would provide accommodation and a degree of weather protection for a loved one, but did not provide a sociable conveyance.

In his budget speech of April 1909, David Lloyd George announced that roads were to be made self-financing and cars would in future be taxed to use the road. The tax was determined by a scheme devised by the RAC and based on piston area. This was very favourable to the smaller, lightweight vehicle and helps to explain the growth in the number of light cars and the development of cyclecars from this date. The system was revised by the Roads Act 1920 and a charge of £1 per RAC horsepower introduced. Three-wheelers of whatever capacity were classed with motorcycle combinations and paid a flat rate tax of just £4 per year. This concessionary rate of tax was a major Morgan selling point and often emphasized in the company's advertisements and sales brochures.

Edward Bradford Ware, an ex-London University lecturer, joined the J. A. Prestwich company in the experimental shop under chief designer Val Page at the end of 1913. Ware was already an established racing motorcyclist and had set 750cc motorcycle and sidecar records with a Zenith-JAP of 744cc. In January 1914 he commissioned a special streamlined Morgan to be fitted with the same engine for further record attempts. By July he had established new records for the flying kilometre and flying mile in the 750cc class at 65.10mph (104.16km/h) and 63.09mph (100.94km/h).

The new Pickersleigh Road works was used initially as an extension of the original Worcester Road factory. There was no attempt to introduce a continuous production line of the type pioneered by Ford in America and incorporated into the new Model T production plant at Trafford Park in Manchester. To do so would have involved significant borrowing to fund the investment in plant and would have reduced the family's financial control. It would also have created a production capacity greatly in excess of the likely market. HFS preferred to rely on traditional craftsmen-based production methods to build cars to demand; a

E. B. Ware with his single-seater, JAP 1, at Brooklands in April 1914. The machine was fitted with a 744cc sv JAP for record breaking.

other machine was a special racing car developed for the proposed Cyclecar and Light Car Tourist Trophy Race to be held over ten laps of the old, 15.8 miles (25.3km), Isle of Man motorcycle course in September 1914. It was based upon the Grand Prix model and the seats, placed either side of the torque tube, were only $4\frac{1}{2}$in (114mm) above the ground. The rear forks were widened to accept a larger brake drum. A cylindrical 6-gallon fuel tank was placed behind the seats and pressurized using a dashboard-mounted hand pump. The bodywork was of all-wood construction and of striking appearance, with flat sides and a wedge-shaped toolbox behind the engine. The engine was an ohv eight-valve air-cooled MAG of 1078cc (82mm × 102mm), which was claimed to produce 30bhp. The full potential of the machine was never realised, as the Great War caused cancellation of the event. However, after the war it found some success in speed hill climbs.

Disruptions of War and the Development of New Post-War Models

HFS and George Morgan would have looked forward to 1914 with high hopes. Within three years the Morgan Motor Company had grown from a sideline garage business to become the third largest British motor manufacturer. Without outside financial support, the company had been able to fund expansion and show a good return on investment. Profits in 1911, the first year of production, had been nil, but in the second year the company returned a profit of £1,314 and raised this to £4,797 in 1913. By 1913 the company had a work force of about seventy and was producing almost 1,000 cars per year, which were distributed through a network of fifty dealers. Success in the French Cyclecar Grand Prix had opened an overseas market and Morgans were now being exported not only to France, but also to India, Russia and North and South America.

policy remaining in force to the present day. The complete rolling chassis, including engine and all running gear, continued to be assembled in Worcester Road before being taken to Pickersleigh Road to be united with the bodies, which were also made in Worcester Road. They then passed through paint and trim shops before returning to Worcester Road for despatch. The movement of vehicles between works appears an inefficient process, but represented only a small overhead on the manufacturing cost. It had the benefit of allowing the new factory extension to come on line with little disruption to vehicle manufacture.

Two rather special Morgans were produced about this time, including the very first four-seater. The machine is thought to have been built about 1913, although the surviving photograph is dated several years later. It was based upon the Standard model and the frame appears to have been lengthened to an impractical degree to fit the second row of seats. The

With the new factory under construction and strong demand, it was hoped to raise production to 1,500 cars per year in 1914. However, the outbreak of war in August 1914, shortly after the new factory had commenced operation, meant the target would not be achieved within the next five years. Nevertheless, 1914 was a good year for the company with profits increased to £10,450. Car production amounted to almost 1,000 and, amongst British manufacturers, was exceeded only by Wolseley with 3,000 vehicles and Austin with 2,000. (In the same period Ford, who dominated the British market, assembled 8,300 Model Ts at the Trafford Park plant.)

Production of cars did not stop immediately upon announcement of hostilities, but orders were cancelled and demand fell. One of the first casualties of war was motor sport. Denied the publicity afforded by competition successes and recognizing the mood of austerity in the country, Morgan chose to publicize the other major attribute of the Runabout: its frugality. The advertisements in the press made the extravagant claim of '60 Miles per Hour. 60 Miles per Gallon' and stated 'The MORGAN RUNABOUT is the Car of Economy'. Despite these endeavours, production of cars continued to fall from the planned thirty cars per week to barely a trickle. Very soon the factory would be made over largely to the pro-

duction of shells and other munitions for the war effort.

The commercial production of new vehicles finally came to a stop at the end of 1916, as a result of two new measures imposed by the government. The first restricted the supply of petrol for private vehicles to those required for work of national importance. The second, more drastic measure, prohibited the manufacture or assembly of any new motor vehicles from 16 November without a military permit.

The repair shop would remain in operation throughout the war and the development of new models continued. A lightweight military machine was designed and a prototype built. Although a very basic design, it provided seating for three persons and machine-gun mounting platforms. Like similar machines offered by other cyclecar and motorcycle combination manufacturers, it found little favour amongst the military. A new sports model, powered by a MAG water-cooled engine, was developed in 1916 by combining styling features of the Grand Prix and Sporting models. It proved popular with servicemen home on leave but few were produced and it was not given a model name. However, the machine served as the prototype of the Aero model, which was announced in 1919 and finally entered production in 1921. A four-

The rear quarter view illustrates the stark simplicity of the bodywork of the TT Morgan, intended for Vernon Busby to race in the 1914 Isle of Man Cyclecar TT.

Liscater 1918

The 1918 photograph of the four-seater prototype outside the rectory at Stoke Lacy. HFS is at the wheel with Ruth alongside. The passengers are HFS's sister, Dorothy, and Ruth's brother, Geoffrey Day.

seater Family model was also developed and announced in 1917. HFS was photographed with his wife, daughter and three small children in the car for publicity purposes in late 1918.

Whilst HFS was committed to the three-wheeler from the earliest days of the company, he had retained an open mind about future four-wheel models. A prototype four-wheeler was under development at the start of the war. The design was based upon a three-wheeler chassis with a cross member, located in front of the bevel box, for attachment of the quarter-elliptic rear springs and the swinging arms locating the rear axle. The axle was a simple tubular affair without differential, which called for use of a narrow track. The twin chain trans-

mission of the three-wheeler was retained. Patent application drawings were submitted in September 1914 and the patent granted in May of the following year. HFS's decision not to enter four-wheeler production would have been influenced by a quirk in the taxation system, which taxed three-wheelers at a lower rate than four-wheelers.

The government munitions contracts provided for an agreed but fairly generous fixed profit and allowed the Morgan Company to operate profitably during the war years. However, with car production reduced to a trickle, the return on investment was considerably reduced. The most profitable of the war years was 1916, when profits amounted to £6,133.

The military prototype, produced during the Great War, had flat platforms, front and rear, for mounting machine guns. The forward mounted, rear facing, third seat provided accommodation for a second passenger.

42

4 Boom and Very Nearly Bust

The Great War had been the first mechanized war and for most servicemen it provided a first taste of motorized transport, a taste they found to their liking. Having fought for freedom and survived, they now wished to enjoy it and for many that meant acquiring a motor vehicle. The desire was fuelled in part by the service gratuity and, whilst this was unlikely to run to a conventional motorcar, it would buy a motorcycle or, for the family man, a motor-cycle and sidecar or a cyclecar. It resulted in a period of unprecedented demand for motor vehicles.

The signing of the Armistice on 11 November 1918 had lead to the immediate cancellation of all government contracts and manufacturing companies were forced to reorganize quickly to resume civilian production. For some companies this meant a return to vehicle manufacture, whilst others would commence vehicle manufacture for the first time to provide work for factories expanded to meet wartime demands. HFS anticipated the likely demand for vehicles and was shrewd enough to appreciate that there would very quickly be surplus manufacturing capacity. It was, therefore, vital to begin Morgan production as quickly as possible. In fact, the Morgan Motor Company was better able than most of its competitors to re-establish peacetime car production. The company was in good financial shape, due to the fixed profit government contracts, and had ample reserves to fund expansion. It was better equipped than pre-war, as the new machinery, purchased with the aid of government subsidies for the military contracts, was readily adaptable for car pro-

duction. Also it had the advantage of relying on a labour force of craftsmen and, unlike most other manufacturers, did not have a moving production line to convert back to car production. The Morgan factory was amongst the first to recommence manufacture.

The first Runabouts announced immediately after the Armistice comprised the following pre-war models:

Sporting, with air-cooled MAG engine	£132
De Luxe, with air-cooled MAG engine	£137
De Luxe, with water-cooled JAP engine	£145
Grand Prix with JAP engine	£137

The machines were fully equipped with hood, screen, lamps, generator, horn, mats, tyre pump and tools. Extras included wheel discs at £2 15s, special colours at £2 10s, speedometer at £4, hood cover at £1 and painting number plates at 5s. A deposit of 5 per cent was required upon placing the order, but delivery dates were not quoted as the entire output had been pre-booked by Morgan agents. The prices were considerably greater than those applying in 1914, which had ranged from £85 to £115, but even these would soon appear cheap, as the high inflation of the post-war years took effect.

The return to vehicle manufacture was not without its difficulties. The company was not beset by supply difficulties to the same degree as its competitors, as most of the manufacture was carried out in house. It was, however, dependent upon outside suppliers for engines and tyres. In February 1919 an announcement was made that the MAG engine was unavailable

Not "MARKING TIME" But "MAKING PROGRESS"

An Early Return to Something like the "Good Old Times."

HOLDERS of stocks of petrol or petrol licences can use their Morgans for any purpose within 30 miles of their home or business address from the 1st December. In January, licences will be issued to all applicants, and motoring for any purpose will then become possible for all who have and can obtain cars. Those who require delivery of a Morgan in the near future should place their names on the list AT ONCE.

Morgan Runabout

— 1918 —
GRAND PRIX MODEL,
£137 Plus 5% Fully Equipped.

Special Features:
Extreme Simplicity of all Working Parts.
Very Light on Tyres.
Motorcycle Tax.
Special System of Springing, giving Great Comfort.
Consumption, 50 M.P.G.
No Belts or High speed Chains.
Accessible Position of Engine.

Write for Descriptive Leaflet:
MORGAN MOTOR CO.,
LIMITED.
MALVERN LINK.

The first post-war advertisement appeared just two weeks after the signing of the Armistice. It fully summarized the current situation and wisely recommended prospective purchasers to place their order 'at once'. It was not long before the waiting list exceeded several thousand.

and that in future either air-cooled or water-cooled JAP engines would be fitted. The availability of these was no doubt due to HFS's friendship with E.B. Ware, and Ware's enthusiasm for the Morgan. Tyres presented a greater problem. As late as April 1919, the *Light Car and Cyclecar* reported:

About 50 [Runabouts] are rapidly nearing completion, the work being suspended in the majori-

ty of cases owing to the difficulty of obtaining certain component parts, whilst at the new body and finishing works, situated about half a mile from the old works, a number of other cars are being finished off. Chatting to Mr Hales, the works manager, I was told that one trouble at present was to obtain tyres. Apart from the components referred to and the JAP engine, the Morgan Motor Co. make the complete car, and as the difficulty of obtaining parts is rapidly being surmounted, a steady output amounting to about fifteen cars per week should soon commence.

An unfortunate occurrence was reported in a subsequent news item in the same issue of the magazine under the heading 'Mr H. F. S. Morgan's Mishap'. HFS slipped on a patch of grease whilst passing a capstan lathe in the turning shop at the Worcester Road works. Instinctively he threw out his hand to save himself and was caught up in the machine, causing injuries requiring amputation of the first two fingers of his right hand.

A New Works and New Optimism

The new Morgan works in Pickersleigh Road was completed by September 1919. By this time the importance of the Morgan Motor Company to the local economy had been recognized and the opening ceremony, on 16 October, was attended by the local press. HFS gave a speech (an undertaking he would normally shy away from) in which he summarized the brief but eventful history of the company and his aspirations for the future. By this time the company had orders for more than 5,000 Runabouts.

The new works incorporated offices and stores, together with the brazing, erecting, finishing, upholstery, painting and varnishing shops. The offices and stores were located in the former body-shop adjacent to the road, where they would remain until 2003. The new chassis brazing shop was formed as an extension of this building. The next building down the yard, formerly the original upholstery and painting shops, was also lengthened and formed the chassis building and finishing shops. Continuing down the yard, two new buildings, of the same length as the extended buildings, provided accommodation for the trim and painting shops. The new works extended to over 38,400 square feet. The original Worcester Road works retained the machine, carpentry and tinmen's shops and increased the overall works area to more than 50,000 square feet. With the new factory the company had the capacity to produce 2,500 cars per year.

A second event of equal importance for the future of the company occurred on 3 November 1919 with the birth at Chestnut Villa of HFS's son Peter. HFS and Ruth already had a family of four daughters, Sylvia, Stella, Brenda and Barbara.

It was not long before the new works were operating flat out in an attempt to satisfy demand. Full production, however, came too late in the year to recoup the earlier losses due to production hold-ups and the costs of the new factory building. As a result, 1919 was the first year the company reported an operating loss. Disappointing, perhaps, but little cause for concern, as the loss was adequately covered by returns on the investment of the profits from earlier years, allowing the Morgan family to retain full financial control. Furthermore, the company had a new factory and full order books. And so it proved over the next few years as production climbed, reaching a peak of 2,300 cars in 1923.

The popularity of the Morgan Runabout in France, consequent to McMinnies' victory in the Amiens Grand Prix of 1913, had survived the war and led to a continuing demand for Morgans in that country. To meet the demand, the French agents, Darmont et Badelogue of Paris, were granted a licence at the end of 1919 to manufacture the cars in France. This both reduced pressure on the Morgan works and avoided the heavy duties imposed by the French government upon imported vehicles. Darmont manufactured several hundred cars a year before demand petered out during the late twenties.

Wartime petrol restrictions were gradually relaxed and competition motoring was allowed again from January 1919. It would be Easter 1920 before the Brooklands track was returned to a suitable state for racing, but trials commenced immediately. H. Denley was the first Morgan owner to achieve post-war successes, driving his Grand Prix Morgan to a silver medal in the Victory Cup Trial and a win in the Midland Cycle and Athletic Club's 200-mile trial. Other successes quickly followed.

The speed trial of the Essex Motor Club, held over a one-kilometre length of the

E.B. Ware created a great deal of interest during the early part of 1919 when he was out and about, with Mrs Ware and family, in his special four-seater Morgan. The public interest confirmed the need for an additional model to be added to the Morgan range. Ware noted that the additional weight on the rear wheel made no difference to the handling.

Interior views at Pickersleigh Road during the early 1920s, when the factory was working to full capacity. The views show the chassis assembly, body shop, and final erection and finishing.

seafront at Westcliffe-on-Sea in July, saw the first appearance of W. Douglas Hawkes with a Morgan. Hawkes was already an established racing driver.

During 1919 industry returned to normal peacetime production, but inflation remained high and car prices were forced to rise. By the time of the Motor Cycle Show, held at Olympia in November 1919, the post-war prices of the Runabouts had increased by about 30 per cent over the year. Eight models and a chassis were displayed at the show. They comprised two Sporting models, one with an 8hp JAP engine and one with a 10hp Precision engine, two Aero models, fitted with 10hp water-cooled engines of either JAP or MAG manufacture, two De Luxe models fitted with JAP engines, either air-cooled or water-cooled, a Grand Prix with water-cooled 10hp MAG engine, and a four-seater with a 10hp water-cooled JAP engine.

The show was the first public appearance of the four-seater Family model. Although included in the 1920 sales catalogue produced at the time of the 1919 show, the demand for other models was such that it would not be generally available until the following year. The Aero, which had first appeared in 1916, was fitted with twin Auster screens. It would remain

The 8-valve MAG-engined car, developed for the 1914 TT, was successfully used by HFS for speed hill climbs during the early post-war months. The picture shows HFS with Ruth in August 1919 at the Stile Cop Open Hill Climb.

available only to special order for a further four years. The catalogue listed JAP engines as standard, whilst MAG engines were listed under extras and, having regard to the possible supply difficulties, a note was included to the

Ware modified his pre-war single-seater JAP 1 record breaker to be both wider and longer. The radiator was shortened and a tubular fuel tank positioned behind it. The pre-war 'slipper' body was at first retained but, by the time of the BARC Brooklands in May 1920, a proper bonnet panel had been fitted. The engine was a water-cooled 976cc KT JAP.

effect that special prices would be quoted. The basic prices of the 1920 models were:

Sporting a/c	£170	Family a/c	£190
De Luxe w/c	£185	Grand Prix w/c	£185
De Luxe a/c	£175	Aero w/c	£190

The quoted prices contained a hidden increase, as the standard equipment no longer included lamps and acetylene generator, for which an extra £5 8s was asked. Other extras included a mechanical horn at £1 17s 6d, wheel discs at £4, special colour at £2, speedometer at £6, hood cover at £1 10s, clock at £4 10s, and painting number plates at 5s. A four-speed gear option was also available at £17.

Industrial Recovery and Over-Production

Rising material and labour costs were a continuing problem through 1920 and most British motor manufacturers were forced to raise prices. By the end of the year, new cars had become readily available but prices had risen beyond the reach of most buyers. However, the sporting successes of the Morgan and its economy ensured that demand for the

Runabout remained high. HFS was forced to raise prices again in November 1920, at the time of the Motor Cycle show. The Sporting and Grand Prix models with JAP 8hp engines cost respectively £206 and £218, whilst the De Luxe was priced at £215 or £228 depending upon whether an air-cooled or water-cooled JAP engine was fitted. The price of extras was also increased and Lucas electric lighting was also offered for the first time at a cost of £25.

The post-war boom conditions collapsed rather earlier in the United States than in Britain and by the end of 1920 the prices of American cars were tumbling. Ford reduced the price of the Model Ts made in both the United States and at Trafford Park in Britain. By this time the Model T was already an old-fashioned eccentric design, but it was a full five-seater made of high quality materials and with an excellent reputation for reliability. Furthermore, it was made using modern production methods at a price the British industry could not match. It sold for £195, compared with £170 asked for the cheapest Morgan.

In February 1921, William Morris became so alarmed by the accumulation of unsold cars at his works that he took the decision that was

E. B. Ware carrying out repairs at the 1921 French Cyclecar Grand Prix at Le Mans in September 1921. Ware had been unfortunate the previous year when his Morgan was dropped onto its nose as it was lifted aboard ship en route to Le Mans. He was forced to return to JAPs for engine repairs and arrived at the circuit too late to practice. In the race he suffered overheating and, continuing on one cylinder, finished outside the time limit. He was no more fortunate in 1921 when he hit and killed a dog during practice. Straightening the machine took most of the night and Ware was exhausted before the start of the race. First gear-change problems, then tyre problems resulting in the collapse of a front wheel, forced his retirement.

destined to move him to the forefront of British car manufacturers. He cut the prices of his cars by up to £100. This was a bold move, as some months earlier Bean had made similar price reductions to boost sales, but without success. The move was, however, well received and Morris quickly cleared his backlog of cars and was able to expand production. Morris's competitors were initially reluctant to follow his lead, but by the time of the October 1921 Motor Show had been forced to do so and prices were down by an average of 17 per cent. Morris's response was to announce a further reduction on the eve of the show. The four-seater Cowley model now cost £341 against its price of £525 at the start of the year. It was still significantly more expensive than the ageing Ford Model T at £195.

Against competition of this strength most light car and cyclecar manufacturers were forced out of business. Morgan continued to prosper and still enjoyed full order books. However, HFS realised that this situation could not last and that orders could as easily be lost as gained. He decided to introduce a new, bottom of the range, economy model in time for the Motorcycle Show. Called the Standard Popular model, it was derived from the Standard model first introduced in 1911, but withdrawn from the catalogue for 1915. The price, inclusive of acetylene lighting equipment, was a competitive £150; cheaper than most motorcycle combinations on the market. Morgan folklore suggests the 'Popular' name derives from a pun on the word Poplar, referring to the black Poplar timber bought cheaply from a local timber merchant and used in the body construction. The truth is that the name was intended to reflect the popular appeal of an economic machine.

The Standard Popular featured amongst a total of nine machines and a chassis displayed at the 1921 Olympia Show. The Family four-seater, making its second appearance, would become generally available during the coming year and was priced at a competitive £191. The Aero, with its ship's ventilators, snake

The advertisement placed at the time of the 1921 Olympia Show for the new Standard Popular model. The machine was fully equipped and represented exceptional value for money. The new body was not only stylish, but also was cheaper to construct.

horn, aero screens and nickel fittings, was a striking and greatly desired machine but available only to special order. The Sporting model was dropped from the 1922 range, which comprised:

Standard Popular	£150	De Luxe a/c	£175
De Luxe w/c	£185	Grand Prix w/c	£185
Family a/c	£191	Aero w/c	£235

The Light Car Challenge

The death knoll for the cyclecar and many light-car manufacturers would sound with the arrival of Sir Herbert Austin's Austin Seven. Sir Herbert had designed the car as a private venture without the approval of the Austin board of directors. Stanley Edge, a talented young

The 1914 TT racer was acquired by Douglas Hawkes and modified for short distance races by removing the large fuel tank from behind the seats and replacing it by a smaller torpedo-shaped tank containing both fuel and oil. Renamed 'Land Crab', the machine suffered severe engine reliability problems. It is seen at Brooklands in 1921.

Mr Blackwell, of Reading, with his Grand Prix model purchased new in 1922. He was so disappointed with the factory finish that he immediately dismantled the car in order to build it properly!

draughtsman at Austin's Longbridge plant, was installed at Austin's home, Lickey Grange, to prepare the drawings and the design was completed during the later months of 1921. The first public announcement of the car was made in January 1922 at the annual dinner of the Birmingham Motor Cycle Club. An inappropriate occasion in view of Sir Herbert's comment, as guest speaker, that the Seven would 'knock the motor cycle and sidecar into a cocked hat and far surpass it for comfort and passenger carrying capacity'.

The first models of the Austin Seven were demonstrated in July 1922. Sir Herbert announced the price would be £225, but in December of that year, as the first models were being distributed to dealers, the price was reduced to £165. At this price the Seven was assured sales despite public reservation over its diminutive size. However, Sir Herbert, like HFS with his Runabout some twelve years previously, recognized that full public acceptance would only be achieved once the car had been proven in competition. Within months Captain Arthur Waite, Sir Herbert's son-in-law, had won the Small Car Handicap at the

Easter Monday meeting at Brooklands, followed by the 750cc class of the Cyclecar Grand Prix at Monza in April. Very soon Gordon England was enjoying similar success with a record-breaking single-seater. This was the sort of publicity Austin craved and the Seven began to sell in increasing numbers. By October 1923, a total of 1,936 Austin Sevens had been produced.

The threat from the Austin Seven was perceived rather than real in 1922 and the Morgan order books remained full. Nevertheless, HFS appreciated that this could not continue and that both competitive pricing and sporting successes would be required to maintain sales. In July 1922 he substantially reduced the prices of his best selling models. The Standard model was offered for £135 and the Family for £165. The new prices provided little margin for profit and for production to remain viable it became essential to improve efficiency. One way that this could be achieved was by bringing the entire manufacture onto a single site. During 1922, HFS began the extension of the Pickersleigh Road works with the construction of two extra buildings at the bottom of the yard. The first of the new buildings, and the fifth in line, became the sheet-metal shop and despatch department. The second building, which extended the row of buildings to six, was used as the body shop. It included its own wood mill located adjacent to a new

wood store in the yard. Previously the bodies had been transferred between sites on an army surplus Crossley truck. With the new buildings completed only the machine shop remained at the original Worcester Road works. It would be 1929 before the entire manufacture was finally concentrated on a single site.

Racing and Record Breaking

Morgans were prominent in trials and speed events throughout the year. Douglas Hawkes returned to Morgan racing after a four-wheeler interlude with a new single-seater Morgan at Brooklands on 29 July 1922. The machine, nicknamed 'Flying Spider', had been constructed at the works during 1921. It employed a special long-wheelbase chassis constructed with a beefed-up central tube and dispensed with the two lower tubes. The narrow single-seater body was tailored to fit Hawkes and required a removable off-side panel to allow him to get in. Fitted with the 8-valve MAG engine previously used in 'Land Crab', the machine achieved second place in the three-lap handicap for 1500cc machines. It achieved its first win the following weekend in the Light Car and Cyclecar Handicap.

A further striking Morgan was that of Colonel A. Horrocks, the Morgan agent for Blackburn. Horrocks had persuaded MAG to loan him an 8-valve MAG engine, which he

Horrocks' 'Kettle'. The photo was taken in March 1923 and shows the Morgan fitted with an 8-valve Anzani engine.

fitted into a new chassis constructed, with soldered lugs for strength, by his assistant Chris Shorrock, later of supercharger fame. The machine was fitted with a streamlined, light, aluminium body with curved nose. The machine, affectionately known as the 'Kettle', achieved an easy victory on its first outing at the speed trial on the newly built Lancaster–Morecambe road.

Three Morgans were entered for the JCC 200-mile race at Brooklands on 19 August 1922. E.B.Ware drove his special narrow-bodied two-seater, JAP II, which was adapted for the purpose with an extra torpedo-shaped fuel tank attached to the near side of the body and a second extra tank in the scuttle. Harry Martin entered his Anzani-engined racer. Douglas Hawkes drove a new machine based upon a wide-tracked Aero chassis. The body was flat sided and a pointed petrol tank replaced the bonnet. The oil tank was located across the flat tail behind the seats. The engine was a special air-cooled 8-valve ohc Anzani. All three machines were fitted with a loop over the rear wheel to provide anchorage for a Hartford shock-absorber. In the race, the machines suffered a variety of mishaps and all were forced to retire before half distance, Hawkes with a blown engine, Martin with a misfire and Ware with a cracked water-jacket.

Despite the disappointments of the JCC 200-mile race, by and large fortune smiled on the Morgan entrants throughout the year with numerous wins and best times. In the ACU Six-Days Trial, for example, gold medals were won by the entire team, comprising the two-seater models of HFS with a 978cc JAP, S. Hall with a 1096cc MAG and W. Carr with a 1090cc Anzani. Hawkes made amends for the 200-mile race failure by taking his car back to Brooklands, prior to its closure for winter repairs, to attack class H2 records. The records for 5 miles, 10 miles, flying $\frac{1}{2}$ mile and flying kilometre were obtained at 85.14mph (136.22km/h), 81.7mph (130.72km/h), 87.89mph (140.62km/h) and 86.94mph (139.1km/h) respectively.

Price reductions were announced in October. The air-cooled Standard, De Luxe and Family models were made available for £135, £155 and £160 respectively, whilst the Grand Prix, De Luxe and Family models with a water-cooled engine, either 8hp JAP or 10hp Blackburne, were priced respectively at £160, £165 and £170. Alternative engine options with the water-cooled models were the 10hp MAG at £7 extra or the 10hp ohv Anzani at £5 extra.

The 'flat-sided' or '200-mile' Aero displayed at the 1922 Olympia show was based upon the machine used by Hawkes in the JCC 200-mile race at Brooklands. It was finished in polished aluminium and nickel with black mudguards and fitted with a water-cooled Anzani engine.

Eight separate models and a stripped chassis were exhibited at the 1922 Olympia show. Particularly striking amongst the range on display was a new sporting Aero model, based on the lines of Hawkes' 200-Mile racer. Subsequently referred to as the 'flat-sided Aero' or '200-mile Aero', it featured a flat-sided body with flat top to the tail and was finished in polished aluminium and nickel plate with black mudguards. It was powered by an ohv 8hp water-cooled Anzani engine fitted with a Binks two-jet carburettor

Further price reductions were made to coincide with the Olympia show and the range of Morgan models for 1923 comprised:

1923 Standard Popular.

Standard a/c	£128	De Luxe a/c	£148
Family a/c	£153	Grand Prix w/c	£155
Aero w/c	£200		

An additional £10 was asked for the De Luxe and Family models fitted with a water-cooled engine. Acetylene lighting was fitted as standard, although a Lucas dynamo lighting set could be provided for an additional £10. Engine options comprised JAP, MAG, Blackburne and Anzani.

Despite the economic pressures and the downturn in demand for motor vehicles, no less than seven manufacturers, including Morgan, displayed cyclecars at Olympia. Not surprisingly, single-seat utility machines, powered by the 269cc Villiers two-stroke engine, were offered by two manufacturers, Harper and Xtra, at about £100. Most manufacturers, however, preferred to use the ubiquitous 8hp JAP V-twin. Soundly engineered machines were offered by L.S.D., New Hudson and Scott, with prices starting from £146 9s, £195 and £176 8s, respectively.

Compared with other cyclecars and light cars on the market during 1923, the fully equipped Morgan was competitively priced. HFS's policy of selling a sporting cyclecar of high quality and excellent value continued to appeal to potential buyers. Thus, whilst other manufacturers suffered declining sales, resulting in many ceasing trading, Morgan continued to prosper. The company could no longer enjoy the commercial buffer provided by long waiting lists, but was still able to sell all the machines that could be produced. No doubt sales were obtained as a result of the Morgan's established reputation for reliability and value for money. The appeal of the machine, however, lay in its sporting potential. During the year there would be no shortage of competition and record-breaking successes to maintain public attention.

Performance, Economy and Retardation

Ware, driving a Standard model fitted with the then new KTC engine, had missed overall victory in the JCC General Efficiency Trial in March 1922 due to losing marks in the braking test. The rear wheel had locked on the slippery surface, causing the car to skid to a halt and victory, together with the prestigious Westall Cup, to pass to Godfrey driving a GN. No similar misfortune could be entertained in future and for the 1923 event Ware's Standard model was fitted with internal expanding front

brakes operated by a hand lever and Bowden cable. The Morgan lapped the Brooklands circuit at 55.71mph (89.14km/h) and averaged 13.4mph (21.4km/h) up the test hill, was best on standing start acceleration and top gear acceleration and achieved 56mpg (5.05ltr/100km). It was also best in the breaking test! Ware scored 1,743 marks out of a total of 2,000 and convincingly won the Westall Cup; a performance he would repeat the following year. Immediately following Ware's success in the 1923 event, Morgan offered front wheel brakes as an option on all existing models at a cost of £6.

Other successes quickly followed during the year. The Morgan team of HFS, Bill Carr and George Goodall won the team prize and individual gold awards in the Victory Trial. The London–Lands End Trial saw seventeen Morgans entered and seven gold and three bronze medals won. Morgans were also in the forefront when speed trials got underway in April. The machines to beat in the early events were the wide-track flat-sided Aeros of HFS, Norman Norris and Goodall. The dominant power unit was the 8-valve Anzani, which was favoured by all the fast drivers. Norris, driving the ex-Hawkes 200-mile race Aero, began the season with an Anzani engine but was able to persuade Blackburne, through his friendship with Cecil Burney, a director of the company, to supply him with a special racing engine. This was fitted to his Aero at the Morgan

works and proved successful on its first outing at the end of April when it won the Brooklands Short Handicap race at 76mph (122km/h).

Morgan sporting successes throughout the year must have raised HFS's expectations for the JCC 200-mile race held at Brooklands on 13 October. The event, however, proved there was no room for complacency. The Morgan team comprised Beart and Norris, both Blackburne powered, and Hawkes, who was using the 8-valve ohc water-cooled Anzani engine from 'Flying Spider'. In addition, private entries were made by Ware, with his JAP II powered by an extended bore (85.5 × 95mm) KT water-cooled side-valve engine, and by Horrocks, who failed to start. Beart suffered engine problems during practice and was forced to retire as he approached the start line. Hawkes was well down the field when forced to retire after thirty-one laps with a broken valve collar. Norris lapped consistently at 84mph (134km/h) and pressed the leading three Salmsons hard before falling back and retiring with stripped timing gears on the forty-fifth lap. Only Ware completed the race, but was well down the field having made pit stops to repair a puncture and to replace a steering connection.

Ware and Hawkes had for several years been competing to set speed records. Ware had achieved more than 86mph (138km/h) in the 1100cc (H2) class in his single-seater and by the end of 1923 Hawkes raised the British Class H2 flying-start kilometre and mile records to 92.17mph (147.47km/h) and 90.38mph (144.6km/h).

In October 1923 Norris was winning races at Brooklands at 86.77mph (138.83km/h) with his Aero model fitted with a new racing Blackburne engine. In November he captured British and World records at 91.94mph (147.1km/h)

Two newcomers, who would go on to make their mark in Morgan circles, made their first competition appearances in 1923. Eric Fernihough, a young student, entered his stripped-down De Luxe with air-cooled side-valve JAP for the Spread Eagle Hill Climb near Shaftesbury. He went home with six cups and made fastest time. Clive Lones, a power-station engineer, took his side-valve Blackburne-powered Grand Prix to the Madresfield Speed Trials in July. The engine, which had been self-tuned, proved to be the equal of the 8-valve Anzani units and allowed Lones to be up with the leaders.

HFS could look back on 1923 with some satisfaction. Despite a downturn in the cyclecar market, Morgan had achieved a record year with 2,300 cars produced and a profit of £40,851. The year would prove to be the peak year of three-wheeler production.

The Aero, which for several years had been available only to special order, was finally listed as a catalogue model at the Olympia Show in October 1923. The model was now fitted with a rounded tail and featured an external gear-lever alongside the brake lever. It was fitted with a side-valve water-cooled engine and, at £150, cost £5 more than the Grand Prix model. The earlier body style remained available to special order and was known as the 200-mile Aero. A further un-catalogued model on display was a special single-seater with a Blackburne engine: priced at £160, it came with a 75mph (120km/h) guarantee. Price reductions were offered across the range and the cheapest Standard model, complete with acetylene lighting, was available for £110.

HFS, accompanied by Ruth, tackles a ford during the 1924 ACU Stock Machine Trial.

Further small price reductions were made in December and the Morgan range for 1924 comprised:

Standard a/c	£110	De Luxe a/c	£130
Family a/c	£135	Grand Prix w/c	£138
Aero w/c	£148		

Either a JAP or Blackburne engine could be specified. The Aero with an ohv racing Blackburne engine was listed at £160; the same engine was available for an extra £12 on other models. The De Luxe and Family models could be supplied with a water-cooled engine for an additional £10. The option of a 10hp British Anzani engine, either air- or water-cooled, cost an additional £5.

An electric lighting set cost an additional £8 on the Standard model, but was included in the specification of the other models. Hoods were standard on all models except the Aero, for which it was a £3 extra. Front wheel brakes were still listed as extras on all models.

To put the prices into perspective it is worth noting that at this time the Ford Model T was available, fully equipped, for £110 and the Austin Seven cost £165. Certain primitive cyclecars were available for less than £100, whilst £60 would purchase the LAD, a machine similar to a motorized sidecar with tiller steering.

Unsafe or Too Competitive?

The sporting events of 1924 opened on 23 February with the Colmore Trial. Seven Morgans were entered and, despite difficult conditions, won five medals. These comprised gold medals for Carr, Horton and HFS, a silver medal for Chippendale and a bronze medal for Goodall. Three weeks later, Ware achieved his second consecutive win in the JCC General Efficiency Trial with a score of 330 marks out of a total of 385. The season continued with gold medals for HFS, Goodall and Carr in the ACU Stock Machine Trial.

Other successes followed in rapid succession

Clive Lones

Clive Lones, an electrical engineer, was an enthusiastic motorcyclist, having first ridden a bike at the age of fourteen. However, new wife Nel, a Malvern girl, took exception to continually getting wet on Clive's Indian motor-cycle and persuaded him that a Morgan was much to be preferred. A 1913 Runabout was the outcome and provided transport for thousands of miles in all conditions. Two years later, in 1923, the couple bought a new Grand Prix model with side-valve Blackburne engine.

Left *Lones racer at Brooklands, 1932.*

The Lones racer with some of the awards gained. The car had previously been successfully raced at Brooklands by Robin Jackson; it was about to have further use as Mrs Lones' shopping car.

and, as in previous years, Morgans dominated the sporting calendar. However, past achievements were overshadowed by an accident in the Junior Car Club's 200-mile race, held at Brooklands on 20 September, which was to have a profound effect on Morgans and three-wheelers in general. The race was contested by three Morgans, each reputed to be capable of lapping at over 90mph (144km/h). HFS

Learning of the Madresfield Speed Trials he decided to enter, but first needed to tune the Blackburne for more power. This he carried out following the do-it-yourself advice given in a book by George Newman of Ivy Precision Motorcycles. Up against an entry of eighteen Morgans, including ohv and 8-valve Anzani-powered machines, he came second to George Goodall driving the factory's racing Aero with ohv Blackburne. The bug had bitten and Clive went on to buy one of the ex-200-Mile Race cars from HFS. Thus began the extraordinary career of an owner/driver and of his intrepid passenger, Mrs Lones. Such was his enthusiasm that Clive spent his holidays in the experimental workshops of JAP His many achievements with Morgans included:

- Obtaining over 200 firsts in speed events
- Winning the Light Car Grand Prix in 1928, 1929 and 1930 and gaining second in 1932 and 1934
- Obtaining thirty-seven world records at Brooklands in a single season
- Being the only person awarded a Brooklands Gold Star for a 100mph (160km/h) lap in a 750cc un-supercharged Morgan
- Being one of only two persons awarded a Gold star in the 1000cc class
- Achieving 68mph (109km/h) with a 350 cc JAP single

In 1936 Clive created a four-wheel special Morgan, named 'Tiger Cat', for sprinting, by grafting a GN rear axle and quarter-elliptic rear-springing to run with the Morgan two-speed transmission. Post-war he enjoyed success in 500cc racing with his 'Tiger Cat' and 'Tiger Kitten' specials; the latter comprising an inverted Austin Seven chassis with Morgan independent front suspension and a Speedway JAP engine.

entered two wide-track flat-sided Aero Morgans, with ohv Blackburne engines, to be driven by Norman Norris and Harold Beart. A third, similar, car was commissioned by Ware and privately entered. It was fitted with a prototype ohv water-cooled JAP engine. All three cars were fitted with additional five-gallon fuel tanks under the chassis backbone tubes and small oil-tanks on the tails. Large external silencers were fitted to comply with new track regulations.

The Morgans were beset with problems from the start of the practice sessions. Beart and Norris were both working to the last minute before the race to rectify problems of ignition and overheating. Ware suffered with blown head-gaskets and experienced trouble with the drive chains. His passenger during the practice sessions was a young JAP apprentice, but Prestwich considered a more experienced passenger was needed for the race and chose motorcycle racer, T.R. Allchin, to accompany Ware. The race started badly for Ware, as his engine refused

E.B. Ware at the pits, prior to his accident, in the 1924 JCC 200-mile race.

to pick up and he was immediately amongst the tail enders. It was not long before a broken top gear dog forced him to pull into the pits. Further troubles followed requiring the car to be pushed into the pits. For adjustments. He was followed in by Beart, with a flat tyre, and Norris, who coasted in with a broken top gear chain. Once back in the race, Ware settled down and began lapping at around 90mph (144km/h), to improve his race position. On his thirty-third lap the rear wheel began to wobble. Ware, despite looking anxiously behind, continued at the same pace until two laps later, when the car swerved across the track and collided with the iron fencing opposite the pits. The car spun several times, flinging out the occupants, before overturning. Ware landed on grass, but Allchin was less fortunate and landed on the concrete.

Beart's engine initially refused to restart following the tyre change. When it did restart he deemed it wise to return after two laps to increase the clearance between the rear tyre and bodywork. Norris was still running at the end of the race, but well out of contention with the winners.

The accident to Ware's car occurred when the tread, stripped from the rear tyre, became entangled with a rear drive chain and caused the rear wheel to lock solid. Both Ware and Allchin required hospitalization but eventually recovered. Ware sought compensation from his employers, JAP, from tyre manufacturers Dunlop, and from Morgan for the extensive surgery required and for convalescence after the crash. All the firms denied liability and Ware lost his claim.

The immediate repercussion of the accident was a ban placed by the JCC on three-wheelers racing alongside four-wheelers in future 200-Mile Races and the General Efficiency Trial. The BARC and other sanctioning clubs fully supported the ban, thus bringing to an end an era when the diminutive Morgan could humble expensive racing cars. Not surprisingly the ban was the subject of considerable controversy in the correspondence columns of the magazines. George Morgan, writing to the *Cyclecar*, expressed surprise that the Junior Car Club, which had started life as the Cyclecar Club, would no longer admit to membership owners of the one remaining cyclecar. Others surmised that the ban would give four-wheelers a chance to win the Westall Cup, as three-wheelers had proven unbeatable in any general efficiency trial. The JCC were insistent, however, that the ban was for safety reasons and remained adamant. It would be another four years and require creation of the New Cyclecar Club before three-wheelers would again race against four-wheelers at Brooklands.

The model range for 1925 remained largely unchanged from the previous year, although prices were again reduced. At the bottom of the range, the Standard model, without the acetylene lighting of the previous year, could be purchased for £95; the first time since the war that it was possible to purchase a Morgan for less than £100. Equipped for the road with electric lighting, the price of the Standard increased to £105. Other models in the range were reduced by between £10 and £13. The following were catalogued models for 1925:

Standard a/c	£95	De Luxe a/c	£120
Family a/c	£123	Grand Prix w/c	£128
Aero w/c	£135		

The JAP 8hp engine was fitted as standard to all models. An alternative water-cooled engine could be supplied with the De Luxe and Family models for an additional £10. The ohv Anzani engine remained an option on all models except the Standard for an additional £5, but the ohv racing Blackburne was only listed as available with the Aero and cost an additional £12. A self-starter was listed as an extra for the first time and cost an additional £12 if ordered with a new machine. Front wheel brakes remained optional at £6 extra. Balloon tyres were also listed for the first time and cost £2 per wheel.

At the time of the Olympia Show, the *Motor*

George Goodall makes light of passing an immovable obstacle during the 1925 ACU Stock Machine Trial and leaves the motorcycle combination struggling in his wake.

Cycle described the Morgan as 'the sole survivor of the British three-wheeler' and added that 'the Morgan preserves its simple mechanical features unchanged, because it has justified itself in every class of competitive event'. The Aero models were particularly well liked. They were described as being the last word in racy appearance, although somewhat lacking in room for both the occupants and in the provision for carrying luggage. It was noted that for purely sporting use the Aero Morgan compared in performance with high-powered semi-racing cars of five or six times the price.

The cause of the remark in the *Motor Cycle* review was the first appearance at the show of a new sporting French tri-car of advanced design. Described by its makers as a car on three wheels, the D'Yrsan was fitted with a 4-cylinder, water-cooled, engine of 750cc. It was fitted with a conventional three-speed and reverse gearbox with central control. The chassis was of tubular construction and very Morgan-like in appearance, with enclosed propeller shaft, rear bevel box and chain final drive. Two transverse, inverted, semi-elliptic springs supported the steering pivots to provide independent front suspension, whilst the rear suspension used quarter-elliptic springs in

the manner of the Morgan. Shock absorbers were fitted all round. The machines, which were fitted with front wheel brakes, Dunlop Cord tyres and acetylene lighting, were priced from £150 up to £160 for the Sports Model with its claimed 70mph (112km/h) performance. The D'Yrsan could already claim sporting successes in its native France by the time of its show appearance and would no doubt have been the subject of close scrutiny by HFS. It is interesting to conjecture the influence it might have had on the future 4-cylinder Model F.

The JCC ban on three-wheelers did not prevent Morgans from taking part, with their usual measure of success, in all competitive events for which they remained eligible. For several months these had included public road speed trials and Morgans had continued to demonstrate that they were more than a match for any four-wheeler. Speed events on public roads had technically been illegal, but were run with the consent of the local police provided public inconvenience was minimal. The events came to an end, however, when the RAC and ACU decided to discontinue the issue of permits following injury to a spectator, struck by Giveen's Bugatti, at an event at Kop, organized by the Essex MC on 28 March 1925.

More Racing and Record Breaking – the First 100mph Cyclecar Record

Beart and Norris entered their 200-mile race Blackburne Aeros in the BMCRC three-wheeler championship race at Brooklands in October 1924 and each was keen to demonstrate who had the faster Morgan. Although Norris led in the initial stages, Beart took the lead on the final lap and proved the victor at an average of 83.99mph (134.38km/h). Beart returned to Brooklands during the record breaking spree held in the period preceding the 1925 Motorcycle Show and successfully attacked British and world records in the 1100cc classes. His best speed, of a little under 95mph (152km/h), demonstrated that the magic ton was now in sight. It whet his

The advertisement from October 1925 could rightly claim the Morgan Runabout to be unrivalled!

Mr. Beart on a Morgan at Brooklands, beat all 1100 c.c. records for mile and kilometre at the amazing speed of

104·6 m.p.h.

For Speed, Comfort, Economy and Reliability combined

The **Morgan Runabout**

is unrivalled.

Prices from £95 (with electric light). Tax £4.

A Morgan driven by Mr. Carr, selected to represent Great Britain in the **6 days International** won a Gold Medal with loss of 1 mark only and was one of the Motor Cycle Championship Team.

In the 3 great Six Days Trials of 1925 (English, Scottish, and International) 4 Morgans were entered and all obtained Gold Medals.

MORGAN MOTOR CO., LTD. - - - MALVERN LINK.

appetite to become the first person to record a speed of over 100mph in a three-wheeler. The only problem was that he considered the Malvern product to be insufficiently robust to withstand the pounding it would receive at this speed from the bumpy surface of the Brooklands track. Undeterred, he decided to construct his own version of a properly engineered Morgan suitable for racing and record breaking.

His first outing with the new 'Morgan' netted Class H2 (three-wheel cyclecars, with passenger, not exceeding 1100cc) records for the standing 10 kilometres, flying 5 kilometres and flying 5 miles at 88.78mph (142.05km/h), 99.62mph (159.39km/h) and 99.10mph (158.56km/h), respectively. The figures were tantalizingly close to the magic 100mph (160km/h) and Beart returned to the track a few days later, on 24 July 1925, to complete the task. The flying 5-miles figure raised the record to 99.67mph (159.47km/h) but was still short of his objective. The flying 5-kilometres figure, however, raised the figure to 100.4mph (160.64km/h), to break the 100mph barrier for the first time by a cyclecar.

Beart continued with his record-breaking endeavours throughout the year. On 19 August he raised the Class H2 for the flying mile and kilometre to 102.65mph (164.24km/h) and 103.37mph (165.39km/h). The speeds were the average of runs in opposite directions and one such run of the flying kilometre was at a speed of 104.68mph (167.49km/h), which placed Beart's Morgan as the fastest un-supercharged car in the world under 1500cc. On 12 September he again took to the track to take the long distance records. The 100-mile record was taken at 91.54mph (146.46km/h), annexing in the process the 50-kilometre, 50-mile and 1-hour records. The weight of Beart's Morgan made the machine unsuitable for the short-distance standing-start record attempts and left the door open for Robin Jackson. On 7 October Jackson seized the opportunity and, driving his stripped Blackburne Aero without passenger, established Class H1 standing-start

Harold Beart and the 100mph Record Breaker

Harold Beart's involvement with Morgans began during the early 1920s whilst he was still an engineering apprentice. Keen to put into practice his engineering theory, he rented two lock-up garages near Croydon railway station, to be used as workshop and garage accommodation, and began tuning Morgans for racing at Brooklands. His first outings on the track were with a tuned Blackburne Aero and in a short space of time he became established as one of the faster drivers. In recognition, HFS helped him to set up as a Morgan agent in Kingston-on-Thames. Success nurtured an ambition to be the first person to exceed 100mph in a three-wheeler and for this he needed a specially strengthened racer.

Beart built his car, along Morgan lines, during 1924. Beefed-up chassis lugs were cast and the chassis assembled using heavier-gauge tubing. The front cross tubes were spaced apart more than normal to allow greater spring travel. Sliding axles of cast steel replaced the standard bronze units and incorporated a forward projecting bracket used to attach a Hartford shock absorber. The lower mounting of the Hartford was a steel bracket located below the cross tube, free to swivel about bronze bushes. The tubes, about which the sliding axles moved, were replaced by hardened and ground Ubas steel pins screwed into position and arranged for pressure-gun lubrication. The rear quarter-elliptic springs were each constructed of seven leaves of graduated thickness. A single Hartford damper was positioned over the rear wheel and attached to a bracket fitted to the top of the bevel box and a stirrup fitted to the fork

ends. Spring-loaded ball joints were used for the steering connections and an epicyclic steering reduction box, ex-Ford T, fitted. Braking was on the front wheels only and controlled by a hand lever, alongside the gear lever, outside the body.

The gear selector mechanism was spring loaded to prevent the drive dogs springing apart at high speed. A press button cut-out switch for the M.L. magneto was fitted to the top of the gear lever. Depressing the button momentarily slowed the engine to allow instant gear changing without slipping the clutch or changing the throttle opening. A pressurized drip lubrication system provided a constant oil feed to the chains and bevels.

The engine was a water-cooled ohv Blackburne of 1098cc (85 × 96.8mm) fitted with racing cams and high compression heads. The carburettor was a B & B 'mouse-trap' operated by a foot pedal and Bowden cable. The gear ratios of 3.33 and 5.95 to 1 allowed in excess of 60mph (96km/h) on the bottom ratio and 100mph (160km/h) at 4,300rpm on the top ratio.

The streamlining of Harold Beart's record breaker followed aircraft practice. The car incorporated few, if any, genuine Morgan components.

A 7000-Mile Road Test of the Aero

The *Light Car and Cyclecar* carried out a road test of the Aero Morgan in May 1925, followed in November by an article titled '7,000 Miles in a 1925 Aero Morgan' in which 'Shacklepin' described experiences with a Blackburne-engined model. The article, unusually for its time, included as many brickbats as bouquets.

The journey home from Malvern Link was interrupted to discover the cause of stiff steering and a harshness, which was traced to the majority of moving parts, such as steering joints, dog clutches, clutch thrust races, and so on, being in need of lubricant.

The hood was disliked as it created appalling draughts and restricted vision to an alarming extent. Subsequent experience suggested it was better to keep the hood furled and maintain a reasonable speed to sweep the rain over one's head.

The clutch thrust race required frequent lubrication and excess lubricant was flung over the friction linings causing clutch slip.

The front brakes were praised, but the application of either rear brake on greasy roads involved a risk of skidding. 'Shacklepin' toyed with the idea of redesigning the braking to provide a coupled system.

The dynamo output was inadequate, as the use of the headlights resulted in a slow discharge from the battery.

It was considered that more padding was required to the seat squab and possibly 2in greater body width was required for touring.

On the plus side the performance was good with 70mph (112km/h) available in top gear and 48–50mph (77–80km/h) in second gear. The paint, varnish and plating of the body were also considered of the very best.

'Shacklepin' concluded:

> To sum up, I can say, without fear of contradiction, that the Aero-Morgan is a cyclecar which is particularly well adapted to the high-speed touring enthusiast, and at the same time it is a sufficiently all round vehicle to be suitable also as a hack, but one which, nevertheless, can at all times be relied upon to make drivers of other cars 'sit up and take notice'.

kilometre and mile records at 64.30mph (102.88km/h) and 69.70mph (111.52km/h), respectively. He immediately returned to the track with a passenger to claim the corresponding Class H2 records at 64.04mph (102.46km/h) and 71.03mph (113.65km/h), respectively.

The 1926 model range announced at the Olympia Show held during October 1925 was again unchanged. The cheapest model, the Standard, could still be purchased for £95 and electric lighting was now included within the specification rather than at £10 extra. The Family model was reduced by £7 and the remaining models by £5. The catalogued models for 1926 comprised:

Standard a/c	£95	De Luxe a/c	£115
Family a/c	£116	Grand Prix w/c	£123
Aero w/c	£130		

Side-valve 8hp JAP engines remained the standard fitment. They now incorporated the larger valves and ports of the single-camshaft sports KTC engine and the water-cooled version was given a revised water jacket. An ohv Anzani engine was still offered on all models, except the Standard, for an additional £5. The Aero fitted with the Blackburne engine cost £142. Prior to the show, JAP had announced a new 1096cc LTOW engine, which was based upon the ohv water-cooled engine used by Ware in the 1924 200-mile race. In standard trim it was claimed to produce 32bhp at 3,000rpm, whilst the use of domed pistons, to raise compression, was expected to boost output to over 50bhp! The LTOW engine could be fitted to the Aero, but was not catalogued.

Eleven models, including a nickel-plated chassis, were displayed on the Morgan stand. The *Motor Cycle* considered the three Aero models on display to be very racy and the colour schemes were described as 'very striking, not to say startling'. The Blackburne model was in a delicate sky-blue, picked out in red, with a red chassis. The Anzani model was painted cream with a red chassis. The side-valve JAP

Morgans were also able to show their paces against four-wheelers on the Southport sands. The photograph, dated from July 1926, shows Clive Lones and Syd Keay, with Mucklow's G.N. in the foreground.

model was finished in a peculiar dark grey, having the appearance of glittering carborundum powder, which was described as crystalline grey. The remaining models on display comprised two each of the Standard, De Luxe and Family models, illustrating the various engine options, and a Grand Prix with water-cooled JAP. The bodies of the De Luxe and Family models were revised with 1in higher sides and fitted with improved hoods for easier access and double-pane windscreens. Front wheel brakes remained an extra, but were now reduced to £4; they were fitted to only one machine on display, an Aero.

Despite the increasing availability of cheap light cars, the three-wheeler, and Morgan in particular, continued to retain a popular appeal. Only two three-wheeler cyclecar manufacturers, Morgan and D'Yrsan, had exhibited at the 1924 Motorcycle Show. At the 1925 show they were joined by Omega and Coventry-Victor, who each displayed a single model.

Morgans continued to enjoy successes in record breaking and trials. Eric Fernihough, whilst an engineering undergraduate at Cambridge, built himself a single-cylinder Morgan special using a 1925 push-rod ohv JAP of 494cc. This proved highly successful, providing

Fernihough with victory in the 600cc class and a second place, to Robin Jackson, in the unlimited sidecar class on its first outing at the inter-varsity speed trials. The machine was subsequently used for racing and record breaking at Brooklands. On 31 March 1926 he obtained Class I flying start 5-mile and 5-kilometre records at 73.12mph (116.99km/h) and 73.37mph (117.39km/h), respectively, and standing start records for 10-mile and 10-kilometre at 69.65mph (111.44km/h) and 70.37mph (112.59km/h), respectively.

A Sporting Four-Seater and Chassis Improvements

In 1926, Arthur Maskell, a London Morgan agent, took delivery of a Blackburne-engined Aero with a sporting four-seater body comprising the rear part of a Family model grafted onto the front of the Aero. Maskell lost no time in entering the machine in trials with a full complement of three passengers. He obtained a silver medal in the London–Land's End Trial in April and a gold in the London–Edinburgh in May. The machine proved popular with enthusiasts, but it would be 1931 before it was offered as a catalogued model.

'Sportsman, Family Man, Tourist or just an average Motorist – there is a Morgan Runabout to suit you' was the claim made in the 1927 sales brochure. The Grand Prix model was discontinued, but the remaining machines

Another Morgan agent to recognize the advantages of the Family Aero was Freddie James. The car was manufactured in 1926 although the photograph dates from two years later.

HFS, with Ruth as passenger, approaches a hairpin bend and an intrepid photographer during the 1926 Derbyshire Trial. The weights on the rear panel of the Aero were used to aid traction.

catered for all tastes and represented excellent value. At first glance the models appeared to be unchanged, but closer examination revealed numerous technical refinements. The chassis of the De Luxe, Family and Aero models had been lengthened and widened allowing more commodious bodies to be fitted with greater leg-room. The bevel box had been redesigned to accept a larger pinion bearing, the counter-shaft, dogs, rear fork bearings and rear axle had been strengthened, and there was now ample clearance between the chains and tyres even when the largest tyres were used. All the models, except the Standard, now featured 7in front brakes. Grease gun lubrication was provided and 4in Dunlop tyres fitted. The internal appearance of the cars was enhanced by use of mottled aluminium dashboards.

Prices for 1927 were reduced across the range. The bottom of the range Standard model, now fitted with electric hooter and double-pane windscreen, was reduced by £6 to £89. The De Luxe and Family models were reduced by £5 to £110 and £111 respectively, with an additional £10 for the JAP water-cooled engine. The Aero was available with the ohv Anzani engine for £127, or with a 10/40hp Blackburne or ohv JAP engine for £140. An electric self-starter was available on all models for £10 extra.

The display of 1927 models at the Olympia Show, held in October 1926, also included two additional machines available to special order. Prominently displayed were two 'Super' Aeros fitted with V-section mudguards and one-piece bodies. The bonnet sills were dispensed with and the bonnet formed in-unit with the body to create a clean line from radiator to tail. The model was offered with either JAP or Blackburne engine at £145, with delivery taking two or more months. The second machine was a Family Aero based upon the machine driven by Maskell in the London–Land's End and other trials. The front of the machine was exactly similar to the ordinary two-seater Aero and the body was constructed on the lines of the Family model. It was priced at £142.

At Olympia, Morgan faced competition from three other three-wheeler manufacturers. Both Coventry-Victor and Omega were making their second show appearance. Coventry-Victor offered touring, chummy and sports models; prices ranging from £99 15s to £125. Omega displayed touring and sports models. The newcomer to the show was the Hilton-Pacey, which was powered by a 500cc single-cylinder engine and priced at £65, without lighting. The *Light Car and Cyclecar* reporter, 'Shacklepin', in his review of the three-wheelers at Olympia, bemoaned the fact that one was still unable to obtain a model fitted with a reverse gear:

To my certain knowledge the absence of a reverse in the specification of three-wheelers drives very large numbers of motorcyclists when they seek added comfort to take a four-wheeler car right away, when a three-wheeler would be more suitable both for their requirements and their pockets. It is not the effort so much as the indignity of pushing a car which is the principle objection.

In the spring of 1926, the Motor Cycling Club imposed a ban on its trade members from competing in its trials with effect from the London–Exeter trial at Christmas 1926. This must have proved a disappointment to HFS, who was a regular and successful competitor.

Selling the Morgan Three-Wheeler

Probably the greatest difficulty which confronts the trader who is endeavouring to secure a sale for the Morgan three-wheeler, is the apparent prejudice which the average person has against the three-wheeler. That such a prejudice exists there can be no doubt; that it is unreasonable all who are familiar with this handy little vehicle will agree.

The above were the opening remarks to an article on selling the Morgan three-wheeler, which appeared in the *Motor Cycle and Cycle Trader* in July 1926. It is of interest now as it gives an insight into the public perception of the machine in the mid-twenties; a period of gradually declining sales. Rather than extol the technical features to effect a sale, the salesman was advised first to scotch popular misconceptions concerning safety, namely a tendency to skid on greasy roads or wet tramlines and instability resulting in the vehicle being easily turned over. A test ride with an experienced Morgan driver was suggested to demonstrate that stability and roadworthiness are selling features rather than points to be smoothed over. Skidding due to tramlines, a common bugbear, was considered no more of a problem than with a four-wheeler, whilst the direct steering of the Morgan facilitated the correction of any tendency to skid when attempting to pull the wheel away from the tramline. The test ride would also demonstrate the comfort of the machine, its exceptional liveliness and its ability to climb hills in top gear. Mention should also be made of 'reliability which can become positively monotonous'!

Once acquainted with the performance of the Morgan it was time to draw attention to its sporting achievements and the many competition successes against motorcycle combinations and cars. It was then appropriate to discuss technical matters; emphasis being placed upon the simplicity of the design. 'There is no complicated mechanism of any description, in fact, nothing which even the most unmechanically minded could fail to understand.' The power units utilized, either JAP or Blackburne, were considered a recommendation for the machine.

The last objection to the Morgan to be addressed was rear tyre trouble. This bugbear had inconvenienced Morgan owners since the early days. However, the position was now improved and the prospective purchaser should be shown the new design of rear fork, which allowed the wheel to be removed with ease without removal of the drive chains.

Finally, it was suggested the machine should be identified as the link between the sidecar combination and the car, providing the comfort of the latter with the low initial cost and upkeep of the former. Detailed technical improvement, without major revision of the design ensured minimum depreciation and excellent value for money.

The Morgan Standard, with its short chassis, had for many years been the favoured machine for trials use. By 1927, however, the ohv J.A.P. Aeros were gaining popularity. This photograph is of HFS and Ruth in the 1927 Victory Cup Trial.

It did little, however, to stem the tide of Morgan successes. In the 1926 London–Exeter no less than twenty-one Morgans entered and the total medal count comprised eleven gold, three silver and a bronze. Even greater success followed in the London-Edinburgh when fourteen Morgan starters came away with eleven gold and three silver medals.

Learning the Lessons to Create the Super Sports

The importance of a low centre of gravity had been appreciated ever since the first Cyclecar Grand Prix in 1913. Further lessons on the benefits of ultra-low build, combined with a widened track, were learnt during the 1927 racing season.

It required Dick Caesar, a Cambridge undergraduate, to demonstrate the advantages of an ultra-low build. For his twenty-first birthday, Caesar's parents had bought him a Blackburne Aero, which he used in the 1926 Intervarsity Trial. With the trial over, Caesar modified the car by widening the front track and lowering the tail by about 6in. The latter was done by the simple expedient of reversing the rear spring hangers to reside below, rather than above the rear wheel spindle. A hole was cut in the top of the tail panel, to give clearance for the rear wheel, and fitted with a special cowl. Once completed the car was offered

for sale to a friend, Steward Brownbill, who farmed near Liverpool and had expressed an interest in racing at Southport. The Aero was entered at the Southport meeting on 9 April and, as Caesar had built it, his friend offered him the first drive whilst he rode as passenger. During practice for the 10-mile sidecar race the car hit a gully in the sand at high speed and Brownbill was lucky to remain in the car. Thoroughly shaken by the experience, Brownbill persuaded a third member of the team, Geoffrey Armitage, to take his place and became a spectator as his car gained an easy victory. The success of the widened and lowered Aero was noted by the other racers, who were quick to introduce similar modifications to their own Morgans.

At an earlier Southport meeting in September, Ron Horton had overturned his JAP-powered racer in the 10-mile car race. The Morgan was rebuilt at the factory with a widened and strengthened wide 'B' chassis. The front was lowered by cranking the top axle tube and inverting the lugs for the lower tube. When the machine was returned in May it had been fitted with a slim streamlined two-seater body of beetle-back style. Vertical side-panels fully enclosed the rear wheel and the rear panel was hinged to allow access to the wheel and transmission. The style would subsequently be adopted for the Super Sports Aero.

The cranking of the front cross tubes in order to lower the front of the car was introduced following an incident when Lones broke the crosshead tie-bar on his Aero during a Brooklands race meeting in July. The breakage allowed the front chassis tubes to bend but, far from upsetting the handling, Lones found the bend actually made handling easier; indeed the greater the bend, the better the handling. Lones passed this information onto HFS and a few days later was invited to the factory to see a new chassis with cranked tubes set-up on jigs. The chassis was built into an Aero for Lones.

Ronnie Horton with his new beetle-back Morgan. It is fitted with a Blackburne KMB engine.

Racing Against Four-Wheelers – The New Cyclecar Club

The ban, imposed by the JCC following Ware's accident in 1924, remained a subject for resentment by Morgan owners keen to compete on equal terms against four-wheelers at Brooklands. Expression of the resentment was voiced by 'Shacklepin' and 'Grand Prix', writing in the *Light Car and Cyclecar*, who claimed the ban had resulted in reduced enthusiasm for three-wheeler racing. The remarks brought forth a flood of correspondence and led to the three-wheeler world taking action on its own behalf. On 4 August 1927, the Morgan Club, previously a predominantly social organization, was reconstituted to allow membership to any three- or four-wheeled cyclecar of under 8cwt and 1100cc covered by the ACU definition. To reflect the broader interests, the club was renamed the Cyclecar Club. However, following complaints from the JCC, which was originally called the Cyclecar Club, the name was changed to the New Cyclecar Club. The new club was chaired by Prof. A.M. Low and a racing committee, comprising H. Beart, J.J. Low, E.B. Ware, Capt. A. Frazer-Nash and G.E. Tottey, was appointed to organize the club's first Brooklands meeting to be held mid-1928.

The Southport sand races had continued to offer three-wheelers the opportunity to

George Goodall and Freddie James were the drivers of Number 42 and 7, respectively, in the ACU Stock Machine Trial held during March 1928.

compete against four-wheelers. However, from August 1927, three-wheeler cyclecars were restricted to racing amongst themselves or with sidecars; thus confirming the importance of the new club to the Morgan racers.

One of the most enthusiastic advocates of three-wheelers being allowed to race alongside four-wheelers had been Jim Hall, who claimed to have covered more than 1,600 high-speed miles at Brooklands without any anxiety. Hall had gone record breaking on two wheels before moving onto three wheels with a 1096cc Omega-JAP and later with an HP fitted with a 350cc JAP engine. On 20 September he returned to the track with a Morgan, prepared by Beart and fitted with a special 731cc JAP engine, to attack long distance, Class J, records. A burst back-tyre at around 80mph resulted in the car somersaulting along the Railway Straight and Hall and his passenger, Vic Derrington, were both thrown out suffering head injuries. The timing of the accident was inopportune but did not dampen enthusiasm for the new club; as Beart remarked: 'an Amilcar or Austin Seven might be safer in a 200-mile race as they would be unable to attain anything like the speed'.

Two new models were exhibited alongside the long-established Standard, De Luxe, Family and Aero models on the Morgan stand at Olympia in November 1927. One was a smart Commercial variant of the Family model fitted with a 20cu. ft luggage box with load capacity of 3cwt, which could be converted back to a family runabout in five minutes. The second model, and the focus of attention for most visitors to the stand, was the Super Sports Aero. The machine was intended for racing and incorporated experience gained during the past racing season. It featured a chassis $2\frac{1}{2}$in (60mm) lower and 6in (150mm) wider than standard, a beetle-back body with hinged tail-section and staggered seating, and a specially tuned version of the overhead-valve JAP 10/40hp engine fitted with high-compression pistons. Although the model was listed as the Super Sports Aero, it was more often referred

to as the Super Sports or, occasionally, Super Aero. Fully equipped with lights and Watford speedometer, but without hood, the new machine was priced at £155, an exceptionally keen price for a car with an 80mph potential.

Prices were again reduced for 1928. The Standard model was reduced by £4 to £85 and the De Luxe, by now with a very dated body style, was reduced by £10 to £100. The Family and Aero models were reduced by £9 and £8, respectively. The Convertible Carrier variant of the Family model was available for £112. The 1928 models are listed below:

Standard a/c	£85	De Luxe a/c	£100
Family a/c	£102	Convertible Carrier	£112
Aero w/c	£119	Super Sports Aero	£155

JAP engines were standardized across the range, although a water-cooled ohv Vulpine (Anzani) engine was offered with the Aero as an alternative to the JAP side-valve at no extra cost. The Aero with the 10/40 JAP ohv engine cost £132, and the price included large exhaust-pipes and silencers. The De Luxe and Family models could be fitted with a water-cooled JAP for an additional £10.

The factory continued to offer improvements to the models. All machines were fitted with an improved dynamo drive taken from the bevel-box counter-shaft. This allowed the starter motor to be fitted in the earlier dynamo position adjacent to the engine; self-starting was by now becoming more popular but remained an £8 extra. A steering reduction box, offering 2 to 1 reduction, was announced at the show but did not feature on the models displayed; it was offered for an additional £2. Tapered, anti-wobble, steering pins were by now being fitted to the track-rod ends. Other listed extras for 1928 included wheel discs in black for £2 10s, speed indicator £3 10s, Rotax side-screens for Standard, De Luxe or Family models £1 15s, hood cover 15s and Aero hood £3.

Despite the remorseless lowering of prices to maintain sales, the Morgan Company was

Jackson's aluminium-bodied special with 546cc Blackburne engine.

able to return a profit of £21,060 in 1927. The present prices, however, were only viable whilst sales were maintained, and sales were now falling at an increasing rate. The profitability of the company was destined to continue to fall.

The Supremacy of Three Wheels or Four at Brooklands?

Morgan drivers rounded off the 1927 season with eight gold medals in the London–Exeter trial and continued to enjoy their usual measure of success during the new year in trials, racing and record breaking. However, the main sporting interest for the year was the eagerly awaited New Cyclecar Club's Brooklands meeting held on 25 August. Entries had been invited from three- and four-wheelers with engine capacity of less than 1100cc. A 'Grand Prix' course had been devised with S-bends constructed using sandbanks in the Finishing Straight and at the start of the Railway Straight. Racing began with a two-lap novices' handicap, which was won by Major Gardner from scratch in his supercharged Salmson. This was followed by a three-lap handicap race for

three-wheelers, which was contested by seven Morgans and a Coventry-Victor. The race was won by Jackson, driving his aluminium-bodied special fitted with a V-twin Blackburne engine of 546cc, at 67.85mph (108.56km/h) with Horton second and Lones third. Horton gained victory in the following three-lap handicap race for all comers at 92.4mph (147.84km/h), leading home Maskell and Lones by a quarter of a mile. This margin of victory was considered too great and Horton was duly re-handicapped for the next race, a 5-lap handicap. He responded by lapping at 98mph (156.80km/h), and averaged 94.5mph (151.20km/h), to lead home Jackson and Lones with a margin doubled to half a mile!

The next race was the long awaited Cyclecar Grand Prix, which took place over twenty laps of the special course, a distance of fifty miles. Gardner's supercharged Salmson was a favourite, but retired on the second lap with a fractured petrol pipe. Horton then took an early lead, but oil on his brakes forced his retirement on the fifth lap. This left Lones and Maskell as the front runners for a brief period before Maskell suffered the handicap of a gear lever broken off in top gear. From this point on Lones, accompanied by his wife Nel, was able to build up a commanding lead and, despite stopping to refill the small radiator, came home an easy victor. He was followed home by Wilkinson's Riley, Smythe's Amilcar and Vidler's Coventry-Victor. Lones won the Light Car and Cyclecar Cup for the overall winner, the Greenway cup for victory in the 1100cc class and the Jackson cup for the first private owner to finish.

The event proved popular with the public and the performance of the Morgans was a revelation. Many people had been conditioned to expect the return of three-wheeler racing to result in a crop of accidents, but the only serious incident during the event occurred when Martin's Austin Seven overturned following collision with one of the artificial sand banks.

The Standard model was deleted from the Morgan range for 1929. It was replaced as the cheapest model of the range by the De Luxe, which was now fitted with the same smooth-sided style of body as the Family model. In basic form, with braking on the rear wheel only and direct steering, it was priced at £86. With front-wheel brakes and geared steering it

was available for £92, the same price as the Family model. Both the De Luxe and Family models could be supplied with electric start, speedometer and side screens for an additional £10. If purchased individually the prices of these items were £8 for the starter, £3 10s for the speed indicator and £1 15s for side screens. The Convertible Carrier variant of the Family model, with its limited load capacity, was also discontinued. It was replaced by a conventional van with a more commodious body, but still with a maximum 3cwt (152kg) capacity. The 1929 model range comprised:

De Luxe		De Luxe a/c	£92
(standard)	£86	Delivery Van	£105
Family a/c	£92	Super Sports	
Aero w/c	£115	Aero	£150

JAP engines remained the standard option, with alternative engine options as the previous year. However, a reduced extra charge of £8 was made for a side-valve water-cooled JAP or ohv Anzani with the De Luxe or Family models. A premium of £12 was required for the Aero model fitted with the 10/40 JAP ohv engine. Disc front wheel covers, which had been a popular styling extra on Morgans since pre-war days, had not been featured on the cars illustrated in the 1928 sales catalogue and were

Maskell in car number 12 rounds one of the sand bank chicanes in 1928 Cyclecar Grand Prix at Brooklands.

not identified as an extra for 1929. A new addition to the list of available extras, at £2 15s, were Newton front-wheel shock absorbers for all models other than the Super Sports, for which they were now fitted as standard.

Only Morgan and Coventry-Victor displayed machines at the Olympia show in November 1928. Both HFS and Mr W.A. Weaver of Coventry-Victor expressed the view that a little more competition would be welcomed and would be distinctly good for the three-wheeler cause. Matters were little better in France. The French motorcycle show had included examples of the Darmont-Morgan and the Morgan-inspired Sandford, plus the Villard, a utility machine with two-stroke power unit, variable-friction gearing and chain drive to the single front wheel. In passing it is worth noting that Coventry-Victor were now fitting a reverse gear mechanism outside the bevel box and controlled by a centrally placed lever.

More Racing and Record Breaking

Racing and record-breaking successes again provided much valuable publicity for Morgan during 1929. The first Brooklands meeting of the New Cyclecar Club had proved popular and a second meeting was held on 31 August 1929. The meeting followed the form of the previous year, but this time Morgan swept the board in all five races despite strong four-wheeler opposition. The two-lap novices' handicap went to Sydney Allard's LTOW Super Aero at 73.37mph (117.39km/h). The second race, a three-lap handicap for three-wheelers, was led from start to finish by Tom Rhodes in his Blackburne Aero, who won at a speed of 87.9mph (140.64km/h). Victory in the third race, a mixed three-lap handicap, went to Ron Horton in his 496cc Blackburne engined Morgan at 71.15mph (113.84km/h) despite strong competition from blown Amilcar, Austin, Salmson and Ratier cars plus various fast Morgans. Rhodes was re-handicapped for the five-lap all-comers handicap race fol-

Assembly of the Wide 'B' chassis frame during the late 1920s.

Panelling the bodywork in the sheet metal shop.

lowing his earlier victory. He, nevertheless, again took the chequered flag, this time at 89.74mph (143.58km/h).

The 20-lap Cyclecar Grand Prix attracted twenty-one starters. The course had again been laid out with artificial bends created by sand banks and these proved to be an irresistible attraction to several of the competitors. A Salmson and an Amilcar both narrowly avoided overturning and an Austin damaged its front wheel. Maskell, suffering braking and engine problems, broke one of the crosshead tubes when he clipped a sandbank. He was forced to retire two laps later when he lost control due to the damaged chassis and came

Morgan stores manager, Cecil Jay, with chief tester, Charlie Curtis, as passenger prior to the practice session for the 1929 Cyclecar Grand Prix. Curtis refused to accompany Jay in the race.

to rest on top of a sandbank. Cecil Jay, the Morgan stores manager, had his close encounter with a sandbank during the practice session when he misjudged a turn and flipped the car over. He had been entered for the race by George Goodall and was driving George's 731cc Beart engined 'Jim', with Charlie Curtis as passenger. Curtis had joined the Morgan Company in 1917 and had become chief tester, remaining with the company for almost sixty years and testing almost every car produced during that period. However, he found the experience during the practice session more than testing and refused to passenger for Jay. As a result Jay was forced to carry sand ballast rather than an acrobatic passenger during the race. Machines of less than 850cc were credited with three laps and this provided Jay with a more than adequate margin. Driving a cautious, steady, race he averaged 64.7mph (103.52km/h) to maintain his lead and came home almost two laps ahead of the Amilcar Six driven by scratch-man Gardner.

Record breaking remained as popular as ever. Clive Lones enjoyed a successful year gaining three-wheeler cyclecar records in Classes H (not exceeding 350cc), I (not exceeding 500cc) and K (not exceeding

1100cc). It was, however the exploits of one of the most famous lady racing drivers of the inter-war years, Gwenda Stewart, which provided Morgan with much more glamorous publicity. Gwenda enjoyed a record-breaking spree at the banked Montlhéry circuit near Paris with a Super Sports Aero with JTOR engine prepared by Douglas Hawkes. By the end of the year Gwenda could claim a total of

Cecil Jay receives the cup and congratulations from HFS upon winning the 1929 Cyclecar Grand Prix at Brooklands.

over sixty records in Classes H, I, J and K. Most noteworthy was the achievement on 7 September when Gwenda became the first cyclecar driver to cover more than 100 miles – actually 101.4 miles – in an hour.

The machine shop was transferred from Worcester Road to the Pickersleigh Road works during the year bringing the entire manufacture of the Morgan onto a single site. The company sales were declining at this time, although production for the year would be an acceptable 1,002 machines and result in a profit of £12,343.

A New Sporting Chassis – The 'M' type.

A new chassis, identified as the 'M' type, was announced immediately prior to the Olympia show in November 1929. It would be made available early in 1930 as an alternative to the 'B' type and, although intended for use with the Super Sports Aero, it was offered on all models at an additional cost of £6 10s. The new chassis comprised a total redesign of the rear end of the two-speeder chassis and was, arguably, long overdue for the sporting machines. The stated objective of the design was to simplify tyre changing whilst strengthening the rear forks and making the transmission quieter and free from vibration, but it offered many other real advantages, including constant chain tension.

A Super Sports Aero fitted with the new 'M' type chassis featured prominently at the Motorcycle Show and was offered for sale at £150. Also featured, but available only to special order, was a replica of Gwenda Stewart's record-breaking machine, which at the time of the show had recently accomplished 106.3mph (170.08km/h) for 5 miles (8km) to record the fastest speed ever attained by a three-wheeler. It was fitted with a special 8/55hp ohv air-cooled JAP engine.

In other respects few alterations were made to the model range for 1930, although prices were again reduced:

De Luxe a/c	£87 10s	Family a/c	£87 10s
Super Sports Aero	£145	Aero w/c	£110
Super Sports Aero 'M'	£150	Delivery Van	£100

The alternative option of a side-valve water-cooled JAP or an ohv Anzani engine with the De Luxe and Family models was made available for an extra £7 10s.

Despite the passing of the cyclecar craze, Morgan had continued to face competition from other manufacturers of three-wheelers. The three-wheeler market was in decline, but it was not infrequent for two or three other firms to display machines alongside the Morgan stand at Olympia. Their presence helped to generate interest in three-wheelers and actually helped Morgan, with its unrivalled reputation, to gain sales. However, no such complacent attitude was appropriate when an altogether more formidable competitor in the form of the industrial giant, BSA, was encountered at the 1929 show. BSA was the major manufacturer of motorcycles in Britain. They had taken over Daimler some years earlier and had previously produced four-wheeled

The rear section of the 'M' type two-speeder, introduced for the 1930 season, bolted to a flange at the rear of the propeller shaft tube and was held by U-bolts to the longitudinal tubes. The rear fork, comprising substantial forged beams, pivoted concentrically with the cross-shaft ensuring constant chain tension.

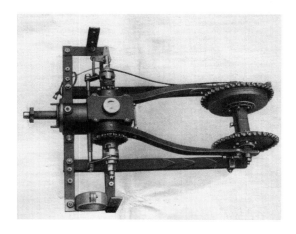

Gwenda Stewart

As the daughter of Sir Frederick Manley Glubb and sister of John, better known as 'Glubb Pasha' of Arab Legion fame, it is hardly surprising that Gwenda Glubb possessed an adventurous spirit. This first found expression during the Great War when she was an ambulance driver on the Russian and Rumanian fronts. Post-war thrills were found in the male dominated, and dangerous, world of motorcycle and motorcar record-breaking. Her first exploit took place in November 1921 under her married name of Gwenda Jansen. It comprised a thousand-mile trial, under ACU observation, of a two-stroke friction-drive Ner-a-Car, accomplished without stopping the engine. This was followed by a 'double Twelve-Hour' class A record at Brooklands at an average speed of 44.65mph (71.44km/h), achieved riding a 249cc Trump-JAP motorcycle.

Later, when the Brooklands authorities banned women motorcyclists from the track she teamed up with new husband, Lt Col. Neil Stewart, for further racing and record attempts at the Montlhéry Autodrome on the outskirts of Paris. It was here she met Douglas Hawkes. Douglas had raced motorcycles pre-war and, in the early twenties, had achieved success racing and record-breaking with Morgans. He was now concerned in the design and preparation of cars for record breaking and the organization of the attempts. It was at his suggestion that she switched to record breaking on three wheels, driving

Gwenda Stewart.

Morgans prepared by Douglas and his mechanic Fred Cann. Douglas offered to prepare a Morgan for record breaking if HFS supplied the car; HFS declined. The MEB concern proved less reluctant and Gwenda was soon acquiring cyclecar records with a 730cc MEB-JAP three-wheeler. It was not long before HFS contacted Hawkes with the offer of a Super Sports Aero.

The year 1929 was a period of frantic record breaking for Gwenda and Douglas. The ease of exchanging engines meant that, once one record had been obtained, only a few minutes work with the spanners would have the Morgan available to attack records in a different class. As well as 996cc and 731cc twins, 500cc and 350cc JAP singles were used to such good effect that, by the end of 1929, Gwenda and Douglas between them held almost all the available records. A particularly notable achievement was the first one hour record at over one hundred miles an hour in a three-wheeler; achieved using an air-cooled 996cc JAP running on alcohol fuel.

The Morgan was returned to Malvern for overhaul and Douglas requested a new single-seater should be developed for short-distance record attempts. For publicity purposes, HFS would have preferred Mrs Stewart to continue using a near standard car, similar to those available to the public, rather than a special. He did, however, agree. In the meantime the Super Aero, now fitted with a new 1096cc air-cooled JAP racing engine developed by lengthening the stroke of the JTOR, returned to the track on 21 March 1930. Its return was rewarded with middle distance records in class K. Other records soon followed including a praiseworthy 24-hours record, achieved jointly with S.C.H. ('Sammy') Davis. All went well for several hours until the nearside piston seized during Sammy's second three-hour driving spell. Whilst the drivers rested, Hawkes replaced the engine and the record attempt was restarted. All went well until a suspension spring broke after twenty-one hours, but by this time the distance covered was equivalent to an average of 64.85mph (103.76km/h) for twenty-four hours and the record had already been broken.

The new single-seater was powered by a JAP JTOR engine and based upon the 'M' chassis. The propshaft was divided into two with a central universal joint to prevent propshaft whip, which had become a recurring problem at the speeds now being achieved. The machine was handed over in July 1930 and made its first record attempt on 6 August at Montlhéry. Although delayed until the evening by squally weather the first outing successfully netted the 5-kilometre and 5-mile records at

113.52mph and 107.51mph (181.63 and 172.02km/h) respectively. On 24 August, the machine took the flying kilometre record at 115.66mph (185.06km/h) on the narrow, and heavily cambered, road at Arpajon, near Montlhéry. Gwenda described the run as a nightmare ride and suggested that the two factors enabling her to achieve the record were the distinctive design of the Morgan controls and stark terror! Vibration at high speed caused the throttle to close but was cured by giving the lever a stiff setting. Above 110mph, the car snaked violently down the road in an apparently uncontrolled manner as the rear wheel was affected by the road camber, but she dared not take her hands from the steering wheel to alter the throttle.

By the end of 1930 Gwenda held over sixty three-wheeler cyclecar car records. These comprised six in class H (350cc), ten in class I (500cc), twenty-six in class J (750cc) and thirty-four in class K (1100cc). Eight years later Gwenda Hawkes, she had married Douglas in 1937, was the fastest woman on four wheels and the fastest person on three wheels. She also held the outright lap record for Montlhéry at 147.2mph (235.5km/h) and the woman's record for the Brooklands outer circuit at 135.95mph (217.52km/h).

Above *The advertisement placed following Gwenda Stewart's record run at Arpajon.*

Gwenda seated in her racing Morgan at Montlhéry. Douglas Hawkes is standing behind the car.

rear-drive cars. They now announced an advanced, front-wheel driven, three-wheeler powered by a proven ohv air-cooled 90-degree twin of 1021cc capacity and with a three-speed and reverse gearbox. The new FWD model was conventional in appearance and extremely well engineered. It was competitively priced at £115 and came fully

equipped with Lucas electric lighting, starter and speedometer. Production of the new car was slow to get fully underway and must have provided HFS with a breathing space and time to consider the future development of the Malvern product. Once in full production, from 1931 to 1935, the BSA FWD outsold the Morgan almost four to one.

The BSA FWD

The BSA three-wheeler was announced in November 1929, at the same time as Morgan introduced the improved, 'M' type, two-speeder chassis. Whereas the Morgan chassis was an attempt to make a nineteen-year-old design acceptable by the standards of the day, the BSA design was ultra modern. Having two wheels at the front and a single rear wheel was the accepted three-wheeler configuration for the period, but the BSA company did not wish to drive through a single wheel. The answer was to adopt front-wheel-drive, which was at that time little used on production cars.

The machine developed by the BSA engineers used an air-cooled ohv 90-degree V-twin engine of 1021cc, which had been designed by Hotchkiss and first fitted to the RWD BSA car in 1922. The engine was fitted with its cylinders across the car and drove forward through a cork clutch and conventional three-speed and reverse gearbox to a differential mounted between the front wheels. Final drive was by shafts, flexible couplings and Hooke joints to the front wheels. The chassis frame was of pressed-steel construction with a large-diameter central steel-tube. Coupled brakes were fitted and comprised a rear-wheel brake and a single in-board front brake. Independent front- and rear-wheel suspension was featured and the wheels were easily detachable and interchangeable. A spare wheel was carried. Shock absorbers formed part of the specification in 1931.

The original two-seater became available in sports or touring versions in 1930. These were joined in 1931 by a four-seater Family model and a short-lived van model. Four-wheel derivatives were also offered for 1932, but were soon replaced by a more ambitious four-wheeler fitted with a water-cooled 4-cylinder 9hp engine of 1075cc. This engine would find its way into an improved three-wheeler for 1933. The V-twin models remained in production alongside the 4-cylinder machines through to the end of three-wheeler production in 1936. The BSA Scout, a more refined four-wheeled sports car, was introduce in 1935 and was a direct competitor to the Morgan 4-4.

When announced in 1929, the BSA FWD with all-weather equipment and speedometer cost £115. The corresponding price of the De Luxe and Family model Morgans was £97 10s. Morgan was able to retain a small price advantage during the BSA production period and the final BSA FWD 4-cylinder models cost £125 or £128 for standard or de luxe models compared with £120 15s or £128 2s for the 8hp or 10hp Model F Morgans The total production of BSA trikes over the period from 1929 to 1935 was approximately 6,650 machines.

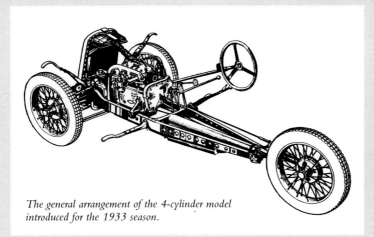

The general arrangement of the 4-cylinder model introduced for the 1933 season.

Further Sporting Successes

The Hawkes/Stewart record-breaking partnership continued to generate excellent publicity for Morgan throughout the year. On 15 May, Gwenda, with S.C.H. 'Sammy' Davis as co-driver, took the 24-hours Class K record at their second attempt at an average speed of 64.85mph (103.76km/h). In July, Gwenda, driving a special single-seater powered by a long-stroke JTOR engine, gained the 5-kilometres record at 113.52mph (181.63km/h) and the 5-miles at 107.51mph (172.02km/h). The car was taken next to Arpajon, a straight section of road a few miles from Montlhéry, to attempt the flying kilometre and mile records. A terrifying ride resulted in Gwenda establishing a record average speed for the kilometre of 115.66mph (185.06km/h).

The New Cyclecar Club changed its name to the Light Car Club at the beginning of the year and extended membership for cars up to 1500 cc. The move resulted in the performance of the racing Morgans more closely matching that of the four-wheeler competition. The club's annual Brooklands meeting was held at the end of July. The novices race was not contested by the Morgan drivers, but the second race, the three-lap handicap, provided a victory for Sydney Allard driving his 1096cc JAP Super Aero. The five-lap handicap race proved to be too long for the Morgan drivers and victory was taken by the car entrants. The Grand Prix was run over the Brooklands Mountain circuit without the addition of sandbanks to create artificial bends. In a change to previous procedure, qualifying heats, each of twenty laps, were run to determine entrants for the two classes. The only Morgan entrant in the first heat, for the under 850cc Class, was Cecil Jay, who despite an early lead was forced to retire on the eighth lap with a twisted bevel box countershaft. The second heat for the 850cc to 1100cc class was contested by six Morgans. Horton took an early lead but experienced plug problems and eventually retired. The lead then passed to Lones, who finally finished second to the supercharged Salmson of Bartlett. In the final, Lones, the only Morgan driver to qualify, took the lead at the end of the first lap and went on to win at 58mph (93km/h) from Bartlett's Salmson.

Preliminary details of the 1931 Morgan range were released in September 1930. Most machines were to be available in either 'Standard' or 'De Luxe' versions according to whether they were fitted with the old 'B' chassis or the new 'M' chassis. The possible confusion with the earlier two-seater De Luxe model was avoided by identifying that model specifically as the '2-Seater'. The cheapest models of the range were the Standard Family four-seater and the 2-Seater Standard models built on the 'B' chassis. The windscreens were now angled back and the coalscuttle bonnets slightly modified, but otherwise the models were little changed from the previous year. They were reduced in price by £2 10s to £85. The water-cooled side-valve engine now cost an additional £5, but the ohv Anzani engine was no longer listed.

An Owner's Impression

An interesting insight into Morgan ownership was contained in a letter by 'H.A.' published in the *Motor Cycle* at the end of November 1929. 'H.A.' had purchased his Super Aero Morgan the previous February and had, by the date of the letter, covered some 3,200 miles. He considered the comfort to be the equal of any other small car he had driven and was pleased with the performance; according to his Watford speedometer he had achieved over 60mph in bottom gear and 84mph in top at Brooklands, whilst gentle running gave a fuel consumption of better than 50mpg. He was a mechanic by trade and kept the machine in perfect condition, but was concerned that he had to spend more time repairing the machine than driving it. During his ownership he had spent £13 on new parts, which he considered excessive. He nevertheless concluded: 'in spite of its rather high cost of upkeep, it is by far the best machine in the car line I have ever driven. I don't think I should change it for anything else.'

FAMILY MOTORING •

• AT MOTOR CYCLE COST

And in addition a standard of comfort and dependability that will surprise you at current prices. The "Family" model now listed at £85 seats two adults and three small children in full comfort and is equipped with coverall all-weather hood. The air-cooled J.A.P. S.V. engine will do 50 m.p.g. and 50 m.p.h. and in addition entails only a £4 annual Tax. Why not send for particulars of this "car at motor cycle cost" —there are models for touring and sport and your local dealer can supply on payment of a small initial deposit.

Morgan Runabout

MORGAN MOTOR CO., LTD.,
Pickersleigh Road, Malvern Link,
WORCESTERSHIRE.

By 1930 Morgan were emphasizing economy rather than sporting successes in the quest for sales. The battle for sales was no longer against the small car, typified by the Austin Seven and the Morris Minor, introduced in 1928, but against the motorcycle and sidecar.

The models on the 'M' chassis were now identified as the Family De Luxe and the 2-Seater De Luxe models. They were fitted with new longer bonnets, which hinged just below the windscreen and eliminated the scuttle. The windscreens were sloped back and the bodies made more commodious. Close-fitting cycle mudguards replaced the flat-topped mudguards, which had been used during previous years and retained on the standard models. Several models on display had ribs running along the centre of the mudguard. An additional £5 was asked for the De Luxe versions.

The Aero models now featured cycle mudguards and a V-windscreen. The price of the Standard model with a side-valve water-cooled JAP engine was reduced by £5 to £105, whilst an additional £14 was required for the Aero with a water-cooled ohv 10/40 JAP engine. The De Luxe versions of the Aero

cost an additional £5. The Super Sports Aero, now identified simply as the Super Sports, was unchanged in price and specification except that it was now fitted with a V-screen.

The new Morgans created a fine display on stand No. 1 at the Olympia Motor Cycle Show in November 1930, with twelve different models and bold colour schemes, plus a chromium-plated chassis. The display models comprised nine De Luxe versions and three Standard versions. A new sporting four-seater, known appropriately as the Sports Family, was displayed. It featured two small seats, one on either side of the rear wheel, which were accessed by tilting forward the passenger seat. The body styling dispensed with the enveloping bonnet of the earlier family models, instead being fitted with the Aero style of bonnet and radiator with the engine exposed. The body turned inward behind the windscreen and was fitted with a launch pattern tail. The machine used a version of the 'M' chassis lengthened by 4in (100mm). The change involved lengthening the propeller shaft, which in turn necessitated splitting the shaft to fit a central universal joint and support bearings to prevent vibration. The chassis variant was known as the 'C' chassis. The Sports Family was priced at £129 with an ohv 1096cc JAP engine.

The 1096cc JAP engine was also fitted to the two Super Sports machines and Aero De Luxe on display. The Super Sports models were strikingly painted in either red-and-white or green-and-white and finished in matching red or green upholstery. The Aero had a cream chassis, pale-blue body and cream trim. Side-valve JAP engines were fitted to the remaining models on display. Water-cooled machines comprised an Aero De Luxe finished in bright yellow with a black chassis, a 2-Seater finished in coffee and cream and a Family De Luxe in blue and black. The air-cooled De Luxe models comprised a 2-Seater in blue and grey and a family model in saxe blue and dark blue. The models on the 'B' chassis were air-cooled Family and 2-Seater models and a water-cooled Aero. They were painted in the standard colour schemes of red or blue with black. Chromium plating of the bright parts of the cars had been an optional extra in 1930; it was standardized across the range for 1931.

Standard Family	£85	Family De Luxe	£90
Standard 2-Seater	£85	2-Seater De Luxe	£90
Standard Aero	£110	Aero De Luxe	£110
Super Sports	£145	Sports Family	£129

Pricing and the Downward Spiral

Debate was raging in the motoring press at the time of the 1930 Olympia show as to which manufacturer would be the first to produce a genuine motorcar for less than £100. *Motor Cycling* magazine concluded its review of the Morgan display with the comment: 'With such well-tried and reliable models as these already in existence one cannot help wondering why there should be a periodical outcry for a £100 car. Surely it already exists!'

Despite an already aggressive pricing policy, Morgan sales continued to fall to the extent that, by July 1931, HFS took the decision to introduce further price reductions. A cut of £10 was made across the range. The cheapest Morgan, the Standard Family model with 980cc air-cooled JAP engine, was now available for £75, the lowest price ever for a Morgan. The new pricing represented a desperate bid for survival as, without higher rates of production to provide the company with economies of scale, cars were now being sold at less than cost price. The modest profit of £4,080 in 1930 was replaced by an operating loss in 1931. This was only the second time in the company history that annual profits had been in the red, but they would remain in the red for the rest of the thirties. During this period the Morgan Motor Company would survive upon investment income.

The Problem of Traction

In the early days of the Morgan, HFS would often carry a suitcase on the rear of his Run-

about during trials. Observers assumed it contained overnight clothes, but in reality it was filled with bricks to increase the weight over the back wheel in order to obtain better grip. Over the years less covert methods to improve grip were adopted and in slippery trials conditions it was usual to add ballast to the rear of the car and to fit the rear wheel with Parson's chains. This was not an entirely satisfactory solution, as Lionel Creed discovered when he was denied a gold medal in the 1930 Colmore Cup Trial due to the Parson's chains becoming entangled with a drive chain. He had experienced similar problems before and decided he could obtain adequate grip without the use of wheel chains by fitting wider tyres. He communicated his ideas to Dunlop and plans were drawn up for two wheel rims to be affixed side by side on a single rear hub. The development was taken up by HFS, but was not without problems as it was found that the twin rear-wheel arrangement placed too great a strain on the bevel box. The design that finally evolved was based upon the 'C' type bevel box with extended bearing housings for the cross shaft.

The rear appearance of a twin rear wheel Morgan.

This allowed the use of a pair of bearings, rather than a single bearing, on either side of the bevel. Standard 'C' type forks were retained and pivoted at the outside of the extended bearing-housing. A bronze rear-wheel hub was manufactured with two outer-spoke flanges and a single central flange was used for lacing in place two 19in wheel rims.

The first twin rear-wheel car, an Aero with louvred bonnet sides and fitted with a special LTOW JAP, was tested by George Goodall's son, 'Jim', in minor trials. These were successful and a second twin rear-wheel Aero was constructed. It was fitted with a racing 996cc air-cooled JAP with compression plates to lower the compression for trials, a dummy radiator and 'D' cut-outs in the bonnet sides. The first major outing for the two machines was the Colmore Trial held during February 1931. Geoff Harris, driving the prototype twin rear-wheel machine, won the Carr Cup for best performance by a three-wheeler and George Goodall in the air-cooled machine gained a silver award. Goodall's next outing with the air-cooled twin rear-wheel Morgan netted him a third class award in the Cotswold Trial despite overturning the car at one stage.

The eagerly awaited Brooklands meeting of the Light Car Club, held on 25 July 1931, proved to be a disappointment for Morgans. The club had decided to replace the Grand Prix by a relay race for teams of three cars over ninety laps of the Brooklands Outer Circuit. Each team was collectively handicapped and the fastest car of the team started first. A maximum of thirty laps could be covered before its place was taken by the second fastest car, which in turn could raise the lap count to a maximum of sixty before passing over to the final member of the team. The Morgan team comprised Lones, Maskell and Rhodes. In practice Rhodes suffered a seized engine and spun, which probably resulted in the team gaining a five-minute concession on handicap. A modest gain, as the Morgans still conceded time to all other teams, including the works Austin Sevens and a team of supercharged MG Midgets. The race opened well for the Morgan team, with Lones lapping in spectacular style at speeds up to 93mph (149km/h). However, by the time Lones handed over to Maskell it had started to rain and very soon afterwards the rain became a downpour. Maskell was soon in trouble with ignition problems due to the wet and was forced to make frequent pit stops. Rhodes faired little better and it was not long before the rain and flooded track reduced him to one cylinder. Under the appalling conditions the Morgan team did well to average of 71.84mph (114.94km/h), compared to the winner's speed of 65.01mph (104.02km/h), but had to settle for twelfth place on handicap.

George Goodall in the 1930 London–Exeter.

Victor were pleased with the interest shown in their products at Olympia, but the interest was not reflected in sales. Morgan sales continued to fall during the year. The sporting models still offered outstanding performance and reigned supreme in their price range but sold to a restricted market of enthusiasts. The touring models represented outstanding value for money. The advantages of the Family Morgan were summarized in the 1932 sales brochure:

> The Two-Speed Family Model provides the cheapest possible form of transport for the family man. Designed to carry four people with a maximum weight of 40 stone, all being protected when the hood is in use; has adjustable front seats and will do all that it is intended to do.

The company might have added the advantages of a £4 annual road tax, the same as a motorcycle. The two-speeders were comparable in price to a motorcycle and sidecar, and cheaper than the light cars being mass-produced by companies such as Austin, Ford and Morris. They had also proved themselves in trials and competition to be rugged and reliable. Against this, however, the design had been on the market, unchanged, for twenty-one years and now lacked popular appeal. The implementation of the three-speeder chassis had represented an attempt at modernization

but the added refinement had resulted in an increased price, now only a little less than that of a Ford 8 or Morris Minor.

The twin rear-wheel machines continued to compete successfully. Both machines were entered in the London–Exeter Trial held at the end of 1931, resulting in a gold award for Geoff Harris. George Goodall entered the trial with a three-speed model fitted with a 60-degree ohv JAP engine and boat-tailed body. The machine was the prototype for a new Sports two-seater model, which was announced in May 1932 and was marketed as a replacement for the Aero model.

Against the background of falling sales, the decision was made in October 1932 to catalogue only the three-speeder models. There was a reluctance to kill the old model, perhaps due to HFS's affection for his original design, and the two-speeder chassis with an air-cooled engine and Family body continued to be available to special order for £80.

1933 Standardized Chassis and Detachable Wheels

The 1933 model range saw the introduction of 18in Dunlop Magna wheels and a standard chassis with a 1in drop on the front cross tubes. The combination of wheel and chassis changes raised the Super Sports by about 1in (30mm),

Harry Jones driving a twin rear-wheel two-speeder in the London–Lands End Trial during Easter 1932.

providing improved ground clearance, and resulted in the other models being lowered by $1\frac{1}{2}$ in (40mm). The Magna wheels were detachable and greatly reduced the inconvenience associated with a rear-wheel puncture. The benefits must have been appreciated by the scribe of *Motor Cycle* magazine, who titled his article previewing the 1933 models 'Morgans with Detachable Wheels'.

The use of detachable wheels meant that there was now a requirement to carry a spare. This in turn required modification to the bodywork of the various models to provide a spare-wheel mounting. The Family model was entirely redesigned to be more roomy and comfortable. The bonnet included a new design of dummy radiator and a sloping panel was fitted at the back to carry the spare wheel. Similar modifications were made to the rear of the Sports Family model. The Aero model was discontinued and replaced by a Sports two-seater with a new design of two-door body styled along the lines of the Sports Family. No changes were made to the beetle-back body of the Super Sports and the spare wheel was initially located on the rounded tail of the car at 45 degrees to the horizontal. It was quickly moved to a less precarious looking position at the top of the rear panel.

Other modifications for 1933 were the use of a single-plate clutch of the normal car type and improved steering. JAP engines were used across the range.

The model range for 1933, which is listed below, included a delivery van with double rear-doors and a load capacity of 4cwt.

Family	£98	Sports Family	£115
Sports 2-seater	£110	Super Sports	£135
Delivery van	£98		

The Family and Delivery van models were fitted as standard with the air-cooled version of the 1100cc 60 degree JAP engine. The Family model with the water-cooled version of the engine, which was standard on the other models of the range except the Super Sports, cost an additional £5. The Sports two-seater and Sports Family fitted with the 10/40hp ohv engine cost an additional £10.

Despite reliance upon JAP engines, Morgan was far from satisfied with the JAP products, which were considered to be rough and relatively expensive. Alternatives were sought and attention focussed on the Matchless Model X, 990cc air-cooled side-valve engine. The engine had been in production since 1929 and was a thoroughly tested product of modern

Several owners had their own view on the ideal body for a Morgan. This streamline saloon body was built in 1932 by Jack Sylvester, the Nottingham Morgan agent, on a Super Sports chassis with ohv JAP engine. A Crouch gearbox was grafted on to cope with the extra bodyweight.

A consequence of the introduction of Dunlop Magna detachable wheels was the requirement to provide a mounting for a spare wheel. On the Super Sports the spare was fitted on top of the beetle back. On the other models, including the new Sports two-seater, illustrated, a barrel-back styling was adopted with a sloping rear-panel to support the wheel.

design with enclosed valve gear. Furthermore it was commendably quiet and smooth running. With the assistance of Donald Heather of Matchless, a water-cooled version of the engine was developed at the Matchless works in Plumstead, London specifically for Morgan. The front timing-cover was modified for coil ignition and a starting-handle boss incorporated. Prototype engines were fitted to the Morgans of Goodall and Bradshaw for the London–Lands End Trial at Easter 1933. The claimed output of the engines, 27.5bhp at 4,000rpm, proved inadequate for some sections of the trial, but both drivers were successful in obtaining silver awards.

The first production Morgan to be fitted with the new Matchless 'MX' engine was a Sports two-seater announced in May 1933. The engine proved well suited to the Morgan and gave smooth delivery of power and adequate performance over a wide rev range. It provided smooth acceleration from 15mph in top gear and a top speed of about 65mph. The new machine was priced at £110.

Two months after the announcement of the MX engine, George Goodall was out testing an air-cooled ohv conversion of the Matchless X engine in the London–Scarborough Trial. The engine used the same bottom end as the side-valve MX, but was fitted with air-cooled barrels and head and overhead-valve gear. The engine was the prototype of the MX2 engine, which would be announced to the public in October 1933.

BETTER THAN EVER
for
1934

See the 1934 Morgans and you must admit there's nothing their equal in design, performance and price. All the comfort and refinements of the 4-wheel light car compacted into 3-wheel design. High road-speed with absolute safety at all times. Cushioned clutch mechanism with velvet drive—improved cooling—improved streamlining—a New Model with air cooled O.H.V. Engine specially manufactured by Matchless Motor Cycles (Colliers) Ltd. to Morgan requirements—and . . . . hush ! !—yet another surprise . . . . No, we *can't* tell you now, but you'll see it at

O L Y M P I A
STAND No. 54
(Opposite Addison Road Entrance)

N.B.—If you can't visit Olympia, write us for the NEW Morgan Catalogue . . . . shortly available.

The CLASSIC 'three WHEELER

The **Morgan**

● ────────
THE MOST LUXURIOUS THREE-WHEELER EVER
────────

proudly built by

**MORGAN MOTOR CO.
MALVERN LINK,
WORCS.**

5 Four Cylinders and a Pressed-Steel Chassis – The Final Years

HFS had recognised several years previously that in order to maintain the sales of his three-wheelers he would need to make the machines more acceptable to car owners. Paramount in this strategy had to be the replacement of the V-twin engine, with its motorcycle associations, by a 4-cylinder water-cooled car unit. Studies were begun in 1930 and focused initially on the use of a small side-valve proprietary engine from Coventry Climax. Tests were carried out with the engine installed in a modified two-speeder tubular chassis, but proved unsatisfactory. A new chassis with Z-section side members, which resulted from these studies, was every bit as innovative as the original Morgan chassis of 1910. Furthermore, its method of assembly and incorporation into the car was compatible with established Morgan, hand crafted, production methods.

Development studies were completed using Coventry Climax engines of various sizes before finally settling on a 750cc unit. However, before production commenced, the decision was taken to switch to a totally new 8hp 4-cylinder engine derived from the Ford Y-type. The Ford Y was the first small Ford and had been developed specifically for the British market. It was introduced in August 1932 and was the first car to be produced at the new

Ford plant at Dagenham in Essex. Ford had set an ambitious first year target of 45,000 units, but this proved hopelessly optimistic due to delays in the supply of body shells and teething problems associated with the new design and production plant. As a result the new engine was being produced faster than the rest of the vehicle and it is likely that Ford welcomed a customer for some of the surplus during the first year of production. In the longer term the demand from Morgan was never likely to be great and could be easily accommodated by Ford even with the model Y in full production. Nevertheless, obtaining supplies of the Ford engine was a coup for HFS; it provided him with a more powerful unit than the Coventry Climax engine and at a cheaper price.

The new Ford-powered Model F Morgan was to be produced for the 1934 season. However, the 1934 model range, which was announced several weeks in advance of the Motorcycle show at Olympia in November 1933, made no mention of the new car and offered few surprises. Sales experience had shown that the air-cooled engine was by now considerably less popular than the water-cooled engine in the Family model and the air-cooled side-valve JAP engine was no longer made available. Water-cooled side-valve engines of either JAP or Matchless manufacture were listed for the Family, Sports two-seater and Sports Family models. Prices were respectively £105, £110 and £115. The Sports and Sports Family models were also

Opposite The advertisements issued by the Morgan Motor Co. at the time of the 1933 Motor Cycle Show made no reference to the new 4-cylinder model announced one week earlier.

offered with the water-cooled ohv JAP engine for an additional £10. The Sports two-seater fitted with a new air-cooled ohv version of the 990cc Matchless engine was announced and priced at £115. The Super Sports, with the ohv 10/40hp 1100cc specially tuned JAP engine, remained available and was priced at £135. The rear bodywork of the Family model had been redesigned with more graceful styling along the lines of the Sports model and an improved radiator fitted. All models were fitted with a modified clutch and a redesigned gearbox with greater oil capacity and improved sealing.

The 'F' type – An Eleventh Hour Surprise

The announcement of the new 4-cylinder Morgan was made a week prior to its debut at the show. *Motor Cycling* magazine, for 23 November 1933, proclaimed: 'A MORGAN WITH FOUR CYLINDERS' and noted 'Eleventh-hour Surprise Model Should be Popular.' The article began:

> For nearly three years *Motor Cycling* has been privileged to see at various times experimental 4-cylinder Morgan three-wheelers. Naturally, it has not been permissible to publish anything concerning these machines until such time as the Morgan company completed its experiments and was in a position to put the model into production. That time has now arrived....

The new Model F Morgan was offered with a four-seater Family body. It was reasonably priced at £120, complete with electric lighting and starting set, windscreen wiper and all weather equipment, as well as the usual tools and fitments.

The Model F was a fine car, but much more tourer than sports car. The Ford engine could match the horsepower of the standard V-twin engines but not their low-speed torque, which was so valuable in trials events. HFS made clear in his advertising that the Model F was a new model and in no way replaced the twin-cylinder model on which the reputation of the name 'Morgan' was built. The Model F was to be family motoring for the family purse. It provided a commodious body for four and, notwithstanding its 4-cylinder engine, remained within the weight limit of the £4 taxation class; still an important factor for the economy minded motorist.

A novelty on the Morgan stand at Olympia was a Super Sports Special fitted with a new water-cooled ohv Matchless engine. The body was of the barrel-backed style, similar to the Sports two-seater, but with the spare wheel set within a recess in the tail. 'Ixion' unkindly commented that 'its tail end looks rather like a

The Morgan 4-cylinder Model F was a last minute surprise at the 1933 Olympia Show. The styling, with cycle mudguards and spare wheel mounted proud of the body, was similar to the twin-cylinder Family models. The first production machine left the factory on 25 April 1934.

1935 Model F4.

worm's eye view of a beer bottle'. The new engine was based upon the air-cooled ohv Matchless, but with forked con-rods, and was guaranteed to produce 40bhp. The new machine was priced at £150.

The new water-cooled ohv engine was identified as the MX4. Together with the previously announced air-cooled ohv MX2 engine and the original water-cooled side-vale MX engine it enabled Matchless to offer a suitable engine for all Morgan V-twin models. It would not be long before JAP engines were phased out in favour of Matchless engines on all machines except the Super Sports. The 1934 sales brochure listed the following body and engine combinations:

Family MX £105
Sports 2-seater MX £110; MX2 £115;
    MX4 £120
Sports Family MX £115; MX2 £120;
    MX4 £125
Super Sports MX2 £125; JAP10/40 £135
Delivery Van MX £105
F type Ford £120

The modifications to the Matchless X engine to adapt it for use with the Morgan had included replacement of the magneto by a coil ignition system. However, the exposed position at the front of the car meant the ignition was very susceptible to moisture and modifications were soon introduced. The high-tension double-ended coil was located under the bonnet, out of the worst of the weather,

and only the low-tension contact breaker remained on the front of the engine.

Three-wheelers enjoyed a modest increase in popularity during 1934. The Ministry of Transport figures for new registrations of three-wheelers produced on the eve of the Olympia show were up 18.9 per cent over the previous year. The annual Morgan sales had increased by a lesser amount, from 591 to 659 machines, but this reflected the more competitive market. The market leaders were BSA with their advanced front-wheel-drive machine, but competition was also provided by Coventry Victor, J.M.B. and Raleigh. The J.M.B. comprised a tubular chassis with a centrally mounted single-cylinder JAP engine in unit with a three-speed and reverse gear-box driving the single rear wheel. In side-valve form it was the cheapest vehicle on the market and at £75 12s was substantially less than the Morgan. The Raleigh, the only three-wheeler with two rear wheels, had originally cost £105, the same as the Morgan, but was later reduced to £99 15s.

The beetle-back body style had remained available alongside the barrel-back on the Super Sports during 1934. For 1935 the Super Sports was available only with the barrel-back design of body common to the other models of the range. This permitted the spare wheel to be carried neatly within a recess in the tail section. A polished aluminium disk covered the wheel, but not the tyre, to further enhance the rear view of the machine. A wooden luggage grid was fitted at the top of the body in the

Factory photograph of the MX2 Super Sports. November 1934.

The Matchless engines, which had been introduced across the range the previous year, had proved popular. For 1935 they were standardized for all V-twin models and, for the first time since the start of manufacture in 1910, the Morgan range did not include a JAP powered machine. The Family, Sports Family and Sports two-seater models were unchanged in both price and specification. The Super Sports cost £127 10s fitted with the air-cooled MX2 engine or £137 10s with the water-cooled MX4 unit. The prices of the Delivery Van and Model F models were also unchanged.

Moving Home and Semi Retirement

In 1925 the Morgan family had moved from Chestnut Villa to a larger house, Fern Lodge, a short distance along Worcester Road. The

position previously occupied by the precariously mounted spare. The exhaust pipes were located at a lower level along the body side to lessen the likelihood of scorched elbows. The F type was also given a more rounded rear section, with the spare wheel mounting slightly recessed within the bodywork. In other respects the model range was unchanged.

90

family moved house for a second time in 1935. The new property, Cannon Hill, was a spacious house dating from the reign of Charles II and designed by the Adam brothers. It was set in twenty-five acres of parkland at Bray near Maidenhead in Berkshire. HFS was by now a wealthy man in his mid-fifties and the move provided the opportunity to start cutting back on his day-to-day involvement in the running of the company. Increasingly the management was passed to George Goodall, who had been appointed works manager in 1927 following the premature death of the company's first works manager, Alfie Hales. HFS still stayed closely involved with the factory and most weeks would travel to Malvern from Bray in a car of his own manufacture in order to assess the new models and the design improvements. He was able to afford luxury cars, and owned several, but these were retained for family use, frequently taking the family on holiday at home and abroad.

Four-Wheeler Salvation – The Introduction of the 4-4

Despite the modest improvement in the sales figures for 1934, it was clear that the day of the three-wheeler was coming to an end and for Morgan to survive as a car manufacturer it would become necessary to embrace the four-wheeler. The new Model F, with its 4-cylinder engine and Z-section chassis, provided an excellent basis for a prototype four-wheeler and it was not long before HFS had a machine constructed. A modified F type chassis with a reduced front-track width was used. The engine was the Ford 8hp unit, fitted to the three-wheeler, and drive was taken through a centrally mounted gearbox. The rear axle was initially suspended on quarter-elliptic springs attached to the outside of the Z-section rear chassis members. This arrangement, however, proved unsatisfactory and the suspension was soon changed to semi-elliptic springs with an under-slung axle.

Development of the four-wheeler had con-

tinued through 1935 and, towards the end of the year, a development machine was fitted with the new Ford 10hp engine, which was about to be offered as an option with the Model F. In this form HFS used the machine for his transport to and from the Motorcycle Show at Olympia. He also entered the car, with son Peter as co-driver, in the MCC Exeter Trial on Boxing Day. The car was entered in a special class for drivers who had competed in the first Exeter Trial held twenty-five years earlier. In 1910 HFS had won a gold medal with his first production Runabout and in 1935 was the only entrant in the class to win a first-class award.

The introduction of the Model F had done little to improve the declining sales performance of the Morgan three-wheeler. The 1935 production figure of 286 three-wheelers was less than half the 1934 total. Clearly company salvation, if it existed, lay in the production of craftsmen-built sporting four-

The F type was much less well suited to trials use than the earlier two-speeder models. This machine benefits from external assistance during the 1938 Exeter Trial.

Henry and Barbara Laird

As the grandson of the founder of the Cammell Laird shipbuilding company, Henry Laird was expected to take up a city job. This offered no appeal to Henry, who chose instead to work with Michael McEvoy and ended up developing and testing vehicle performance equipment. Henry's first Morgan was a 1925 Aero, which was nicknamed Johnny I. Other Morgans followed, each with the same nickname. To celebrate their engagement, Barbara was offered the choice of an engagement ring or a Morgan and chose Johnny IV, a Super Sports with ohv JAP engine. This machine provided a first taste of trials driving in M.C.C. events before being exchanged for a later Super Sports, Johnny V, better known as Johnny Yellow or simply Yellow. The Lairds by this time were taking part increasingly in trials and it was not long before Yellow was returned to the factory to be fitted with straight cross-tubes, to increase clearance, and other modifications to allow it to run in more demanding events. In 1932, Yellow was competing successfully in trials as well as providing everyday transport.

An ex-Maskell racer, basically a three-speed Super Sports fitted with an older dog-eared JAP engine, was purchased in 1933 and christened Johnny Red. Laird gained second place on his first outing with the car at the Easter Donington meeting. In July he joined the works team of Rhodes and Lones to take part in the Light Car Club's relay race at Brooklands. The team managed second place, but the race was notable for Rhodes lapping at over 100mph; Laird managed 89.01mph (142.42km/h). Henry gained his first win with Red at Donington the following year. The same year Yellow obtained a gold medal in the I.S.D.T. in Bavaria.

The association with McEvoy resulted in both Red and Yellow appearing with Zoller superchargers for 1935. The installation on Red had not been without difficulties but, once teething problems had been overcome, the car proved extremely rapid. The first outing at Brooklands resulted in a win in a five-lap handicap race and a new cyclecar record for the mountain circuit. Red then went on to wrest from Gwenda Stewart the world records for the standing-start kilometre at 72.29mph (115.66km/h) and mile at 81.57mph (130.51km/h).

Henry, usually with Barbara as an enthusiastic passenger and able mechanic, was uniquely versatile in achieving success in trials, races and record breaking. The Lairds were amongst the most famous sporting drivers of their day. Both Red and Yellow went into retirement in 1937 when Henry joined *Motor Cycling* as Midland Editor. He was sadly killed in a motorcycling accident during the blackout in 1941.

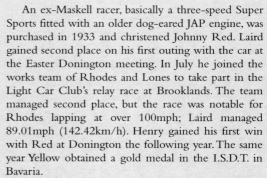

Above *Johnny Yellow — The Laird's trials Morgan.*

Johnny Red — The Laird's racer. The photograph is from August 1936 and shows Red with an air-cooled supercharged JAP.

wheelers. The Morgan agents had suffered just as badly from falling sales as the company. To make amends it was announced in January 1936 that agents who had been faithful to the company in the sale of three-wheelers were to be given preferential opportunity to handle the new car. By the time of its launch in March 1936, the Ford 10hp engine had been replaced by an 1122cc inlet-over-exhaust Coventry-Climax engine. The model was known as the 4-4 to denote four cylinders and four wheels.

A Model F two-seater was added to the Morgan range for 1936. It was fitted with a sporting body styled along the lines of the 2-cylinder Super Sports. The Ford 4-cylinder engine had proved popular and was retained, but was now offered as either an 8hp or 10hp unit, the latter deriving from the De Luxe version of the Ford. Prices for 1936 were quoted in guineas. The 8hp version was priced at 115 guineas (£120 15s), whilst the 10hp version cost an additional 7 guineas (total price £128 2s). The rest of the Morgan model range was unchanged, but prices of all models were substantially reduced. The full model range is listed below:

Family MX £96 12s
Sports 2-seater MX £101 17s; MX2 £107 2s;
  MX4 £115 10s
Sports Family MX £110 5s; MX2 £115 10s;
  MX4 £120 15s
Super Sports MX2 £126; MX4 £136 10s
Delivery Van MX £105
Model F4 Ford 8hp £115 10s.
Model F2 Ford 8hp £120 15s;
  Ford 10hp £128 2s

Morgan took pride of place at the Olympia show and that year had only to compete with BSA for orders. Nine models were exhibited together with a 2-cylinder and a 4-cylinder chassis. Eye-catching colour schemes were the order of the day. The 8hp Model F two-seater was finished in black and cream, whilst a duo-grey scheme was used for the 10hp version. The Model F four-seater was finished in Nile

A MX2 Super Sports competing in the 1936 Lands End Trial.

blue. The two Super Sports were finished in British Racing Green and in red-and-cream, whilst the two Sports two-seaters were finished in red-and-cream and in duo blue.

The Death of HG

In October 1936, a fire destroyed the coach building shop at the Morgan works. Production was maintained by buying in components from local firms and the damage was quickly made good. A sadder event occurred the following month with the death on 10 November of the company chairman, and HFS's father, the Rev. H.G. Morgan. HG was buried in the family plot just inside the entrance of the Stoke Lacy churchyard. The present gate to the churchyard was erected to his memory, in June 1938, by HFS and his sisters. In the fullness of time, HFS and his wife Ruth, with other family members, would be laid to rest in the same family plot.

HG left all his shares in the Morgan Company to his son, who succeeded him as chairman of the company. George Goodall, the works manager, was appointed a director of

The Morgan stand at the 1937 Olympia Show.

the company at the annual general meeting held in July 1937 and the following year succeeded HFS as managing director. He continued as managing director through to the fifties.

The twin-cylinder Family model was dropped from the range for 1937, but all the remaining models were listed with only minor revisions and without any alteration to price. The Ford 10hp engine was made available with the Model F four-seater for an extra £7 7s, and the Sports two-seater body could be fitted with doors for an extra £5.

Total production of three-wheelers during 1937 was a modest 137 cars and increasingly the company was relying on sales of its four-wheeler.

A New 4-cylinder Super Sports

A new super-sports version of the 4-cylinder Model F was introduced for the 1938 season. It was built on a shortened F-type chassis with the Ford 10hp power unit and fitted with a body similar to that of the twin-cylinder Super Sports. The major innovation in the design was the fitting of Girling brakes operated by Bowden cables. The new model was priced at £136 10s, the same as the Super Sports twin fitted with the specially tuned version of the water-cooled Matchless engine. The water-cooled

Sports two-seater model was discontinued. The other models, namely the Super Sports twins and the Model F, both two- and four-seaters, remained available at the same price as the previous year.

Demand for the Morgan three-wheeler continued to fall during 1938 and production amounted to only 110 cars. Further rationalization of the Morgan three-wheeler range for the 1939 season was essential. The model F2 was discontinued. The F4 was listed with the 8hp engine, whilst the super-sports version of the Model F, now known as the F Super, was available with the 10hp engine. The Super Sports model continued to be offered with either the air-cooled MX2 or water-cooled MX4 engine. The prices were unchanged from the previous year.

Announcement was made in June 1939 that the air-cooled MX2 Super Sports would no longer continue in production.

The MX4 Super Sports twin and the 4-cylinder F4 and F Super models were still in production at the start of the Second World War, but sales were few. The total Morgan production figure for 1939, including four-wheelers, was down to 263 machines and of these only twenty-nine were three-wheelers. Wartime petrol restrictions were quickly imposed and initially it was announced that three-wheelers would be classed as motorcycles and restricted to two gallons of petrol a month. This would have represented a significant disadvantage to Morgan owners, but fortunately good counsel prevailed and three-wheelers were grouped with cars and allocated petrol according to horsepower. The Super Sports and F4 were allowed five gallons per month and the F Super a further gallon. This placed the Morgan in an advantageous position, since being of light weight the machines offered good fuel economy; a situation that the firm was quick to publicize in an attempt to clear stock. All the machines on offer had by this time been fitted with Girling brakes with independent operation of the front and rear brakes, by foot and hand, respectively.

Wartime Restrictions

Car production came quickly to an end at the start of the war. The last pre-war Morgan, a Model F, was dispatched in July 1940. Many of the company's workers were called up into the armed forces or transferred to firms carrying out higher priority work. As a consequence the changeover to government contracts was a

gradual process. Ultimately the Morgan company would be wholly involved in war work and manufactured components such as shell cases, anti-aircraft gun components and aircraft undercarriages. The work utilized only part of the Morgan works and the remaining buildings were used either for storage or let to other government contractors. The Standard Motor Company, now run by John Black, who had produced HFS's first patent drawings, used two of the buildings for the manufacture of aircraft carburettors. Flight Refuelling Ltd both rented space and added new buildings on adjacent farmland in Pickersleigh Avenue. These would be incorporated into the Morgan factory after the war.

Post-War Finale

The Matchless MX series of engines proved to be a casualty of war and only the Ford engines remained available by 1945. The post-war Morgan offerings were initially to comprise two four-wheelers, the 4-4 Two-seater and the 4-4 Coupé, and two three-wheelers. The latter were the 8hp Model F4 four-seater and the 10hp Model F Super; and both were

The Model F display chassis at the 1949 Olympia show.

HFS.

unchanged from their pre-war specification. They were now priced at £205 plus £57 13s 10d purchase tax for the F4 and £245 plus £68 16s 1d purchase tax for the F Super.

Steel was in short supply and quotas were rationed against overseas orders. In July 1945 the company obtained official authority to build fifty three-wheelers and seventy-five four-wheelers by the end of the year; many fewer than had been hoped but nevertheless grossly optimistic. No V-twin models were catalogued post-war, but twelve MX4 Super Sports were constructed for export. It is presumed the engines were surplus pre-war units in store at the works. Nine of these were to the order of a wealthy Australian racing driver and were dispatched to Australia during the latter half of 1946. The last machine left the works on the second day of January 1947.

Post-war inflation resulted in the prices of the cars steadily increasing. By 1948 the prices had risen to £246 15s (plus £69 5s 10d pur-

chase tax) for the Model F4 and to £260 (plus £72 19s 5d) for the Model F Super. By 1951 the quoted prices were respectively £270 (plus £75 15s) and £285 (plus £79 18s 4d).

The government guidelines of 'export or die' forced Morgan to expand its overseas sales to the detriment of the home market. In these markets, not blessed with the tax advantages afforded three-wheelers in the UK, three-wheelers proved almost un-saleable. The three-wheeler had become an anachronism in the post-war world and the end was inevitable. The Model F was discontinued in 1952; the last F4 was completed in March and the last machine, an F Super, left the factory in July.

The Death of HFS

H.F.S. Morgan died in Malvern on 15 June 1959 at the age of seventy-eight and some fifty years after he had begun to build his first run-about. Ruth, his wife, had died three years previously in February 1956.

HFS will always be remembered for the small sporting cars that bear his name, yet his love of motorcars was much more general. As a child brought up in a wealthy family, he experienced many of the finest early motor-cars. His own first cars, the Eagle Tandem and Star, may have been of lower quality, but as a garage owner he would soon gain experience of better quality makes such as Wolseley and Darracq. In the early years of car manufacture, HFS drove his own Runabouts. However, with increasing family commitments he drove other cars such as Lanchesters, Hupmobiles and a Prince Henry Vauxhall. By the early twenties, HFS was an extremely wealthy man and could fully indulge his love of fine motorcars. He owned examples of the Rolls-Royce Silver Ghost, Bentley and Rolls-Royce Phantom II. Ruth also owned several examples of the better sporting makes, such as Alvis and Riley. Often the cars were fitted with special bodies constructed in the Morgan factory to HFS's own design. HFS was also a pioneer of the

Family

The 1930 Family model was a fully equipped car for the family man and represented excellent value for money. The styling, however, recalls the Edwardian period of motoring with flat-section mudguards and elaborate coach lining. Later models would be fitted with more rounded bodywork and cycle mudguards.

Below The coal-scuttle bonnet, which was introduced in 1911, remained a feature of the Family model through to the discontinuation of the model in 1936.

Below The front view of the 1930 Family Morgan suggests a conventional, but dated, design. The rear view gives the game away and suggests something rather unusual. The drive chains, either side of the rear wheel, identify a two-speeder.

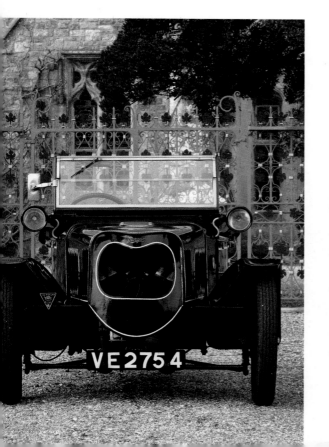

Family

Above left *Dashboard instrumentation comprises a round Lucas switch panel with ammeter, located in front of the passenger, which is matched on the right-hand side by a speedometer. The sight glass for the oil drip feed to the engine is located at the centre. The driver is required to adjust the rate of oil flow according to the load on the engine. The horn button is located below the sight glass.*

Above right *The 980cc, side-valve, JAP KT engine was the most popular engine fitted to Morgans. The use of the water-cooled KTW engine involved mounting a radiator between the engine and fuel tank.*

Left *The fuel tank, with integral oil container, is mounted on the scuttle; re-fuelling involves lifting the bonnet. The gears and external gearbox on the right-hand front wheel provide the drive for the speedometer.*

Below *The Family model offered good weather protection for both the front and rear-seat passengers. Access, via the single nearside door, was as easy with the hood in use as when it was folded. The front side-screens were an optional fitment.*

Super Sports

Right and below left
The beetle-back body of the Super Sports, which dates back to the Super Sports Aero introduced at the end of 1927, was phased out during 1934. The heat shields, to protect occupants' limbs, and the fishtails are popular fitments to the exhaust system.

Far right *The radiator badge identifies the car as a Morgan Super Sports. The Boyce Motometer shows the radiator temperature and is a practical replacement for the Morgan stork.*

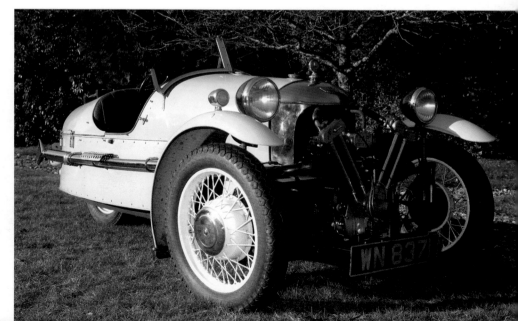

The beetle-back body is especially handsome when not encumbered with spare wheel and hood.

The spare wheel was never an elegant fitment on the beetle-back Super Sports. The wheel carrier on this late model has been replaced by a grid in order that luggage can be carried for touring. The high-level twin exhausts confirm the sporting nature of the car when viewed from the rear.

Left The 1096cc JAP LTOWZ engine, with its aluminium covers for the overhead valve gear and heated inlet manifold, is a handsome unit to adorn the front of the Super Sports. The power output of almost 40bhp is ample for exhilarating performance.

The steering wheel controls comprise a left-hand-operated magneto advance and retard lever, together with right-hand-operated throttle and choke controls.

Above *A light-blue body with matching chassis and cream wheels and wings was one of the four standard colour schemes offered on the Super Sports for the 1935 season. The double 'D' cut-outs in the bonnet sides had been introduced the previous year.*

Below *The dropped chassis and air-cooled, overhead valve MX2 engine of this 1935 Super Sports create a striking and purposeful image. The headlights mounted on the mudguard stays emphasize the low build of the car. Matchless engines had been standardized across the V-twin range by this time.*

The winged 'M' mascot replaced the Morgan stork on the barrel-back Super Sports for the 1934 season.

The barrel back body is terminated by a housing for the spare wheel, which is both functional and stylish.

The main feature of the dashboard is the central switch panel with speedometer and ammeter. The panel includes a dash lamp to illuminate the speedometer at night and a socket for an inspection lamp.

Without doors to facilitate entry, it is necessary to raise and fasten the hood whilst seated in the car. The cockpit, which can best be described as 'cosy', becomes claustrophobic with the hood in place and it is hardly surprising that many owners prefer to dispense with the hood, whatever the weather.

On the right of the dashboard are located a St Christopher plaque, incorporating the car number, and a plate giving instructions for checking the gearbox oil.

'F' Super Sports

Above *The Model 'F' Super Sports, introduced in September 1936, was an attempt to enhance the staid image of the 4-cylinder cars. The chassis was reduced in length by 4in and a larger-capacity (1172cc) engine fitted. The body, with styling based upon the twin-cylinder Super Sports, was reduced in length and made both wider and lower.*

The F-type Morgan does not possess the striking good looks of the V-twin sporting models, but is as handsome as any small sporting car of its day.

Below *Barrel-back styling was featured on all Morgans from the 1935 season.*

Above *The forward view emphasizes the low build of the 'F' Super. The windscreen may be lowered if required.*

Above *The 1172cc, 4-cylinder Ford engine gives a maximum speed of over 70mph (113km/h) and allows indefinite cruising at 65mph (105km/h). The SU carburettor is a replacement for the original Zenith unit.*

The non-standard steering wheel has been cut away to improve driver access. The throttle is controlled by a foot pedal. The Lucas dashboard panel was fitted across the Morgan range.

Below *'For the man who wants speed and acceleration combined with silence, comfort, and the running costs of a motorcycle, we have produced this model.' The statement made in the sales brochure includes a touch of the salesman's hyperbole, but there is no denying the present day appeal of the 'F' Super.*

Above *The photograph is of the Rolls Royce 40/50hp Phantom II with special all-weather bodywork, which was designed by HFS and constructed in the Morgan works during 1930. The mascot depicts the Morgan stork rather than the Rolls Royce flying lady.*

The 1896 Pennington three-wheeler formed part of HFS's collection of historic cars. It was photographed alongside the Model F for publicity purposes.

preservation movement and in the mid-thirties assembled a collection of early light cars and cyclecars.

HFS left the Morgan Company jointly to his son, Peter, and his four daughters. Peter, who had joined the company in 1947 upon demob from the Royal Army Service Corps with the rank of captain, became managing director in 1958. Upon the death of his father he took over as chairman, whilst continuing as managing director. The following years were a difficult period for Peter and the Morgan Company. The viability of a traditionally styled and constructed sports car was no longer certain and Peter was almost alone amongst his family in his determination that the company should survive. He was also beset with problems with the Inland Revenue over the company's liabilities following the death of his father. It was due to his determination and faith in the cars that the company survives to this day.

6 Chassis Design, Development and Innovation

Throughout the period of three-wheeler production the design remained true to the original concept of light construction, with front-mounted engine, rear-wheel drive and all-round independent suspension. That is not, however, to imply that changes were not being made to benefit from engineering developments and to ensure that the car retained its competitive edge and commercial appeal. Three distinct chassis and transmission configurations were adopted, namely two-speeder, three-speeder and F-type. These confer specific driving characteristics to the cars and represent a convenient form of classification. The early cars, the two-speeders, followed closely the design of the prototype and employed a tubular frame with rear bevel box, a two-speed transmission and separate transmission chains for high and low gear. The early two-speeder chassis, without the tiller steering bracket, is known as the 'B' type chassis. The chassis was beefed up from October 1926 to cope with the heavier and more commodious bodies then being fitted. The bevel box was strengthened and made wider, to allow use of larger ball races and stronger rear forks. The modified chassis became known as the 'wide B' to distinguish it from the earlier 'narrow B' type. There was an attempt to update the two-speeder with the introduction of the 'M' chassis from October 1929. This conferred several engineering advantages over the earlier chassis and provided the basis for the three-speeder models introduced in October 1931. The 'M' chassis was phased out upon the introduction of the three-speeder, although the earlier two-speeder 'B' chassis survived for a further year

on the cheapest models. The three-speeder offered a three-speed and reverse gearbox but retained the tubular chassis frame. The F-type, introduced at the 1933 Olympia Show, was constructed on a Z-section girder type chassis and the motorcycle-derived engines of the earlier models were replaced by a 4-cylinder Ford car engine. The F-type would provide the inspiration for the design of the four-wheeled models and the future direction of the Morgan Company.

The sections of this chapter describe the various chassis and detail the major changes made during the production years of the three-wheeler. Numerous different proprietary engines from a variety of manufacturers were fitted and are listed in the following chapter.

The Two-Speeders

General Arrangement of the Early 'B' Chassis

The first cars shown to the public at the 1910 Motor Cycle Exhibition were single-seaters and steered using a tiller operated by the right hand. The main frame member comprised a large-diameter torque tube brazed into a cruciform bracket, referred to as the star lug, at its forward end and soft soldered into a bevel box placed immediately in front of the rear wheel. Lugs brazed to the bottom arms of the cruciform located two smaller diameter tubes below and to the side of the torque tube. These extended forward to provide the lower attachments for the engine mounting-plates and back to the bevel box, where they were brazed

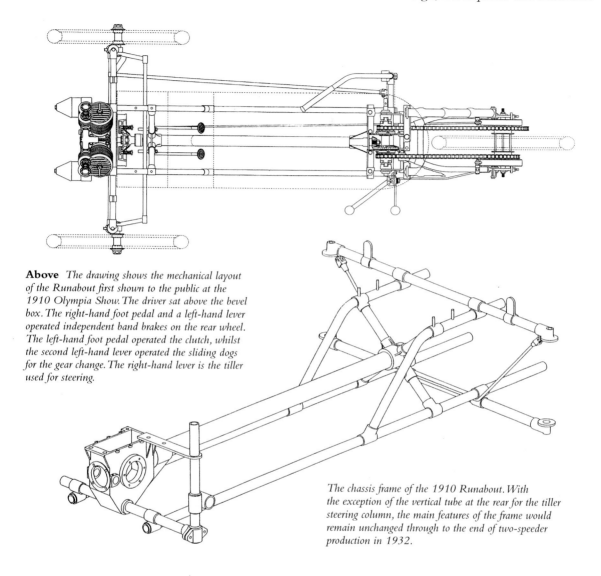

Above *The drawing shows the mechanical layout of the Runabout first shown to the public at the 1910 Olympia Show. The driver sat above the bevel box. The right-hand foot pedal and a left-hand lever operated independent band brakes on the rear wheel. The left-hand foot pedal operated the clutch, whilst the second left-hand lever operated the sliding dogs for the gear change. The right-hand lever is the tiller used for steering.*

The chassis frame of the 1910 Runabout. With the exception of the vertical tube at the rear for the tiller steering column, the main features of the frame would remain unchanged through to the end of two-speeder production in 1932.

into lugs attached to a short length of tube passing through the bevel box. They combined with the torque tube to form a longitudinal frame structure of great rigidity, yet extremely light in weight. Tubes forming the upper attachments for the engine plates passed through the lugs attached to the upper arms of the cruciform before bending down to attach to the lower frame tubes. A pair of transverse tubes, attached one below the lower pair of longitudinal tubes and one above the upper

pair, provided the attachment for the front wheel swivel-pins and suspension. The tubes were braced by a steel tie-rod, attached at the outer ends of the top cross tube and passing diagonally down and under the engine mounting-tubes.

Lugs at the ends of the front transverse tubes were machined to locate vertical tubes, retained by through bolts, which formed the vertical pillars of the front suspension. Steel sliders, carrying the front wheel stub-axles,

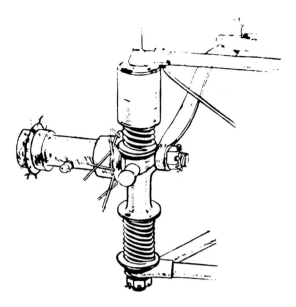

The illustration, from 1912, shows the arrangement of the front suspension and steering. The slider moves both up and down and rotates about a vertical tube clamped between the chassis cross tubes. Total vertical movement is no more than about one inch. The first cars used steel sliders, but these were soon replaced by phosphor-bronze castings to provide an integral bearing surface. At about the same time, the suspension springs were fitted with a top cover, as illustrated, in an attempt to reduce wear due to the ingress of grit. Regular greasing was essential and a grease cup was fitted.

moved up and down the tubes, under the restraint of an upper suspension spring and a lower rebound spring, to provide suspension. Rotation of the slider about the vertical tube provided steering. The steering arms, attached to the sliders by the stub-axle bolts, were linked by a non-adjustable track rod. A long drag link connected the arm at the base of the tiller column to the steering arm at the front wheel.

The propeller shaft rotated within the central chassis tube. It consisted of a hollow tube with solid steel end-sections riveted in position. The front section was machined square and located within the clutch to obtain drive. The rear section was machined to locate within a ball race, at the front face of the bevel box,

and for attachment of the smaller of the bevel gears. The larger bevel gear was keyed to a countershaft, rotating within bearings located in the sidewalls of the box. The drive sprockets were fitted outside the box and were free to rotate about the shaft; the smaller sprocket on the right providing bottom gear and the larger left-hand sprocket the top gear drive. The ends of the countershaft were machined square to provide drive to dog clutches free to move along the shaft and engage with similar dogs forming part of the sprockets. Bottom gear was engaged when the right-hand dogs were meshed, top gear when the dogs on the opposite side meshed. Gears were selected by moving a simple, left-hand operated, lever attached to the gear selector forks.

The rear wheel was located within a swinging arm, pivoted about a rod passing through the rear of the bevel box. It was supported by a pair of quarter-elliptic springs bolted to angle-iron cross members attached to the top of the bevel box. Braking was effected by external contracting bands operating on drums attached either side of the wheel.

The engine, mounted within engine plates, slid onto the four tubes protruding from the front of the chassis frame and bolted in position. The flywheel, which incorporated a cone clutch, was external and located behind the engine. The exhaust comprised aluminium 'coffee pot' expansion chambers, fitted over the ends of the lower chassis tubes, which doubled up as tail pipes allowing the exhaust gases to escape at the rear of the car.

The bodywork of the cars rested on the top chassis tubes, behind the front transverse tube, and the two lengths of angle iron attached to the top of the bevel box.

Although the basic design of the Runabout was sound, several improvements were found necessary. The development of the cars in the early days was a continuously on-going programme as weaknesses were identified and improvements made. Design modifications were very quickly tested on the factory machines and in competition, and just as quickly incorporated into the production models. An early modification was the fitting of diagonal bracing-tubes between the bottom of the steering pin and the lower chassis tubes. Other improvements followed. In some instances the factory was reluctant to make change, perhaps due to manufacturing pressures or the desire not to complicate the design, and it was left to others to offer proprietary fitments to satisfy users' demands.

The following sub-sections consider the evolution of the various component parts of the two-speeder design and explain, as appropriate, the reasons for change.

Steering and Wheel Wobble

Tiller steering proved perfectly acceptable, unless the driver was of a corpulent build, but by 1910 the public perception was that a tiller had become old fashioned. It was replaced by a steering wheel in August 1911, upon the introduction of the first two-seater Runabout. No steering reduction box was fitted and the wheel was little more than a circular tiller, with barely half a turn from lock-to-lock. The steering column was anchored to the wooden bodywork, rather than rigidly mounted to the chassis frame in the manner of the tiller mechanism.

An inherent weakness in the Morgan design of sliding-pillar front suspension is that the stub axle has to be well behind the steering axis in order that the two holes in the slider do not intersect. This increases the castor action and results in heavy steering. Furthermore, as wear sets in it creates a tendency to violent wheel wobble in the manner nowadays familiar with shopping trolleys. Both of these problems would be solved by proprietary attachments before being tackled by the factory.

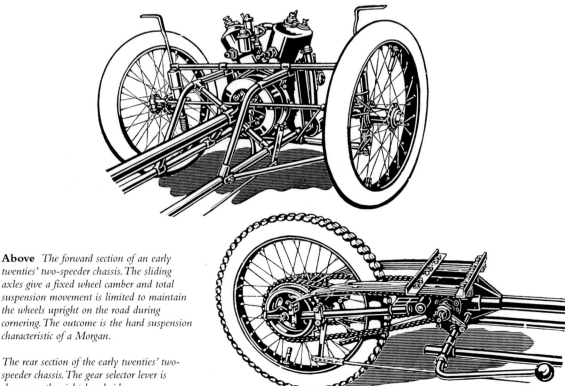

Above *The forward section of an early twenties' two-speeder chassis. The sliding axles give a fixed wheel camber and total suspension movement is limited to maintain the wheels upright on the road during cornering. The outcome is the hard suspension characteristic of a Morgan.*

The rear section of the early twenties' two-speeder chassis. The gear selector lever is shown on the right-hand side.

Whilst the direct steering of the early two-speeders could be a delight under many circumstances, by the mid-twenties it was proving unpopular. The *Light Car and Cyclecar* commented, rather kindly, in a road test of the Aero model in May 1925:

> The direct steering seems a little strange at first to one who has become used to the orthodox geared-down type, but the car did not prove difficult to control, either through traffic or along country roads. It must be admitted, however, that a greater effort was required to steer this Morgan than a conventional light car, and this is noticeable particularly when rounding curves of comparatively large radius at high speeds. We believe that some simple form of steering reduction gear would be a distinct advantage.

A solution to the direct steering problem was found in 1923 by Bernard Whomes, an electrical salesman of Bexley Heath, who fitted his Anzani-powered racing Morgan with the epicyclic steering-reduction box from a Ford Model-T. Other owners soon copied the idea and the modification became de rigueur on racing machines. Harold Beart fitted the Ford box to his 100mph record breaker and offered to install a similar unit to any type of Morgan. It was not until the 1928 season that Morgan began offering its own version of a two-to-one epicyclic reduction box. Initially it was a £2 extra, but by the following year it was being fitted as standard. The use of steering-reduction boxes was not totally trouble free, owing to the ignition and carburettor controls mounted on the arms of the steering wheel.

Right *The Hooley Steering Damper was available from the early twenties and provided a solution to the problem of wheel wobble.*

The Morgan steering-reduction box was fastened to the bulkhead and offered a 2 to 1 reduction. A pinion attached to the upper column was eccentrically mounted and could be adjusted to mesh with the internal cut outer ring attached to the lower column.

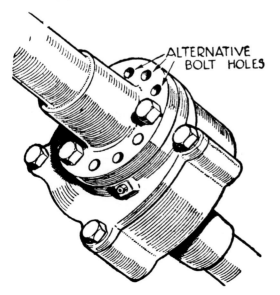

ALTERNATIVE BOLT HOLES

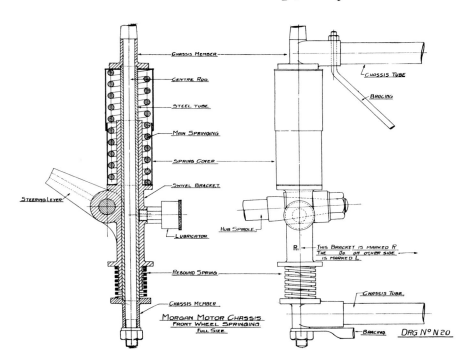

By 1916 the front suspension springs were totally enclosed in a pair of spun-brass covers. It was recommended that the sliders should be greased regularly, at least every 100 miles, using the grease cup provided and the sliding axles renewed every 6,000 miles. Grease gun lubrication was introduced at the end of 1926, but it was 1929 before an internal recess was machined for the retention of grease in order to prolong life.

MORGAN MOTOR CHASSIS
FRONT WHEEL SPRINGING
FULL SIZE.

DRG N° N 20

Rotation of the wheel had the effect of moving the throttle control to the opposite hand and reversing its direction, as well as winding the Bowden cables round the steering column. Some owners devised ingenious methods to mount the controls on the dashboard, but most coped well enough. Beart and many of the other racers adopted the expedient of a foot throttle.

A simple solution to the problem of wheel wobble was to stop it before it began by adding friction to the various linkages. Lesley Hooley, a mechanic at the Nottingham agency of John Sylvester, hit upon the idea of incorporating a friction damper into the joint at one end of the track rod. The device comprised a friction disc clamped between two bronze discs and a coil-spring tensioner. The factory solution to the problem appeared at the same time as the steering-reduction box, on the 1928 season models from chassis number 13981, and comprised tapered anti-wobble steering pins for the track-rod ends. These were spring-loaded

and, provided that they were not lubricated, would supply sufficient friction to damp down steering oscillation.

Adjustable track-rods were first fitted for the 1916 season. Prior to that date, tracking adjustment was only possible by bending the steering arm. Revised steering stops were introduced on the Super Sports Aero from 14 February 1929 and on the other models from 1 April.

The front wheel spindles of the early cars were threaded left and right handed. The cup and cone bearings were fitted with $\frac{1}{4}$in ball bearings. For 1914 the spindles were made $\frac{3}{4}$in diameter and both threaded right-handed. For 1921, larger front wheel hubs were fitted and the wheels were taper fitted into the sliding axles. The wheels were fitted with larger hubs, to run on $\frac{3}{8}$in ball bearings.

The Cone Clutch

A cone clutch was incorporated within the back of the external flywheel behind the engine. The first clutches relied upon metal-to-metal contact and were harsh to operate unless carefully lubricated. The clutch cone was lined with leather for the 1913 season. For 1917 the clutch was increased in size and Ferodo friction linings introduced.

In November 1920, the clutch withdrawal mechanism was redesigned with fibre blocks replacing the operating ring. The operating fork was now pivoted on a removable pin, which once released allowed the mechanism to be withdrawn as a unit, complete with the fibre blocks, in order to facilitate removal of the engine. Two modifications were made to the flywheel at this time. A dust cover for the clutch was screwed to its rear face and a small pulley incorporated at the front, close-up against the crankcase, for a dynamo drive-belt.

An improved dust cover, offering better enclosure of the clutch, was fitted to flywheels with self-starter rings from September 1928 and to all models by the time of the Olympia Show in November.

Chains, Sprockets, Sliding Dogs and Gears

The standard gear ratios on the early cars were 4.5 to 1 and 8 to 1. These could easily be changed by fitting alternative chain sprockets, and special gear sets were available for trials and racing. The low gear used twelve teeth and thirty-eight teeth-sprockets with an eighty-four-link chain, whilst top gear used fourteen teeth and twenty-five teeth-sprockets with a seventy-eight link chain; the bevel gears had sixteen teeth and forty teeth. The high gear sprockets were changed to eighteen teeth and thirty-three teeth at the end of 1920 for the 1921 season, at the same time as other chassis changes were introduced. This allowed an eighty-four-link chain to be used for both gears. It was now necessary to carry only a single spare chain and the harder working high-gear chain could be periodically exchanged with the low-gear chain to even out stretch. The bevel gears were also changed at this time to straight-cut bevels of twelve teeth and thir-

ty teeth. Alternative bevel gears were fitted from the end of 1924 and comprised the option of straight-cut twelve teeth and thirty teeth, or spiral-cut twelve teeth and thirty teeth, or thirteen teeth and thirty-one teeth.

The light weight of the Runabout and the good pulling power of the early V-twin engines meant that the two-speeder arrangement was adequate for all normal road applications. However, notwithstanding the successes of HFS and numerous others, it soon became apparent that two speeds gave insufficient flexibility and handicapped the potential of the car for trials use. Morgan's answer to this problem, announced in June 1913, was a four-speeder chassis for competition use. The twin-chain final drive was retained and an additional two-speed gearbox was brazed onto the front of the main chassis tube immediately behind the clutch. The gearbox was of conventional design, with a layshaft turned by a pinion keyed to the clutch shaft. A sleeve, able to slide along splines machined into the end of the propshaft, carried a pair of pinions. The lower, half speed, gear ratio was obtained when the larger of these pinions engaged with the layshaft. The direct-drive high-gear was obtained when the smaller pinion engaged with the internal teeth of the pinion fixed to the clutch shaft. A separate gear-lever attached to the central chassis tube, to the left of the driver, was used to operate the extra gear-change mechanism and obtain a pair of ultra-low ratios. The four-speed option was priced initially at £10 and would remain available through to the 1923 season.

Another drawback of the Morgan two-speeder arrangement was the omission of a reverse gear. This shortcoming was acceptable in the early lightweight cars, which were easily pushed and had very little bodywork to impede entry and exit. It became less acceptable in more fully bodied cars and as drivers' expectations increased. Although Morgan would not meet the demand until the introduction of the three-speeder, others were less slow in coming forward with solutions.

In November 1922, Mr L. Anderton of Leeds described the use of a bevel box with twin crown wheels to obtain a reverse gear, an idea reintroduced by Jackson & Booth Ltd of Cheshire in June 1926. Two reverse gears and equal performance backwards as forwards could only be considered a recipe for disaster! In August 1923, Frank Boddington, the Worcester Morgan agent, was offering a simple reversing mechanism to fit on the side of the bevel box. The low-gear sprocket was replaced by a double-toothed free-running sprocket wheel. The dog for engaging low gear was replaced by a sliding dog and gear wheel.

A four-speed and reverse gearbox was marketed by the Caton Machine Tool and Engineering Co. of Leeds in June 1923. The complete box was the same size and shape as the standard bevel box, which it replaced without alterations to the frame. Gears were included both inside and outside the box to obtain the various ratios and a single drive chain was used. The first gear ratio gave an emergency low gear, second and third ratios were unchanged from standard Morgan practice and

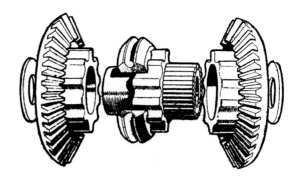

The Jackson and Booth arrangement of crown wheels and central dog clutch to obtain a reverse gear.

the top ratio provided a gear for high-speed cruising on the level. Interestingly, the Caton gearbox addressed a further Morgan deficiency, as it provided means to adjust the mesh of the bevel pinion and crown wheel for quiet running.

A simpler solution offering three gears, but no reverse, was proposed by Mr F.H. Hambling in November 1923. However, it did not

The Boddington reverse gear attachment, fitted to the outside of the bevel box, was operated by an additional lever inside the car. It cost £7 15s inclusive of fitting.

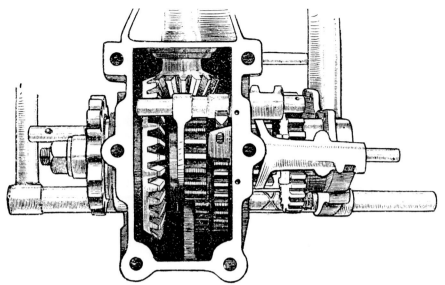

*The Caton four-speed and
reverse gearbox.*

become available until April 1927 and was then priced at £12. The arrangement comprised a heavy-duty motorcycle-style gearbox mounted outside the bevel box on an extension of the countershaft. The sprocket for the single drive chain was concentric with the shaft. The conversion provided an ultra-low bottom gear of 15.2 to 1, but left the other ratios unchanged from standard.

The Morgan is a hands-on car attractive to the amateur engineer. Not surprisingly, there-

The new type of rear fork introduced for 1921.

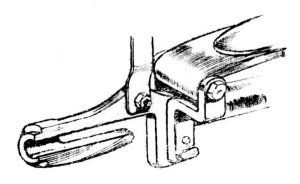

fore, many owners also attempted to correct the perceived shortcomings of the standard Morgan transmission system. Most commonly this was by grafting a conventional three-speed and reverse gearbox from a light car, such as an Austin 7, into the main chassis tube. Some conversions proved successful but most simply weakened the frame and provided unsuitable gear ratios and complications.

Rear Forks, Bevel Box and Frame Variations
Several practical refinements were made to the Morgan chassis for 1921. Notable amongst these was the redesign of the rear fork for rapid removal of the back wheel. With the axle nuts slackened and the brake bands disconnected, it was now possible to slide the wheel forward within the chain adjusting-slots and out of the forks. This action would slacken the two chains, which could then be slipped off the sprockets, and allow the wheel to be removed.

Changes to the design of the bevel box were also made. The central pin of the fork pivot bearings was replaced by tubes, one each side of the gearbox, which were located by taper fit and held tightly in place by a long central bolt.

The rod operating the gear change forks had previously passed through the fork pivot tube and this was relocated to pass through a tube in the base of the bevel box.

Increasing body weight during the early post-war years was found to impose too great a load on the bevel box and forks. In early 1924 the bevel-box housings were made smaller, to take double-row ball races and provide more support. A better solution was adopted at the end of 1926, from chassis number 12,000, with the introduction of the 'wide B' chassis. The bevel box was increased in width from $3\frac{1}{2}$ to 5 inches, to allow the use of wider forks with stronger bearings; the extra width also permitted use of a larger bearing behind the bevel pinion. The final solution to the problem for the two-speeder came at the end of 1929 with the introduction of the 'M' chassis.

The top tubes, used for location of the engine mounting-plates, were originally bent down to terminate at lugs fixed to the lower longitudinal tubes; they were linked to the star lug by additional short lengths of straight tube. To allow greater body clearance on the Family models from the early twenties, the tubes were bent through 90 degrees and connected directly to the star lug. This revision was later adopted on other models and used across the range by 1926. The dropped chassis, using cranked transverse tubes, was first introduced on production models with the Aero Super Sports in November 1927.

Grease-retaining washers and springs were fitted to the transmission shafts from March 1928. Three months later the bevel box side-plates were fitted with felt grease-seals.

Suspension
The basic Morgan suspension on all models up to the introduction of the Super Sports Aero was undamped. This proved perfectly acceptable given the stiff springing and limited suspension movement of the early cars. Shock absorbers, of the Hartford friction type, were first fitted to the various racing Morgans from the early 1920s, to help control the cars over the bumpy Brooklands circuit. The 1922 200-mile racers were fitted with a single Hartford shock absorber anchored to a bracket fixed to the angle-iron cross members of the bevel box and a loop over the rear wheel. The Braddon shock absorber for the rear wheel was marketed in 1923. It was the subject of a 5,000-mile test performed by the *Light Car and Cyclecar*, who recorded the benefits of a damped rear wheel: 'riding comfort is materially improved' and 'steering is improved, stability is increased, the tendency to tailwag is minimized, whilst as a direct consequence, tyre wear is reduced'.

The first production model to be fitted with dampers was the new Super Sports Aero, introduced for the 1928 season, which was fitted with Hartford units on the back forks. By the following year, Newton-Bennet hydraulic shock-absorbers were available for the front wheels. They were included within the specification of the Super Sports Aero and available as a £2 15s extra on the other models of the range. Rear shock absorbers were not offered with the 'M' chassis.

The Braddon shock absorber was priced at 35s per pair, complete and ready for fitting, in 1923.

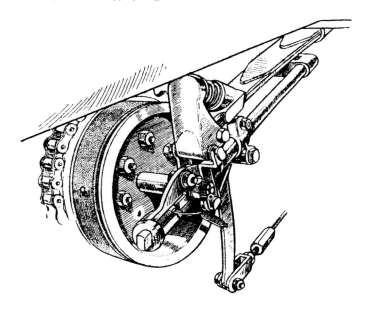

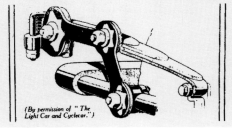

The B&D STABILIZER

Specially designed to suit the back wheel of
The MORGAN RUNABOUT

CHECKS BOUNCING
—
INCREASES ROAD GRIP and **THEREFORE SPEED.**

(By permission of " The Light Car and Cyclecar.")

EASILY FITTED WITH ORDINARY TOOL KIT SPANNERS.

The B & D Stabilizer of the mid-1920s also provided damping for the rear suspension.

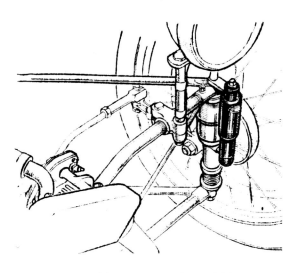

Front suspension of the Super Sports Aero with Newton shock absorbers fitted.

Retardation

To comply with the law, the Morgan required two independent braking systems. Both originally operated on the back wheel and comprised external bands contracting on drums attached to the wheel. The brake on the left of the wheel was operated by hand lever, whilst the opposite side was operated by foot pedal. From the start this was a barely adequate system. Adhesion between the rear wheel of a

Morgan and the road surface is adequate to climb severe gradients. During the descent, however, the vehicle weight is thrown onto the front wheels and any attempt at braking causes the lightly loaded single rear-wheel to scrabble for adhesion, with locked brakes, in a vain attempt to curtail a precipitous downward plunge. A larger brake drum was fitted to the high-gear side of the wheel for 1921 models, but this only gave recognition to the problem and did not provide a solution. The efficiency of front-wheel braking on the Runabout was convincingly demonstrated in March 1923 by Ware's victory in the General Efficiency Trial, just as his failure in the event the previous year had drawn attention to the deficiencies of rear-wheel-only braking. The Morgan Company had been experimenting with front-wheel brakes for over two years by the time of Ware's success. HFS, therefore, lost no time in announcing that a number of cars fitted with front-wheel brakes had already been sold to the public and that front brakes could be fitted to existing cars for £6.

The front braking system was of the internal expanding design, with the brake drums, of 6in (150mm) diameter, integral with the hubs of the wire wheels. It was a hand-operated system with the operating lever mounted on the torque tube. A single Bowden cable passed over a pulley attached to the lever and its ends were connected to the operating arms of the two brakes, thus ensuring equal braking effort on the two wheels. The front brakes were considered for emergency use only and during the first year the hand lever was not fitted with a ratchet to hold the brakes on for parking.

Wider brake linings and dust covers were fitted to the front brakes from June 1929, body No.1732A. Redesigned front hubs with brake cable adjusters were introduced from No.1979A.

The brakes were never more than adequate. A road test of the Family Model in the *Motor Cycle* in 1930 succinctly summarized the brakes:

> The question of brakes is a ticklish one. If they are weak the owner complains bitterly, and if they are too powerful he may get into trouble through over-eager application. The expert can be given powerful brakes, because he knows how to use them, but the novice must be catered for. Those on the Family Morgan were adequate and no more, though the front ones could have had more bite with perfect safety.

The reviewer went on to note that, on a gradient of 1 in 9, the rear brake would pull the machine up in due course, whilst the front brake just failed to do so.

Lighting Equipment – Acetylene or Electric?

Electric lighting had been offered as an optional extra from as early as August 1915, but the equipment, consisting of electric lamps, side lamps, tail lamp and battery, did not include any means of recharging the battery. The preferred alternative was acetylene lighting and this was fitted as standard on certain touring models from 1913 and offered as an extra on others. Acetylene lighting continued to be offered post-war and electric lighting was not listed again until November 1920, when a Lucas dynamo lighting set became available as an extra. The dynamo was fitted to

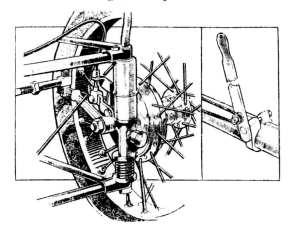

The arrangement of front-wheel brakes first announced in March 1923 as a £6 optional extra. Not until the 1927 season would they became a standard fitment on all models, with the exception of the Standard.

the nearside chassis tube, just behind the engine, and was driven by a Whittle belt from a small pulley incorporated within the front face of the flywheel. The dynamo had an eccentric driving shaft and could be rotated to tension the belt.

The dynamo was initially fitted adjacent to the flywheel and belt driven. The illustration also shows the early design of clutch cover, which was well suited to catching road grit!

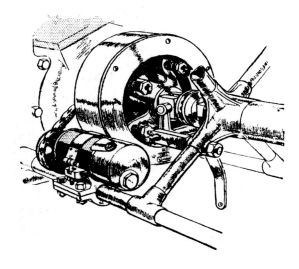

109

In 1921 the Lucas equipment was an expensive extra at £25 when compared with acetylene equipment at £6 10s. However, the price was reduced to £13 10s the following year and to £10 by 1923. By 1924 it was being fitted as standard on all models except the Standard, which was still equipped with acetylene lighting, although electrical equipment could be specified. Electric lighting was finally standardized across the range in 1926. For the 1927 season, from chassis number 13981, the dynamo was repositioned at the back of the car and gear-driven from the countershaft. The drive was improved from 28 June 1928 by fitting a bracing stay to the dynamo bracket and through use of skew gears. A similar bracing stay was fitted to the starter bracket at the same time.

The acetylene headlights on the early models were mounted at the rear of the coalscuttle bonnet. This position, just forward of the windscreen, was common to most light cars and was retained for both acetylene and electric headlamps on all two-speeder models, with the exception of the Aero and Super Sports. The latter were fitted with forward-mounted electric headlamps located between the radiator and mudguard. The electric lamps could not be dipped and were fitted with dimmer mechanisms to avoid dazzle to oncoming motorists. Mudguard-mounted side lamps were never fitted. Only a single tail-lamp was required to satisfy the law and this was mounted on a centrally located bracket attached to the rear of the car. A new tail-lamp bracket, welded to the body, was featured from November 1928.

Starting the Motor

The engines used in Morgans were based on motorcycle units and, without a gearbox and associated kick-start mechanism, lacked any means of starting. The problem was overcome by arranging for a starting handle to be engaged with the countershaft of the bevel box. Cranking a car at the rear was not then as unusual as it now appears and was used on several cyclecars, but has the disadvantage that effort is increased due to the gearing-up of the bevel drive. The use of a valve-lifter to reduce engine compression was essential! It was just possible for the driver to hand-crank the early cars whilst seated at the wheel and a *Motor Cycling* road test of September 1911 illustrated the procedure. An oval steel pressing was being fitted to Morgan bodies from the end of 1920 to locate the starting handle and prevent damage to the bodywork.

The 'Kushi' Starter of the mid-1920s was an attempt to simplify the starting procedure. It comprised a kick-starter on the nearside of the car, which operated with the car in neutral, when the kick-start quadrant engaged with a

The 1928 models were fitted with a countershaft drive for the dynamo. Initially the gears were protected by a metal shield but this was found to be unnecessary.

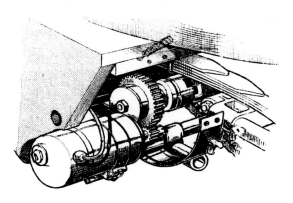

The 'Kushi' Starter offered simpler starting before the introduction of an electric starter.

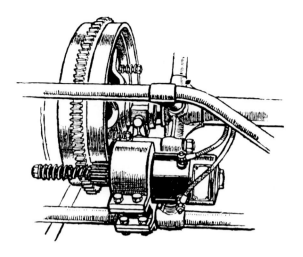

The Lucas electric self-starter.

special sliding dog. A face-cam-operated valve lifter ensured the exhaust valves were lifted as the pedal was pressed and automatically released at the optimum moment.

An electric self-starter was available from 1924. It was fitted to a bracket attached to a lower chassis tube, as the early dynamos, and engaged with a starter ring on the flywheel.

Instrumentation

The dashboards on the early cars were sparsely instrumented and might include no more than a sight feed for the lubrication system. Speedometers were not a legal requirement and were originally offered as an extra, priced at £3 10s. The first instrument was of Jones manufacture, but by 1915 a Watford instrument was listed. In post-war years, Watford, Cowey and Smiths instruments would be offered. The Super Sports Aero of 1930 was the first Morgan to be sold with a speedometer included as standard. A speedometer became a standard fitting on the Aero model of the following year, but would remain an extra on the basic 'B' chassis models through to the end of production. The speedometer drive was via an external gear fitted to the offside front wheel. This arrangement could not be used with the

new wheels and hubs, which were fitted to the 'M' chassis models from 29 January 1931 (frame M443), and was replaced by a Smiths internal speedometer drive.

The switches controlling the electrical circuits were incorporated within a Lucas switch panel. The panel was fitted on the left of the dashboard and included an ammeter and switches for the lights and charging circuit. The early cars used a five-sided panel, but this was replaced for 1927 by the current Lucas round panel. The speedometer, when fitted, was on the right of the dashboard. An oval instrument panel, located at the centre of the dashboard and incorporating the speedometer, was first fitted from 5 February 1931

The 'M' type chassis

By the late twenties the two-speeder chassis was almost twenty-years old and competition events were showing up weaknesses in the transmission and rear wheel suspension. The new 'M' type two-speeder chassis, introduced on selected models at the 1929 Motor Cycle show, was a more soundly engineered design and rectified known deficiencies. The entire rear assembly of the new chassis, comprising the bevel box, rear suspension, chains and rear wheel, formed a separate, removable, unit. This was achieved by flange mounting the bevel box to the rear of the torque tube and using U-bolts for attachment to the longitudinal frame tubes. The bevel pinion shaft on the first cars was fitted with a square end to engage with a square formed within the end of the propeller shaft, but this was soon changed to a dog-coupling. This allowed separation of the two shafts and facilitated a more accurate meshing of the bevels. The propeller shaft could also be shortened and made stiffer.

The tubular forks of the original design were replaced on the 'M' type by heavy forged beams pivoted co-axially with the drive sprockets. This ensured unchanging chain centres and constant chain tension. The underslung rear springs offered greater comfort and allowed for a lower body mounting. In turn

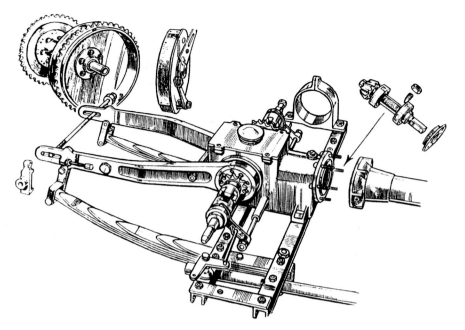

The rear section of the two-speeder, 'M' type, chassis.

this gave a lower centre of gravity and improved stability.

The rear wheel rotated about a knock-out spindle carried in closed slots in the fork ends. Removal of the rear wheel was simply a case of disconnecting the brake control rod and a single nut to allow the spindle to be withdrawn; the chains could be lifted from the wheel sprockets without removal from the car. The rear-wheel brake was now of the internal expanding type and fitted with an 8in diameter by $1\frac{1}{4}$in drum and operated by a flexible cable.

One effect of pivoting the rear fork at the shaft centre, instead of behind it, was to reduce the wheelbase by 3in (80mm) without affecting the body space. Advantage of this was taken on the De Luxe, Super Sports and Aero models only. On other models, such as the Family and Sports Family, a longer wheelbase was introduced to gain more room for the rear seats.

The increasing speed of racing and record-breaking Morgans resulted in serious propshaft whip. Robin Jackson provided an initial solu-

tion to the problem when he turned a piece of ash to insert within the propshaft. Ron Horton had his propshaft dynamically balanced by the Andrews Crankshaft Grinding Company of Birmingham with some success. Clive Lones attempted to balance his propshaft by the addition of lead solder before spinning the propshaft in a lathe at 6,000rpm. Lones discussed the problem with HFS and the two men decided the better solution lay in reducing the length of the propshaft by splitting it in two. Initially the two halves of the shaft were connected by a male and female joint of square section, supported by a ball race slid within the backbone tube. Lack of lubrication limited the life of the bearing but in other respects the experiment was a success. The new divided propshaft first appeared on the Sports Family four-seater introduced at the 1930 Olympia Show. The machine featured the 'M' type chassis of the Super Aero, which had been lengthened by 4in (100mm) to accommodate the new body. The new variant of the 'M' chassis became known as the 'C' type, although it retained the 'M' type chassis number.

The two-speeder 'M' type chassis was in production for 1930 and 1931 only, before being replaced by the new three-speed chassis.

Two-Speeder Chassis Numbers

Factory records for the two-speeders built prior to spring 1928 were lost during the Second World War and precise production and chassis number details are not available for the early cars. From the registry of surviving cars and other sources it appears that the first Morgan received chassis number 1 and successive cars were numbered consecutively up to 14,999 by 1928. The cars were next numbered with the suffix 'A' or 'B' in the sequence 1A to 1999A, followed by 2000B up till the end of 'B' type production. The 'M' and 'C' chassis cars were numbered upwards from M1. The numbers provide only guidance as to the total number of cars produced, as chassis numbers were allocated against orders. If the order was cancelled, as frequently happened during the depression, the number was not reallocated.

'B' type chassis numbers were stamped into the forward section of the bevel box connected to the propshaft tube. The year of manufacture was sometimes noted by stamping in the last digit of the year. Up to about 1914, a car number was also stamped into the engine timing cover and this number is commonly identified on registration documents as the chassis number. The 'M' and 'C' chassis numbers were stamped onto the bevel box mounting-flange. The chassis number was also stamped onto the St Christopher/Morgan Runabout dashboard plaque, which was introduced about the time of the 'A' suffix numbers in 1928.

The Three-Speeder Chassis

The three-speeder chassis was first introduced at the 1931 Motorcycle Show for the 1932 season. It was derived from the 'C' chassis and comprised a three-speed and reverse gearbox, flange mounted, in the position of the two-speeder bevel box. A worm drive at the rear of the box rotated a countershaft, which was

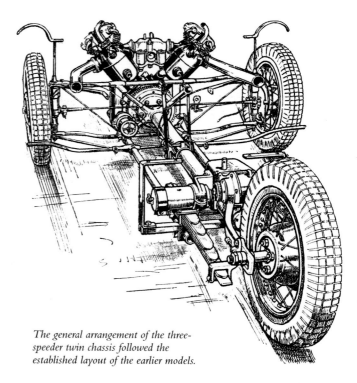

The general arrangement of the three-speeder twin chassis followed the established layout of the earlier models.

fitted with a sprocket on the offside for the drive chain to the rear wheel. A helical-toothed gear wheel on the opposite side of the countershaft provided drive for the dynamo. The under-slung rear suspension of the later two-speeders was retained.

The Burman-designed gearbox followed the conventional practice of the day, with first, second and reverse gears selected by sliding the gear wheels into mesh and the direct top-gear being obtained by means of a dog clutch. The main shaft was well supported by three deep-groove ball bearings, designed to carry both the thrust and radial loads, which were located at the front of the box, between the box and the worm drive, and behind the worm drive. The layshaft was mounted in two long bronze floating-bushes directly above the main shaft. Two gear selectors were used and operated by two steel strips connected to a lever mounted upon the central frame tube adjacent to the brake lever. The standard gear ratios for the Family models were 4.85, 8 and 13.1 to 1, whilst the sporting two-seater models used ratios of 4.58, 7.5 and 12.4 to 1.

The steel worm-wheel was mounted above the bronze worm within a circular aluminium housing forming the end of the gearbox. It was bolted to a cross shaft carried in a deep-groove roller bearing on the nearside and a roller bearing on the drive side. The bearing housings comprised circular bronze plates, the outer surface of which formed the bearings for the rear swinging arms. The worm drive gave a drive reduction of just over 2 to 1.

The considerable heat generated by the worm-and-wheel drive had to be dissipated if the bronze worm was not to suffer rapid wear. This was achieved by circulating the lubricating oil into the forward compartment, containing the gear cluster, where it was more easily cooled by the passing flow of air. The oil enters the front compartment through a hole at the top of the partition, being pumped by the action of the worm wheel, and returns by gravity through a hole near the bottom. On the original box the return flow was much slower than the outgoing and the worm and wheel could be starved of oil. The problem was alleviated to a degree by using good quality oil and Castrol 'R' was recommended. The early gearbox is now known as the 'Castrol "R" Box', often abbreviated to the 'R' type box. This information is cast in raised letters on the lid of the box.

The cooling, marginal at its best, proved inadequate as soon as a layer of mud or oil insulated the front of the box from the airflow. A revised box was announced in July 1932. This had a much wider base at the rear to contain a larger quantity of oil and a larger hole for the return flow of oil between compartments. The Morgan Company stated that, after extensive testing of gear oils, they now recommended Castrol 'D'. The revised box is now known as the modified 'R' box. A number of these were fitted with surplus lids from the early boxes with the letter 'R' chiselled off.

Although an improvement, the modified

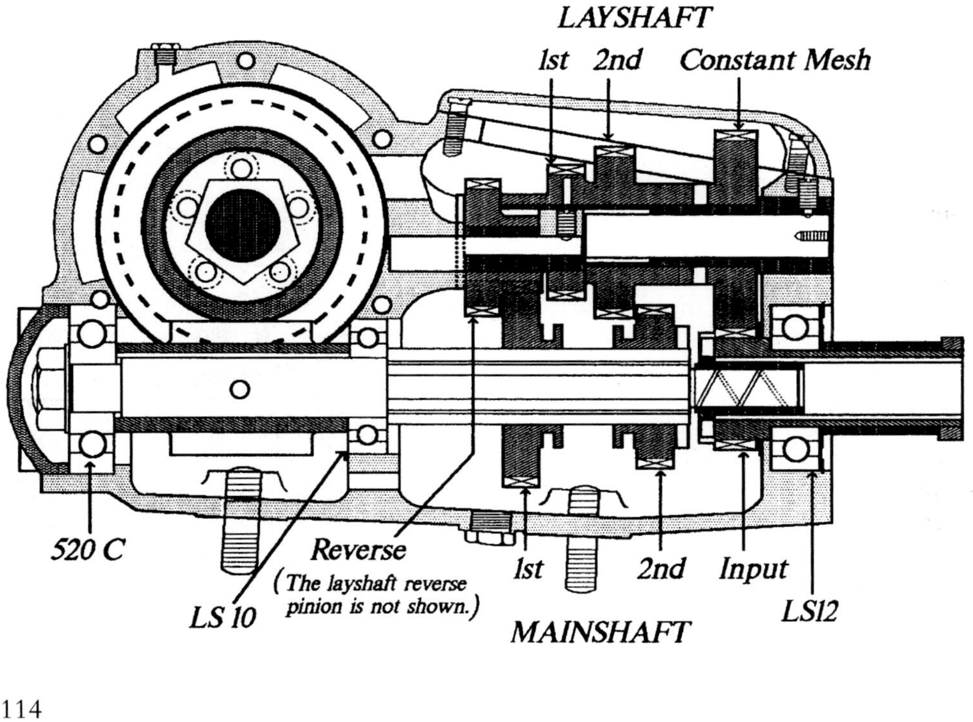

Section through the Castrol 'R' box.

LAYSHAFT

1st 2nd **Constant Mesh**

520 C

Reverse
(The layshaft reverse
LS 10 *pinion is not shown.)*

1st 2nd **Input**

LS12

MAINSHAFT

'R' box was not entirely satisfactory and was replaced by the Castrol 'D' box for 1933. The new box used a redesigned casing. The single aperture at the bottom of the partition was replaced by larger holes on either side of the centre bearing. The modifications resulted in improved oil circulation and more efficient cooling. The new 'D' box was used, without further modification, through to the end of three-wheeler production.

Detachable Dunlop Magna wheels were introduced on all 1933 models, except for certain Van and Family models built to 1932 specification. The wheels used a four-stud attachment and, with the exception of some export models with 19in rims, were fitted with 18in × 3in rims. At the same time, the chassis of all Morgan models was standardized with a 1in (30mm) drop on the front cross-tubes.

The steering also received attention at this time. Modifications were made to the design of the steering arms to comply more fully with the requirements of Ackerman steering principles. A slight reduction in the rake of the sliding axles was also made and the combined effect was to reduce the steering effort. The wing stays, which form the bearing surface for the sliding axles, were increased in diameter to reduce wear.

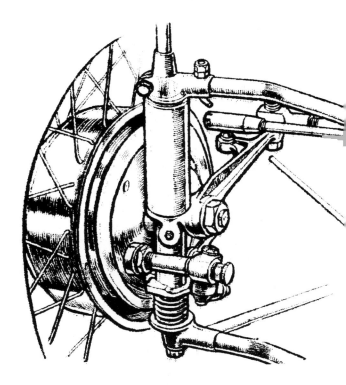

Above *Dunlop Magna wheels, introduced for the 1933 season, were detachable and inter-changeable. The rear hub was located by a knock-out spindle as previously.*

The single plate clutch introduced for 1933.

Arrangement of the front suspension. Revised steering arms were introduced with the new standardized chassis in 1933.

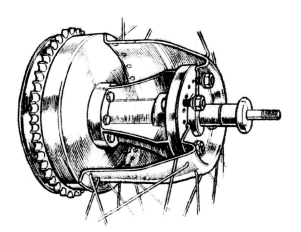

OIL TOGGLE PINS

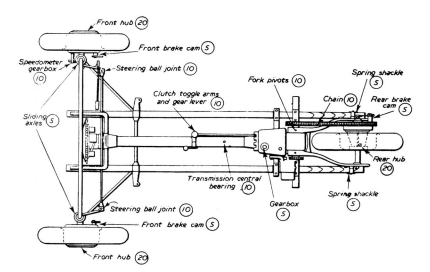

The Morgan three-wheeler required regular lubrication. The figures on the chart are the maximum lubrication intervals, in hundreds of miles.

Three-speeder Chassis Numbers

The chassis number on three-speed Morgans is stamped onto both the lug, which attaches the propshaft tube to the gearbox, and the St Christopher dashboard plaque. The factory records list 356 'R' type and 1,892 'D' type chassis numbers allocated over the full production period. However, numbers will have been allocated upon receipt of orders, and some machines will not have been constructed.

Year	Starting Number*	Number Produced
1932	R 1	352
1933	D 1	591
1934	D 591	659
1935	D 1250	286
1936	D 1536	137
1937	D 1673	110
1938	D 1783	70
1939	D 1853	29
1940–45	D 1882	10

*The prefix letter 'R' or 'D' identifies the R or D type gearbox

The F-Type Chassis

Morgan had always bought in engines and several other components. With the F-type they also bought in the pressed-steel chassis frames. These were purchased from Rubery Owen, Darlaston, Staffordshire.

The advent of the Model F, with its more conventional chassis, introduced a change in the manufacturing process. Previously the rolling chassis were manufactured in the chassis construction shop and united with the completed body, constructed in a separate body shop. The 'F' chassis was assembled in the chassis erecting shop as previously, but the body was now built directly upon it. Firstly the wooden framework was built in the body shop before the vehicle was pushed through to the sheet metal shop for the steel panels to be manufactured and fitted. It then went through to the paint shop before finally passing to the upholstery shop for the seats and trim to be added.

The F-type Morgan, first shown to the public at the 1933 Olympia Show, had been under development since 1930. Although a new model, and drastically different in appearance from the earlier cars, it was clearly an on-going development based upon the design of the twin-cylinder cars. The chassis retained the tubular backbone, which enclosed the propeller shaft, but the side tubes were replaced by Z-section pressed-steel members. The twin-tube front axle with sliding pillar independent suspension was retained. The steering arrangement was revised with the track rod and drag link positioned in front of the axle. A reduction box was fitted to the steering column. At the rear was fitted the Morgan three-speed and reverse gearbox with worm drive and single drive chain to the rear wheel. The latter was located in a forged-steel fork, swivelling about the worm-gear housing, and supported by a pair of quarter-elliptic springs.

The Z-section chassis sides were joined by two channel-section cross-members at the back, onto which were bolted the gearbox and rear springs. Another cross member, of Z-section, was riveted to the side members

immediately behind the engine. The side members were joined together in front of the engine by a pressing comprising two angle-pieces and a pair of diagonal ties. To this pressing were connected the two front-axle tubes and various radius rods. The engine was moved back behind the front axle and a radiator was conventionally mounted, with a slight backwards tilt, in front of the engine and enclosed in a chromium-plated shell.

The 'F' models used the same gearbox shell and rear suspension as the three-speeder models. The 'F' gearboxes are easily identified, as the boss on the nearside for the three-speeder dynamo bracket is not drilled, since the dynamo is mounted on the engine. The gear ratios, slightly different to the three-speeders, are 12.4, 7.5 and 4.58 to 1, and reverse 16.5 to 1.

The brake pedal operated coupled-brakes

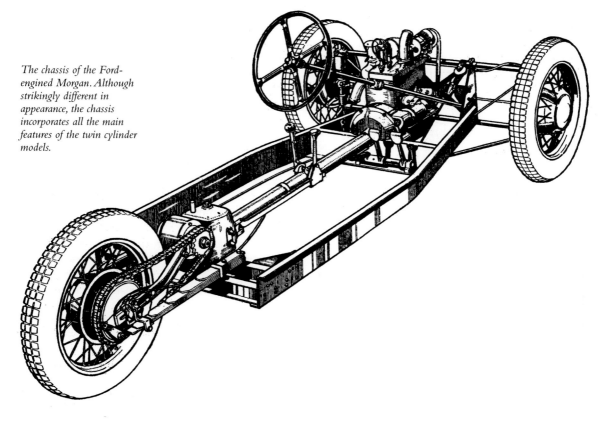

The chassis of the Ford-engined Morgan. Although strikingly different in appearance, the chassis incorporates all the main features of the twin cylinder models.

on all three wheels. The hand lever operated the rear brake only and was fitted with a ratchet for parking purposes.

Other than minor attention to detail, there were very few changes to the mechanical specification of the 'F' models during the production period. The cast iron bell housing for the clutch at the rear of the engine was replaced by an aluminium casting from July 1938. A shortened chassis was fitted to the new Model F Super Sports announced for 1938. At the same time, Girling wedge-type brakes were fitted to all models. All post-war 'F' models were fitted with an accelerator pedal. Straight track rods replaced the earlier curved pattern. Commencing from January 1948 on chassis F880 on the F4 and for all 'F' models from chassis F1100, the centre pins were replaced by a combined centre pin and wing stay. From November 1949 and chassis F1193, longer and softer front springs were fitted to provide a softer ride and improve comfort. This required the introduction of a stepped chassis top lug.

F-type Production Numbers

The F-type chassis number was stamped into the front edge of the gearbox cross member, on the passenger side. The prefix, F, usually precedes the number on early chassis, but not on later models. Pre-war the chassis numbers run from F1 (April 1934) to F592 (July 1940). Post-war the numbers extend from F600 to 1301, although numbers 1059 to 1099 were unused. Other numbers will also have been unused owing to cancellation of orders.

F-type production			
Model	Pre-war	Post-war	Total
F4	424	367	791
F2	113	–	113
F Super	47	265	312
Total	**584**	**632**	**1216**

Colour Schemes and Finishes

It is not wise to be too dogmatic about the colour schemes applied to the various Morgan models, as special colours were usually available at extra cost. The following is a summary of the colour options listed in the sales brochures.

All Morgan models up to 1922 were offered with the choice of grey or green paint. For 1922 through to 1924, the standard colours were listed as grey, red, blue or purple on all models except the Standard Popular, which was finished in grey or, for 1922 only, brown. Green was added to the standard colours for 1925, with the Standard now available only in grey. For 1926 through to 1928, the standard paint options remained grey, red, blue, purple or green across the range except for the Standard, which was available only in grey through to 1927 and in dark red in 1928.

By 1928, more striking colour schemes were offered. The Super Sports Aero, announced for 1928, was supplied with the body and chassis painted any colour to choice. The selection of an alternative colour for the other models cost an additional £2. Bodies could also be painted in two colours at an additional cost of £2 10s, whilst an alternative chassis colour cost an additional £1.

The standard colours for 1929 through to 1932 were dark blue or Panhard red, but these were changed for 1933 and 1934 to a black body and mudguards with red, cream or green wheels. The Super Sports remained an exception. Up to 1933 it was finished to the customer's choice, but from 1934 a choice of striking colour schemes was on offer. Initially these comprised: top of body dark green, inter-panel with wheels and chassis light green; body and chassis black with wheels and wings a choice of red, green or cream; body and chassis bright red, wheels and wings cream; body and chassis light blue, wheels and wings cream.

Revisions for the 1935 season saw the Super Sports finished with the following colour schemes: black body and chassis, with wheels and wings a choice of red, green or cream; all black with aluminium wheels; body and chassis light blue, with wheels and wings cream; body red and cream, chassis and wings red, wheels cream; body British Racing Green, wings, wheels and chassis darker green. The standard finish on the Model F was saxe blue for the body, black wings and chassis, and cream wheels.

The light blue option with the Super Sports was discontinued for 1937. Changes for 1939 saw the model offered in the following colours: black body and chassis with wheels in red, green or aluminium; red body, chassis and wings with cream wheels; British Racing Green throughout. The F Super Sports was offered with the same choice of colours as the V-twin model.

Post-war the F4 was available in saxe blue with black wings and wheels, whilst the F Super was offered in red or British Racing Green.

The Morgan was always attractively presented. Coach-lining, often considered a feature of bespoke bodywork on luxury cars, was extensively applied to even the cheapest models. The De Luxe and Family two-speeders, for example, were finished with a broad black-band highlighted by a white pinstripe at the edge of the body panels, with a similar feature used to highlight the bonnet louvres. The bright parts of the early cars were nickel plated. Chromium plate was introduced on the Super Sports for 1930 and used across the range for 1931.

Machines fitted with a coalscuttle bonnet were identified as Morgans by a transfer script affixed to the front of the bonnet. Upon the introduction of the Grand Prix model, an engraved badge, soldered to the nose of the radiator, was used to identify both the make and model. Wings were added to the badge with the introduction of the Aero model to create the design of badge still used to this day.

The first factory mascot fitted to a Morgan appeared about 1924. It was first identified simply as a flying bird, but later as a stork, and remained available, first in bronze and later in aluminium, through to the mid-1930s. In fact, its appearance was more pterodactyl than stork and it was the subject of considerable criticism. Billy James, the Sheffield agent, had arranged for the first batch to be cast in the city. His son Freddie, also a Sheffield agent and well known trials driver, so disliked it that he commissioned an alternative mascot to his own design and based upon a scaled-down Hispano-Suiza stork.

7 The Power Units

One of the very real advantages of the original Morgan chassis proved to be the ease by which engines of different manufacture could be substituted one for another by the simple expedient of changing the mounting plates. It was only a few minutes work to slide an engine, complete with its mounting plates, off the front chassis tubes and to slide on a replacement. This flexibility was very much to HFS's advantage. He was able to perform comparisons between engines with the minimum of effort and could select the appropriate engine for the task in hand. He could, furthermore, chop and change suppliers for his production machines and was not dependent on any one manufacturer. This placed him in an excellent bargaining position to purchase engines at the lowest possible price. As a result, various different engines were fitted as standard to Morgan three-wheelers, whilst other engines could easily be substituted and often were.

Initially all Runabouts were fitted with side-valve 8hp JAP engines and it was not until 1913 that alternative engines of Blumfield or Precision manufacture were offered. The Swiss MAG engine became available for 1915 and was listed, together with JAP, as an option throughout the war years. Post-war, supplies of MAG engines were initially unavailable and only the side-valve JAP, either air- or water-cooled, was offered until 1920 when the MAG engine was again listed. The choice of engine was widened at the end of 1922 with the availability of the 10hp Anzani and Blackburne units. The 10hp MAG was discontinued for 1924 and Morgans were supplied as standard with either JAP or Blackburne side-valve

engines. However, better performance was now on offer, albeit at extra cost. The 10hp ohv Anzani engine, either air- or water-cooled, could be specified for an additional £5, whilst the 10hp Blackburne racing engine was available for a further £12. The side-valve Blackburne unit was discontinued at the end of 1924.

The side-valve JAP, together with the ohv Anzani at £5 extra, remained the standard engine options for all models during 1925 and 1926. The racing Blackburne engine continued as an option for the Aero. The Anzani engine was not listed as available with the Standard and De Luxe models for 1927, although it could presumably be fitted if requested. It remained the standard fitting for the Aero, which was now also available with either the ohv Blackburne or the new 10/40 ohv JAP engines. The Blackburne engine was not listed following the 1927 season. The Anzani engine remained an option through to the end of 1930.

The discontinuation of the Anzani and Blackburne engines resulted in JAP becoming the sole supplier of power units to Morgan for 1931. They would remain the sole supplier through to the end of 1933 and the introduction of the Matchless MX engine range and the F-type Morgan with its 4-cylinder Ford engine. The JAP side-valve engines, which had been the most commonly fitted engines since the start of Morgan production, were discontinued at this time. The Super Sports ohv water-cooled JAP survived a further year, alongside the ohv Matchless, before being phased out at the end of 1934. The Matchless

Harry Martin in the factory car with 8-valve Anzani at the BMCRC meeting at Brooklands in July 1922.

engines in side-valve and ohv form continued to be offered with the three-speeder chassis up to the advent of war in 1939. The Ford 8hp engine was joined by a 10hp version in 1934 and both 8hp and 10hp F-types were offered pre-war. Post-war, only the 10hp engine was offered up till the end of three-wheeler production in 1952.

All engines fitted as original equipment to the two-speeder chassis were derived from motorcycle power units and were fitted with magneto ignition and total-loss lubrication systems. No provision was made for direct hand-cranking to start the engine. With the advent of the three-speeder chassis hand cranking of the countershaft was no longer possible and a starting handle boss was incorporated into the timing cover of the engines.

Anzani Engines

In 1900, at the age of twenty-three, Alessandro Anzani, an Italian cyclist of some note, emigrated to France to further his cycling career. It was here that his natural engineering talents were recognized and he was offered the use of a workshop to develop a 2-cylinder engine lighter in weight and more powerful than any other engine available at the time. The engine was fitted to a motorcycle and very soon Anzani was achieving racing successes. Spurred on by these achievements, he established a small workshop at Asnières, near Paris. Before long his interests turned towards the fledgling aviation industry and Anzani, a self-taught engineer, was soon the foremost designer of aero engines. His fame was assured when an Anzani engine powered Louis Blériot on his first crossing of the English Channel in July 1909. The British Anzani Engine Company was originally established as an agency of the French company to make aero engines for the emerging British market.

The first V-twin engine produced by the British company was based upon a 500cc single-cylinder French Anzani engine, which had been sent over just after the war. Developed by Hubert Hagens, it first appeared in 1921 and in its various forms would remain in production through to 1938. The engine, designated the CC model to signify its cycle-car application, was an air-cooled unit with roller-bearing big-ends and an aluminium piston. The capacity was 1000cc, but this was soon increased to 1100cc. The engines are recognisable by open parallel push-rods and open rocker-gear. An 8-valve racing version with twin inlet and exhaust valves per cylinder was announced by Hagens in March 1922. A single overhead camshaft per cylinder operated two cams, each of which operated a pair of valves. The bore and stroke were 83mm × 92mm, giving a capacity of 994cc. Douglas Hawkes used an enlarged 1078cc (85mm × 95mm) version of this engine to power his Morgan to the flying 5-mile (85.14mph, 136.22km/h) and the standing 10-mile (81.70mph, 130.72km/h) World Records during 1922.

The 8-valve Anzani air-cooled engine proved fast, but the valve mechanism was unreliable and it was prone to overheating. A water-cooled version was developed and was first seen in Hawkes' Flying Spider when the machine was used for record breaking in September 1923.

British Anzani had suffered mixed fortunes during the latter part of the war and the early

British Anzani 9hp Cyclecar engine. Model CCW
(CCW denotes Cycle Car engine, Water-cooled)
Bore × stroke: 85mm × 95mm
Capacity: 1078cc
Cylinder angle: 57 degrees
Exhaust-heated inlet manifold
Power: 26bhp at 3,000rpm.

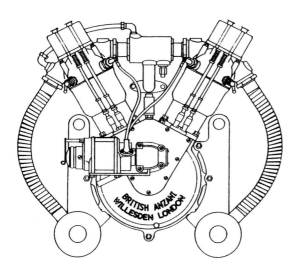

post-war years were little better. It fell under the control of S.F. Edge and A.C. Motors in 1919 and was placed in receivership in January 1925. It soldiered on in receivership until the end of the year, before being acquired by Charles Fox, a director of the company, when it was renamed the British Vulpine Engine Company. At this time, Summit was used as a trade name and the engines became known variously as Anzani, Summit or Vulpine engines.

The new company very quickly ran into fresh problems. Fox's major customer was the Morgan Motor Company, but HFS placed orders by the hundred, rather than give an annual contract, in order to monitor prices keenly. Fox compromised on component quality to reduce prices, with the result that exhaust valves failed within the guarantee period. When the engines were returned Fox simply had the valves replaced by the same poor quality items. Several Morgan agents, concerned about damage to their reputations, refused to take any more Morgans fitted with the Anzani engine and HFS cancelled his current order with Vulpine. Fox sued for breach of contract and lost, putting his company back into bankruptcy. This time Anzani found a rescuer in Archie Frazer Nash Ltd and the company was relocated from its Willesden base to Kingston upon Thames, alongside the Frazer Nash works.

The first Anzani production engine fitted to Morgans was the water-cooled model CCW. Engines up to CCW985 were fitted with the original pattern of cylinder head, with various modifications being made to the pushrods. Later engines, up to CCW1689, were fitted with improved cylinder heads, valves, cams and cam-rocker gear. The M3 engine, commencing from engine number M3/1690, which was quickly introduced by the new company to counteract the adverse publicity arising from the litigation with Morgan, was fitted with revised cam contours and a special double-diameter exhaust valve working in a detachable guide. The changes were widely publicized and owners of the earlier CC and CCW engines were invited to convert to the new, M3, specification. The new engine could also operate at a higher compression ratio and power output; it was claimed to produce 40bhp at 3,000rpm. It was not long before HFS was persuaded to place orders with the new company for Anzani/Summit engines. The M3 engine continued to be fitted by Morgan through to 1931.

Blackburne Engines

The origins of the Blackburne engine can be traced back to aviation pioneer Geoffrey de-Havilland who designed a single-cylinder side-valve engine in 1905. The rights to the engine were sold to the Burney Brothers who, with financial backing from Major Blackburne, formed Burney and Blackburne Ltd for the manufacture of engines and complete motorcycles. After the Great War the motorcycle manufacture was sold to OEC and the firm, which was based at Bookham in Surrey, concentrated on the supply of engines for motorcycles, light cars and industrial applications.

The series of Blackburne V-twin engines, as fitted to Morgans, was the work of Harry Hatch, who had previously been a designer for JAP. The KM engine was introduced at Olympia in November 1922. It was a water-cooled 60-degree ohv engine of 1090cc, which would later be enlarged to 1096cc for production models. Of high specification, it featured inclined valves, aluminium pistons and roller-bearing big-ends. The main bearings comprised four rows of roller bearings on the drive side and ball bearings on the timing side. The power output was a claimed 32bhp.

A side-valve fixed-head engine was available at the same time as the KM engine. This had the same dimensions as the overhead-valve engine and was available either as the air-cooled VCM model or the water-cooled ZCM model. These engines were offered by Morgan during 1923 and 1924 as an alternative to the 8hp JAP KT and KTW engines.

Changes made to the production, KMA, version of the new ohv engine, included the use of four studs, rather than three, to secure the barrel to the crankcase and the option to fit a second sparking plug to each cylinder in place of a compression tap. A power increase to 35bhp at 4,000rpm was claimed. The new engine was tested in a stripped Morgan and, with modest tuning, quickly achieved speeds of 85mph (136km/h). The KMA engine would not, however, be listed by Morgan until October 1923, when it was offered as a £12 extra for the Aero. By this time the company claimed a top speed in excess of over 70mph (110km/h) for the KMA-powered Aero, whilst noting that the machine was similar to the track racers that had circulated Brooklands at speeds of over 90mph (145km/h).

A special version of the engine, designated the KMB, was developed during the latter half of 1923 as a prototype for a future production engine. Steel flywheels were fitted and other modifications made to allow testing to be carried out under racing conditions. The first track appearance was in the hands of Harold Beart at the JCC 200-mile race in October 1923, but it suffered big-end failure in practice and no spares were available to allow repair. The KMB was produced in limited numbers and possibly no more than three in total reached customers. One was supplied to HFS and others were used at various times by Robin Jackson, Clive Lones and Ron Horton.

The final engine of the KM series was the KMC, first produced in October 1926 as a replacement for the KMA. In fact, it was based upon the KMB and announced as a road-going sports version of the KMB. It incorporated strengthened connecting rods, larger crankpin and bearings and an improved oiling system. Speed merchants were offered a 'Special Speed Cam' to convert the KMC to racing specification and in this form over 40bhp at 4,000rpm was claimed using a compression ration of $5\frac{1}{2}$ to 1.

Blackburne racing engines were the popular choice for racing and record breaking during 1926 and 1927, but proved to be unreliable. When three KMB's blew up on the same day, the engines were returned to Blackburnes at Bookham for repair and HFS refused to pay the bill. As a result Morgans no longer offered Blackburne engines after 1927.

The Blackburne V-twin engines were numbered using a prefix to identify the engine type, for example KMA, followed by a number. The latter started at 100 and ran sequentially, regardless as to whether the engine was overhead- or side-valve, air- or water-cooled. The sequence finished at about 530. The table below summarizes the Blackburne engines fitted to production Morgans:

Blumfield Engines

T.E. Blumfield was an early pioneer in the motorcycle industry. By 1908 Blumfield Ltd was established in Birmingham for the production of Blumfield motorcycles and proprietary motorcycle engines. The company was one of the first to supply large capacity V-twin engines to the fledgling cyclecar industry. By 1913 it was offering both 5–6hp and 8–10hp V-twins. The larger unit was of 991cc (81.5 × 95mm) and water-cooled. It incorporated a magneto platform cast in one piece with the timing-gear cover and a crankshaft extended forward to allow the use of a starting handle. The company recorded the brake horsepower of every engine sent out and claimed every

Model	Type	Bore & Stroke	Capacity	V-angle	Power
KMA, KMC	ohv, w/c	85 × 96.8mm	1096cc	60 degrees	40bhp @ 4,300rpm
VCM	sv, a/c	85 × 96.8mm	1096cc	60 degrees	35bhp @ 3,500rpm
ZCM	sv, w/c	85 × 96.8mm	1096cc	60 degrees	36bhp @ 3,500rpm

Left *1927 Aero fitted with a Blackburne KMC engine.*

1913 Sporting model fitted with a 670cc (67 × 95mm) air-cooled Blumfield side-valve. The machine is that driven to a class win in the BMCRC High-Speed Reliability Trial in March 1913 by Vernon Busby.

engine exceeded twice its nominal horse-power figure. Production was discontinued in 1914.

JAP Engines

JAP engines take their name from the initials of John Alfred Prestwich, who in 1894 at the age of twenty founded the J.A. Prestwich Manufacturing Company. Very grandiose sounding, but in reality little more than Prestwich operating as a one-man firm from his father's greenhouse, which had been fitted out with lathe and hand tools. A year later he was able to set up a small factory in Tottenham, North London. He was a talented, natural engineer whose initial interests were in scientific instruments and electrical apparatus. He was involved with William Friese-Greene, the inventor of cinematography, and constructed a number of early cameras. It was not until 1901 that he turned his attention to designing a motorcycle engine and a further two years were to elapse before the first JAP engine was put into production. It was not long before JAP became the dominant supplier of proprietary engines to the motorcycle industry.

The first JAP V-twin engines fitted to Morgans were the work of Harry Hatch. He left the company at the end of 1913 to join Blackburne and was replaced as chief designer by Val Page. Shortly following, E.B. Ware joined the company in the experimental shop under Page.

The most popular engine fitted to production Morgans was the JAP 980cc 8hp side-valve V-twin. It was fitted to all production machines prior to the introduction of the Grand Prix model in late 1913 and thereafter remained the most popular choice for touring machines. An air-cooled version was available continuously from the start of production in 1910 through to 1935. Water-cooled versions of the same engine were offered from 1914 through to 1935.

Overhead-valve engines of 1096cc were

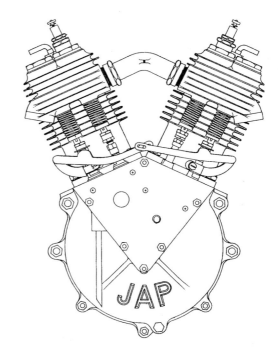

Above *1910 JAP 8hp side-valve engine fitted to the first production Morgans. The external arms above the crankcase operate the exhaust-valve lifter.*

The 8hp ohv 1082cc 90-bore JAP of 1914 as fitted to Grand Prix models. An internal mechanism for the exhaust-valve lifter, improved valve gear and enclosed magneto drive were introduced for 1915.

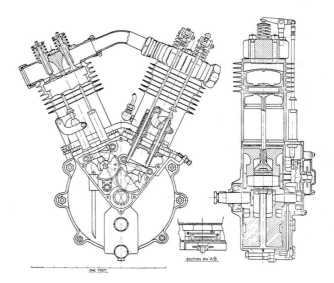

Nomenclature of JAP Engines Fitted to Morgans

JAP stamped a sequence of letters and numbers, partitioned by slashes, into the face of the crankcase to identify the type of engine and its year of manufacture. The numbering code for engines produced prior to 1917 appears not to be systematic, but following on from that date the code sequence fully defines the original specification and age of the engine. The rudiments of the numbering conventions are outlined below.

For engines produced between 1917 and 1920 the engine number is separated by slashes from a preceding symbol, either letter or integer, identifying the year and a following symbol denoting any deviation from standard specification.

Year	H.P.	Symbol
1917	$2\frac{3}{4}$ Single	U/★★★/
1917	$3\frac{1}{2}$ & 5 Twin	H/★★★/
1917	6 Twin	L/★★★/
1917	8 Twin	M/★★★/
1917	8 Twin	Z/★★★/
1918	All	8/★★★/
1919	All	9/★★★/
1920	All	20/★★★/

From 1920 a more systematic approach was followed. The first letter now identified the bore and stroke of the engine. Letters J, K and L are relevant to engines fitted in Morgans. The letter D identifies an industrial engine, which was never fitted to a Morgan but has frequently been adapted for a Morgan in more recent years.

Letter	Bore (mm)	Stroke (mm)	Capacity (cc)	Twin (cc)
J	80	99	487	994
K	85.7	85	490	980
L	85.7	95	548	1096
D	90	104	661	1323

The letters following the bore and stroke symbol specify the engine type.

'T' – Twin cylinder, rather than single cylinder
'O' – Over-head valves, rather than side-valve
'W' – Water cooled, rather than air cooled

The above letters are followed by a slash and, possibly, one further letter to signify.

'Z' – Dry sump, rather than total loss lubrication
'C' – Sports
'S' – Sports (motor cycle engines)
'R' – Racing

The above group of letters is followed by the engine number and a further slash before an additional character, which identifies the year of manufacture. The date symbol letters are:

1920	1921	1922	1923	1924
P	N	E	U	M
1925	1926	1927	1928	1929
A	T	I	C	S
1930	1931	1932	1933	1934
W	H	Y	Z	D
1935	1936	1937	1938	1939
R	V	F	O	G

The sequence of letters for the years 1920 to 1939 was repeated for the years 1940 to 1959.

Thus a 980cc air-cooled side-valve engine of 1930 would be given a number of the form KT/★★★/W, whilst a 1096cc water-cooled overhead-valve engine of 1928 would be given a number LTOW/★★★/C.

first listed in the catalogue for the 1927 season. The engines were water-cooled and intended for the sporting motorist and for racing. They remained available through to 1935. The over-head-valve engines used the same 85.7mm bore as the side-valves, but the stroke of 95mm was 10mm greater. The early engines were 50-degree V-twins and relied upon total-loss lubrication. The later engines, fitted to the three-speeder chassis, were 60-degree twins with dry-sump lubrication and included pro-vision for a starting handle.

The tables below summarize the used JAP engines in production Morgans.

The first engine of the KT series with larger valves to improve engine efficiency was produced in 1921. It appeared in the Olympia show of that year as a sports model and was designated the KTC. The modifications were subsequently incorporated into the KT engine for 1926. The same modifications together with a redesigned water-jacket were also made at this time to the water-cooled KTW engine.

For several years a well-tuned side-valve engine was considered the equal of an ohv unit

The JAP 8hp air-cooled side-valve KT engine. It weighed 91lb. A gear-driven oil pump, mounted on the timing cover, was fitted to engines used on Morgans from 1927. The chamber at the front of the crankcase forms part of an automatic lubrication system, relying on crankcase pressure and non-return valves, which was first introduced in 1914.

Two-speeder Morgan until 1932

Model	Type	Bore & Stroke	Capacity	V-angle	Power
KT	sv a/c	85.7 × 85mm	981cc	50 degrees	25bhp @ 2600rpm
KTW	sv w/c	85.7 × 85mm	981cc	50 degrees	26bhp @ 2600rpm
LTOW	ohv w/c	85.7 × 95mm	1096cc	50 degrees	40bhp @ 4200rpm
LTOWC	ohv w/c	85.7 × 95mm	1096cc	50 degrees	42bhp @ 4200rpm

Three-speeder Morgan, 1932–1935

Model	Type	Bore & Stroke	Capacity	V-angle	Power
LTZ	sv a/c	85.7 × 95mm	1096cc	60 degrees	23bhp @ 2600rpm
LTWZ	sv w/c	85.7 × 95mm	1096cc	60 degrees	24bhp @ 2600rpm
LTOWZ	ohv w/c	85.7 × 95mm	1096cc	60 degrees	39bhp @ 4500rpm

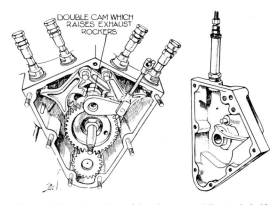

Above *The timing chest of the 8hp engine. The single half-speed timing wheel has two cams cut on the back to operate both the exhaust and inlet rockers.*

The JAP 8hp water-cooled KTW engine was of similar design to the air-cooled engine, with the exception of the water jackets. The sparking plugs are fitted into the inlet-valve caps.

for racing and record-breaking purposes. By 1929 JAP were offering a sports version of the KT engine, designated the KTC and named the 8/30. The company claimed it to be the last word in side-valve engine efficiency and identical to the first engine to have lapped Brooklands at over 100mph.

A new ohv V-twin engine became available in August 1924. The KTOR engine was based upon the JTOR prototype used by le Vack in his racing motorcycle during the 1924 season. The engine in its original form was too high to fit within the standard sized frame of most motorcycles and was reduced

Bert Le Vack with the prototype JTOR engine on dynamometer test at JAP.

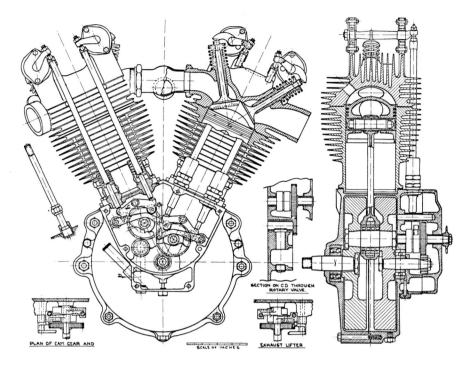

The 980cc ohv JAP of 1924. The 8/45 KTOR engine was intended for racing and incorporated a four-cam layout, hemispherical cylinder heads with domed pistons, and 45-degree inclined valves. The appearance of the overhead valve gear resulted in the affectionate description of 'dog-eared' JAP.

PLAN OF CAM GEAR AND

SECTION ON CD THROUGH ROTARY VALVE

SCALE OF INCHES

EXHAUST LIFTER

in height by adopting the bore and stroke of the KT series of engines. The automatic lubrication system of le Vack's engine was retained in a modified form and included a mechanically timed rotary sleeve-valve to regulate crankcase breathing. The 8/55hp, JTOR, and 8/45hp, KTOR, engines proved highly successful and within a few years JAPs could claim to hold almost every world's record, solo and sidecar.

The water-cooled ohv engine was developed by Val Page. It was based on the earlier 90 bore ohv, but incorporated the main design features of the successful KTOR. When announced at the 1925 show, it was claimed to produce 32bhp on low-compression pistons. This was increased using domed pistons and it was thought that 50bhp would be available for racing purposes. The 1096cc ohv w/c engine was made available from the 1926 show. It could be obtained in standard, LTOW, sports, LTOWC and racing LTOWR tune.

The JAP Eleven-Hundred Sports and Racing engine was introduced in 1926. The quoted horsepower of the LTOW was 10/40hp. The higher compression LTOWC was quoted as 10/50hp. Weight was 128lb.

JAP redesigned the LTOW engine to coincide with the introduction of the three-speeder in November 1931. The cylinder angle was increased from 50 degrees to 60 degrees, in the interest of smoother running, and coil ignition introduced. A dry-sump lubrication system was employed with a duplex Pilgrim pump used, both to feed oil to the engine and return oil to the under-bonnet tank. The front cover incorporated a starter dog, which engaged with one of the two camshafts. Selected engines were specially tuned for use

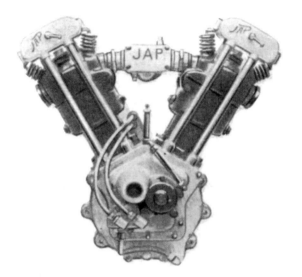

Left *The 60 degree w/c ohv LTOWZ engine developed for the three-speeder Morgan. The capacity, 1096cc, and dimensions, 85.7 × 95mm, were unchanged from the LTOW. The engine incorporated dry-sump lubrication, denoted by the final 'Z' of the engine code.*

The crankcase and timing chest of the 1096cc dry-sump engines.

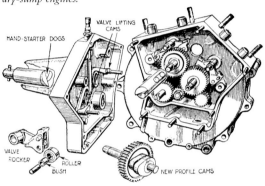

Below *(Left) The 60 degree dry-sump 1096cc (85.7 × 95mm) water-cooled LTWZ and (right) air-cooled LTZ side-valve engines, introduced in November 1931 for use with the three-speeder Morgan.*

by Morgan and are identified by an 'A' stamped on the side of the crankcase opposite the JAP number.

Side-valve versions of the new LTOWZ, both air- and water-cooled, were announced at the same time. The air-cooled LTZ engine was fitted with detachable cylinder heads, a feature not included on the water-cooled LTWZ.

MAG Engines

The Swiss firm of Motosacoche was founded in 1899 by the brothers Armand and Henry Dufaux for the manufacture of clip-on motorcycle attachments; the name derives from 'une moto sa coche' which can be translated as 'a motor in a bag'. Complete motorcycles followed and, by 1914, the company had commenced proprietary engine manufacture under the name MAG, an abbreviation of Motosacoche, Acacias, Geneva. In July 1914 the company announced a new MAG engine for use in cyclecars. This was a 45-degree V-twin, with 82mm bore and 103.5mm stroke, displacing 1093cc. The design was based upon the inlet-over-exhaust valve layout and a notable feature was the enclosure for the inlet valve mechanism, which was lubricated by oil circulated by engine suction. The large diameter valves were operated by three cams, two for the inlet valves and a single large one for the exhaust valves. The engine was of low compression and air-cooled.

The use of MAG engines by Morgan was discontinued when MAG refused to supply HFS at a price he was prepared to pay.

MAG offered the following engines for use in cyclecars:

2C9A air-cooled 993cc (82 × 94mm)
2C13A air-cooled 1094cc (82 × 104mm)
2C20A water-cooled 1094cc (82 × 104mm)

The identification code for the engine is located on the left hand side of the engine.

The quoted output of the 9hp 2C20A engine was 26bhp at 2,600rpm.

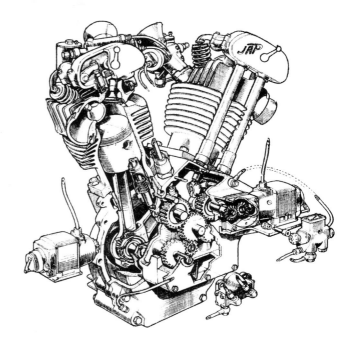

Above *The JAP JTOR 8/75 competition engine was announced in November 1933. It was fitted with two magnetos and two carburettors. The forced lubrication system provided oil to all the bearing surfaces.*

The 1093cc ioe MAG engine developed for use in cyclecars and fitted to Morgans from 1915 to 1923.

Matchless Engines

Matchless dates back to the end of the nineteenth century when H.H. Collier commenced the manufacture of pedal cycles. His sons later joined the company and the first Matchless motorcycle was produced during the early years of the following century. The first V-twin Matchless, with JAP 730cc engine, was produced in 1904. By 1912 the company had commenced engine manufacture with a $3\frac{1}{2}$hp single and, in 1925, the first Matchless V-twin engine was produced for the Model M/3S. The engine was of 990cc and based upon the JAP unit it replaced.

For 1929, Matchless Motorcycles (Colliers) Ltd. replaced the previous Models M and M/3S by new top-of-the-range touring and sports machines, the Models X and X/R. Both machines used the company's own V-twin engine. The engine, which was now designated the Model X, had proved to be a sturdy and reliable unit and was noted for its smooth running and slow tick-over. It was a 50-degree side-valve twin of 990cc with square bore and stroke dimensions of 85.5mm. The valves, which were operated by a single three-lobed camshaft with separate cam levers, were made fully enclosed for the 1930 season. In this form

the engine would also be used in AJS machines from 1933, following the Collier Brothers acquisition of AJS in 1931, and subsequently in Brough Superiors, in both side-valve and overhead-valve, air-cooled form, from 1935.

The engines were adapted for use in Morgans by Donald Heather of Matchless during early 1933. The option of air- or water-cooling was required and changes were necessary to the timing chest cover, as the motorcycle engine had relied upon magneto ignition and a gearbox-located kick-start. For the Morgan, provision was made for a coil ignition system, using a camshaft-driven distributor, and for a hand-operated cranking system with the starting handle engaging directly with the crankshaft. The early distributor systems used a rotor arm, although this was soon changed to a system with double-ended coil.

Three versions of the engine were produced for use in the Morgan. These comprised the side-valve water-cooled 'MX' model and two overhead-valve models, the MX2 and MX4; the MX2 being air-cooled whilst the MX4 was water-cooled.

The MX engine was first offered to the public, fitted to a Sports two-seater, in May 1933. It was withdrawn from the range for the 1938 season. The overhead-valve MX2 and

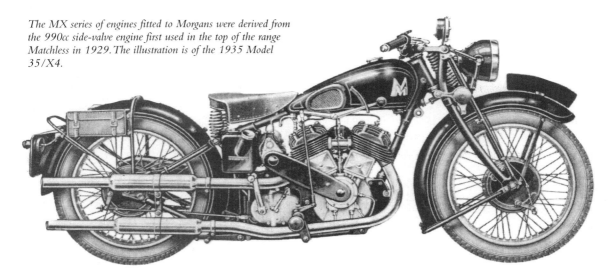

The MX series of engines fitted to Morgans were derived from the 990cc side-valve engine first used in the top of the range Matchless in 1929. The illustration is of the 1935 Model 35/X4.

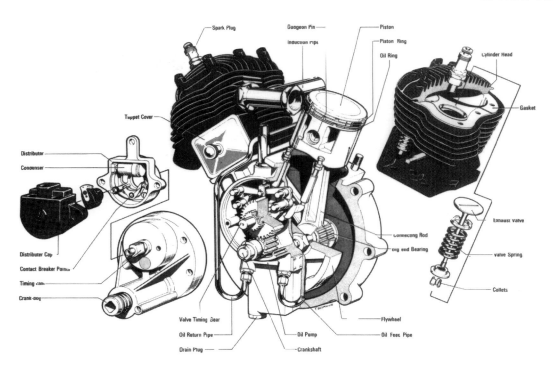

MX4 engines were first introduced at the time of the 1933 Olympia show. The MX2 was discontinued in June 1939, whilst the MX4 remained available up to the start of the war.

The 'MX' Engine

The MX was a highly efficient water-cooled side-valve engine with a compression ratio of 5:1, which developed 27.5bhp at 4,000rpm. The valve gear was totally enclosed and moving parts were lubricated by oil mist, eliminating the necessity for frequent tappet adjustment.

The 'MX2' Engine

The air-cooled ohv MX2 engine with a compression ratio of 6.2:1 developed 39.1bhp at 4,6000rpm. The engine combined a high degree of mechanical silence with an outstanding performance. It could be supplied with high-compression pistons giving a compression ratio of 7.5:1. The crankcase and bottom end were almost identical with that of the side valve. The air-cooled cylinders, cylinder

Above *The illustration is of the air-cooled engine, rather than the water-cooled MX, and has been chosen to illustrate the internal arrangement.*

A factory photograph of the air-cooled ohv MX2 engine.

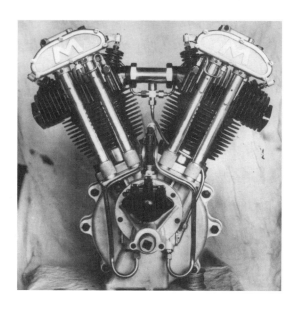

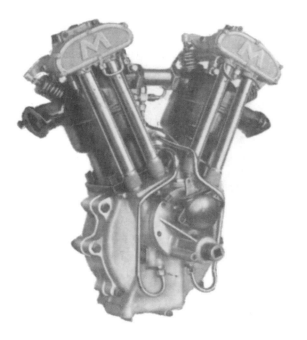

The MX4 engine. The 'M' cast into the tappet covers was appropriate for either Morgan or Matchless.

A Precision ohv engine of 1912.

heads and valve gear were based upon those of the 495cc single-cylinder Matchless motorcycle engine, which would go into production later in the year. The valve gear was totally enclosed and mechanically lubricated.

The 'MX4' Engine

The water-cooled ohv MX4 engine offered slightly improved performance over the air-cooled model. It developed 42.1bhp at 4,800rpm. Again high compression pistons giving a compression ratio of 7.5:1 could be supplied

Precision Engines

Frank Baker established F.E. Baker Ltd in 1906 for the manufacture of bicycle fittings under the Precision name. Motorcycle engines followed in 1910 and proved so popular that no less than ninety-six machines on display at Olympia in 1911 were equipped with Precision engines. About this time Baker acquired

the patents for a novel engine, which was produced as the Green-Precision. Green's idea was to make the water jacket and radiator as a single unit in copper, which could be heat shrunk on to the cylinder. The arrangement had a neat appearance and functioned well.

Frank must have hoped to rival JAP, who for many years had dominated the proprietary engine market, but it was not to be. Post-war the company was renamed Beardmore-Precision, after obtaining new capital from the Scottish firm of William Beardmore & Co. Both proprietary engines and complete motorcycles were produced but, despite sporting successes, sales declined. Finally Beardmore withdrew its capital, causing the closure of the company.

Ford 4-Cylinder Engines

The 8HP Model Y was Ford's first small car. It had been designed in the USA specifically for the British market and was the first car to be

134

manufactured at Ford's new plant at Dagenham in Essex. The plant had been officially opened on 1 October 1931 and the start-up of production was planned for May 1932. However, it would be mid–August before the first cars were completed. Production in the first year fell very far short of the ambitious target of 45,000 cars but, once all teething problems had been resolved, the Model Y quickly established itself as the market leader.

The Model Y was available in two- or four-door versions. Commercial variants were a small van and, of interest in the context of the Morgan, a three-wheeler known as the Fordson Tug, which was designed for door-to-door deliveries towing a trailer.

A larger, 10HP, version of the Model Y was produced from September 1934 and designated the Model C. Both the Models Y and C were replaced by new, all-British-designed

Longitudinal and cross sectional views of the Ford 8 engine. The engine was designed by Laurence Sheldric, the Ford Company's chief engineer at Dearborn, USA.

models, the Model 7Y Eight and Model 7W Ten in 1937. Further redesign for 1939 resulted in the 8HP and 10HP models being replaced, respectively, by the E04A Anglia and the E93A Prefect. The soundness of the basic engine design ensured that few changes were required to either the 8hp or 10hp engines during this period. Indeed the engines would remain in production, without significant redesign, until 1959. A modernized version of the engine, named the 100E, was introduced with the new 100E Anglia and Prefect models in 1953. The earlier engine remained in production alongside the 100E until superseded by the 107/105E ohv range of Ford cars in 1959. The 100E lasted a further two years in the 300E van.

During the years of production the 8hp engine was given the designation Y, E04A or E494A and the 10hp engine was given the designation C, E93A or E493A. Nowadays it is common practice to refer to both the 8hp or 10hp engine as the E93A engine. The engines may be readily recognized by the engine

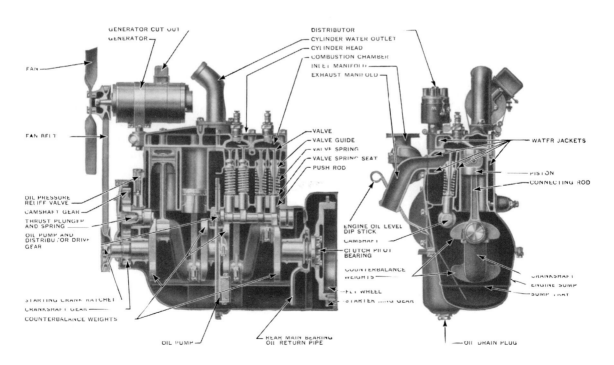

number, which commences with a letter 'Y' for the 8hp engine and a letter 'C' for the 10hp engine. The 100E, which is of the same capacity as the 10hp engine, carries an engine number commencing '100E'.

The F4 chassis exhibited at the 1933 Olympia Show. The Ford 8hp engine is fitted with a 'Silver Top' aluminium cylinder-head.

The Ford 8hp engine was first fitted to the four-seater, Model F, announced in November 1933, and remained available up till the start of the war. The 10hp engine became available as an alternative to the 8hp from 1936 with the new Model F, Super-Sports, two-seater for an additional seven guineas.

	8hp	**10hp**
Type	4 cylinders in-line	4 cylinders in-line
Bore	56.6mm	63.5mm
Stroke	92.5mm	92.5mm
Capacity	933cc	1172cc
RAC rating	8hp	10hp
Brake horsepower	22 at 3,500rpm	32.5 at 3,500rpm
Max. torque	36.4lb ft at 2,300rpm	46.4lb ft at 2,400rpm

136

8   The Two-Speeder Models

Standard, Sporting and De Luxe Runabouts 1910–31

The Runabouts first exhibited to the public at the 1910 Olympia Motor Cycle Show were sparsely bodied single-seaters with tiller steering. They were powered by either a 4hp single-cylinder or 8hp twin-cylinder JAP engine. The machines were well received, but as a commercial venture it was clear that the bodywork would need to be less sparse and to include provision for a passenger. HFS quickly set to and designed a simple two-seater body with the driver and passenger sitting side by side. The bodywork of the prototype, which carried the registration number CJ 743, remained pared down to the essentials and tiller steering was retained. Very quickly, however, the machine was being offered to the public with a full body, including mudguards, a coalscuttle bonnet covering the engine and fuel tank, and acetylene lighting equipment. Tiller steering was entirely satisfactory with direct steering systems but, by 1911, was considered antiquated and was dropped in favour of a steering wheel. The engine fitted was the 8hp side-valve air-cooled JAP twin. This offered a sprightly performance in a car weighing little more than 3cwt. The basic price was eighty-five guineas (£89 5s).

From 1911 the basic two-seater, with open body sides, became known as the Standard model. It was joined in the catalogue by two models, the De Luxe and Sporting, which were built on the same chassis but fitted with bodies with raised sides. The driver and

An early production 8hp JAP single-seater with tiller steering. Ruth Morgan at the controls.

passenger still sat high in the car, above the bevel box, but could now claim to be sitting in, rather than on, the Morgan. The more expensive De Luxe offered the refinement of a door on the near-side, sprung cushions and an upholstered seat-back. The Sporting body was without doors and access was gained by means of a step forming a toolbox.

The Runabouts were supplied without windscreen, hood, lighting equipment and the like; these were available as extras and special prices were offered on fully equipped machines.

Initially the tail section of the body was open and a cycle-type mudguard fitted to the rear wheel for weather protection. The mudguard supports doubled up as a luggage rack. The mudguards were valenced, with a deeper

Right The appearance of the Runabout was greatly enhanced by the adoption of a coalscuttle bonnet and mudguards. The bonnet not only tidied up the frontal appearance, but also offered modest weather protection for the ignition system. The aluminium silencers were replaced by steel units for 1915.

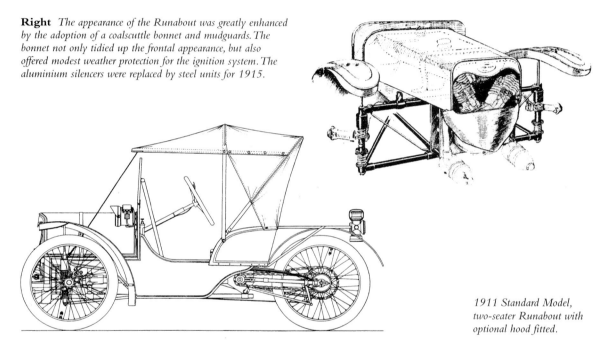

1911 Standard Model, two-seater Runabout with optional hood fitted.

Early sporting model with torpedo fuel tank and exposed engine.

1912 Morgan Runabout – Standard Model

Production period
1911–14. (Standard Popular 1921–28)

Engine

Type	8hp J.A.P. air-cooled
Bore and stroke	85 × 85mm
Capacity	980cc
Ignition	Bosch high tension magneto
Carburettor	B & B two-lever

Transmission

Clutch	Self-contained cone clutch with ball thrust bearings, actuated by foot pedal (lining fitted from 1913)
Final Drive	Enclosed propeller shaft to bevel box. Two-speed final drive by two $\frac{3}{4}$in Coventry chains, selected by dog clutches operated by a side lever

Suspension

Front	Independent helical springs
Rear	Quarter-elliptic springs

Frame

	Special patented design, all metal, very light and immensely strong

Wheels

	Back wheel runs on Hoffmann ball bearings, front wheels fitted with special dust-proof hubs
Brakes	Two band-brakes fitted to back wheel, controlled by a hand lever and a foot pedal
Tyres	26 × $2\frac{1}{2}$in non-skid back tyre. Extra for 3in back tyre £1 15s

Bodywork

	Strongly made of wood and steel-sheet, and entirely separate from chassis. Fitted with mahogany dashboard. Standard colours grey or green
Mud wings	Large and fitted with valances
Luggage carrier	Fitted over back wheel, arrangeable to carry any reasonable weight

Tank capacity 3gal petrol and $\frac{1}{2}$gal lubricating oil

Dimensions 8ft (2,440mm) long, 4ft 2in (1,270mm) wide, 6ft (1,830mm) wheelbase

Weight 3cwt (152kg)

Performance Standard gear ratios of 4.5:1 and 8:1 give about 45mph (72km/h) in top and the ability to climb a 1 in 4 gradient in low

Consumption 60mpg (4.72ltr/100km)

Price £89 5s (special price for model fitted with hood, windscreen, P & H headlamps and generator, horn, kit of tools, tyre pump and floor mats: £100)

Extras Hood: £5, Screen: £2, Horn: 12s 6d, P & H lamps and generator: £3 2s 6d, Tail lamp (not required by law): 14s 6d, Jones' speed indicator, fitted: £3 10s, Tyre pump: 4s, Painting special colours: £1, Upholstered seat back instead of strap: 10s

section valence being used on the De Luxe model. For the 1913 season the bodywork was extended back to form a more substantial rear-wheel enclosure. The redesigned tail-section incorporated space for tools and a modest amount of luggage. The top of the rear section was fitted with a pyramid-patterned zinc sheet to provide additional luggage capacity.

A Commercial Carrier variant of the Standard model was offered for 1914. The luggage container, which fixed over the back wheel, was hinged to tilt forward for access to the rear wheel. Alternatively, it could be removed by unscrewing eight nuts to convert the vehicle back to its original passenger form. The Runabout was not an ideal load carrier. The sales catalogue suggested the maximum capacity of the container was $1\frac{3}{4}$cwt (89kg), but prudent

Left *1912 De Luxe Runabout.*

1913 Sporting model.

Below *A Commercial Carrier body option was offered with the Morgan Standard in 1914. The model was priced at £95, plus an additional £3 for the alternative body. The illustration is of the 1913 Olympia Show car, which was displayed in the livery of James of Sheffield.*

The interior layout of the 1922 De Luxe. A polished-aluminium dashboard was fitted. Instrumentation comprised a speedometer and clock, which were optional fittings, and an oil sight-feed. The oddments ledge below the dashboard was a new feature for the year.

The restyled bonnet with divided front opening was first introduced on the De Luxe model for 1930.

replaced by a two-pane screen with opening top section for 1926. In other respects the styling of the De Luxe remained unchanged through to the 1928 season, by which time it had again become dated. For 1929 through to the discontinuation of the model at the end of 1931, the body was smooth sided with a rounded back. The headlights, previously mounted at the front of the scuttle were moved back to the windscreen.

During the production period of the De Luxe, the public perception of the three-wheeler as an everyday transport vehicle had gradually changed. Once considered a viable alternative to the four-wheeled car, it was now simply an economy vehicle. To refer to a three-wheeler as luxurious had become meaningless! The De Luxe was once the most expensive and luxurious model of the Morgan range, but over the years its status was reduced. With the demise of the Standard at the end of 1928, the De Luxe became the basic two-seater and, alongside the Family, the cheapest model. For 1931 the term De Luxe ceased to be used as a

model name but instead to identify machines fitted with the new 'M' type chassis. The De Luxe became known as the two-seater De Luxe if fitted with the 'M' type chassis or the Standard two-seater if fitted with the old 'B' type chassis.

The bodywork modifications for the 1931 season resulted in the two- and four-seater models being similarly styled. It also meant that the two-seater was largely redundant; it had no pretensions to be a sports model and could not accommodate luggage for touring. The only touring Morgan available for 1932 would be the Family model.

The De Luxe was usually fitted with a JAP side-valve engine, either air- or water-cooled, during all years of manufacture. However, the catalogues list various alternatives, which could be made available at extra cost. These included the 10hp MAG engine for 1921 and 1922, the Blackburne engine for 1923 and 1924, and the ohv Anzani from 1925 to 1931.

The Standard Popular model would be little changed during its period of production.

143

1927 Standard.

The model name reverted back to Standard for 1923 and for subsequent years. The usual engine was always the 8hp JAP side-valve, although for 1923 and 1924 a Blackburne alternative was offered. All Morgan models, including the Standard, were fitted with electric lights from the 1926 season; prior to that time electric lights had been an optional extra. An electric horn was added for the following year. The single-pane hinged windscreen remained in use until 1926 and for the final year of its use was fitted with a glazing bar at the top. For 1927 the two-piece windscreen with opening upper section, already in use on the De Luxe and Family models, was adopted. Finally, for 1928 the styling was improved, to be in keeping with the other models of the range, by use of a longer bonnet and by moving the windscreen closer to the driver. The model was discontinued from the date of the 1928 Olympia Show.

Grand Prix 1913–1926

Within a few days of Gordon McMinnies' victory in the Cyclecar Grand Prix at Amiens in July 1913, HFS was offering replica machines for sale. However, the Grand Prix model was introduced to the public, as a catalogue model, at the Motor Cycle Show in November 1913. Three variants were displayed. The Grand Prix model No. 3, which was identical in all major particulars with McMinnies' race-winning machine, was fitted with a water-cooled ohv JAP engine. It was claimed to be capable of sustained speeds of a mile a minute and was recommended for racing purposes. It cost £115. Grand Prix models No. 1 and No. 2 were offered as touring machines and fitted with water-cooled side-valve JAP engines. Both were two-seaters and differed only in respect of the body width. No. 1 was fitted with a body described as narrow for two, whilst No. 2 was fitted with a wider touring body. They were each priced at £105.

The Grand Prix models incorporated the chassis modifications made on the racing machines. In particular, the chassis was lengthened by 11in (280m) and made more rigid by using larger-diameter bottom tubes. The longer chassis allowed the seats to be placed lower down in front of the bevel box and required increased steering rake.

The machines were initially offered without windscreen and hood, although these were available as extras for £2 and £5, respectively.

The Grand Prix model, with two-seater body, remained in limited production during the early war years. Originally JAP engines were used but, by 1916, all Morgans were being fitted with 10hp MAG engines. The model was little developed during this period. However, it did provide the foundation of the new Sporting model, announced in October 1916.

The Grand Prix model continued after the

144

Above *Identical 1913 Grand Prix models were purchased by the Frys, father and son, of the Bristol chocolate firm.*

A 1924 Grand Prix model providing all-weather transport.

A Grand Prix model ascending Old Wyche Cutting during the early 1920s. The steep hill within a few miles of the Morgan factory formed part of the test circuit for new models.

war as part of a three-model range alongside the De Luxe and Sporting models. It was offered with a water-cooled 8hp JAP engine, which would be the standard option for the remainder of the car's production. The 10hp MAG engine was again offered during 1922 and 1923. Blackburne engines were offered during 1923 and 1924, and Anzani during 1925 and 1926. The model was little changed during its final years of production and was phased out during the 1926 season.

Family 1917–1932

The development of a four-seater Morgan was begun in 1912 with a prototype machine built on an extended Standard chassis. It was 1915, however, before a four-seater three-wheeler was announced and it is unlikely that any machines were produced for sale during the war. The four-seater was re-announced in 1917 as a post-war model. Production was slow to get underway and the machine was not included in the sales brochures for 1918 and 1919. A few machines were produced. HFS was photographed with his wife and daughter plus three other toddlers in a four-seater during autumn 1918. E.B. Ware of JAP also drove a four-seater with a new wedge-shaped oil/petrol tank and fitted with the new 8hp engine.

The four-seater, now named the Family

model, first appeared at the Olympia show in November 1919 and was included in the 1920 catalogue. Production was slow to commence due to demand for other models and surviving copies of the 1920 sales catalogue have the entries for the Family, and also the Aero, models crossed through. The Family model was omitted from the 1921 catalogue, but reappeared the following year when it became generally available for sale to the public. It was destined to be the most popular model of the Morgan range and remained in production in two-speeder form through to 1933 and for a further three years with three-speed transmission.

The bodywork of the production Family model was styled on the Standard Popular, but retained a fixed scuttle region between the bonnet and windscreen. The opening at the front of the bonnet for the cooling air was originally heart shaped. On the early cars this opening was supplemented by four forward-facing louvres on either side of the bonnet, adjacent to the engine. The air escaped from the bonnet via further sets of louvres at the top and sides of the bonnet. The rear section of the body was rounded and the level of the skirt was raised behind the front seats. A single door was provided on the nearside. The front bench-seat could be tilted forward to provide access to the rear and was adjustable, forward or back. The driver could either use the door

The 1918 Family model with HFS at the wheel. Luggage has been strapped on at both the rear and the side.

and slide across into his seat or step over the side of the body. A single running-board, on the offside, was provided for this purpose and to mount either an acetylene generator or a battery. The mudguards were the flat topped, backwards sloping, style used on the Grand Prix of 1917. A one-piece folding windscreen and a hood were fitted. Acetylene lighting was included within the basic specification, whilst electric lighting was available as a £10 extra. The stated weight of the early cars was 4¾cwt (241kg).

When announced, the carrying capacity of the Family Morgan was claimed to be 38 stone (241kg); assumed equivalent to either three adults or two adults and two children. The claim immediately brought forth cries of cruelty to little cars from the motoring press. Morgan's response, made in the 1923 sales brochure, was to increase the allowed load: 'The Family model has been greatly improved during 1922. We have sold hundreds of these machines, which give the greatest satisfaction. We will guarantee this model to carry up to the total weight of 40 stone.'

The most frequently fitted engine was the 8hp JAP side-valve engine. The air-cooled KT engine was the cheapest option, as an additional £10 was required for the water-cooled KTW engine with its associated radiator. The price difference was reduced to £8 in 1929, £7 10s in 1930 and £5 in 1931. Various alternative engine options were listed. These included Blackburne, air- or water-cooled engines, from 1922 to 1924, and, at extra cost, ohv Anzani engines from 1925 to 1930.

The Family, alongside the Standard and later the De Luxe, spearheaded Morgan's battle for survival during the years of depression and against competition from cheap four-wheeled cars such as the Austin Seven, Ford 8 and Morris Minor. When first readily available on the market in 1922, it was priced from £191 and, with the exception of the Aero, which was available only to special order, the most expensive model of the range. By 1929 it had become the cheapest. (The prices of both the

The Family Model exhibited at the 1922 Olympia Show. The running board provided support for the battery and a step for the driver to clamber in. The wheel discs were a popular optional extra at £3 per set.

De Luxe and Family models in 1929 were £92. However, the De Luxe could be purchased without front-wheel brakes and geared steering for £6 less.)

Despite remorseless price cutting, detailed improvements were made to the specification of the Family. The 1923 model was little changed from 1922, but the price was reduced to £153. For 1924 the price was reduced by £18 and electric lighting, previously a £10 extra, standardized. A £12 reduction for 1925 was followed the next year by a further reduction of £7, bringing the price of the 1926 Family model to £116. For 1926 the sides of the body were raised in height by 1in (25mm) and a rigidly attached, vertical windscreen fitted. The screen comprised two panes of glass; the top pane could be hinged outwards to improve ventilation in hot weather and for improved visibility in poor driving conditions. The introduction of the 'wide B' chassis, in November 1926, permitted fitment of more commodious bodies and seats. Interestingly, the load capacity, although remaining unchanged at 40 stone (254kg), was now deemed suitable for four adults. Front-wheel brakes became part of the basic specification at this time. The price for 1927 was reduced to £111. A further reduction for 1928 brought the price down to £102.

Above *This 1927 Morgan Family carries the factory registration CJ 743 and was presumably used for demonstrations and testing. The 1927 Family and De Luxe models were the first Morgans to be fitted with a fixed windscreen with opening top panel. The photograph clearly illustrates the elaborate coach lining that was applied to even the cheapest models. A black band was painted at the edges of the body and on the louvres, and highlighted by white coach lines.*

A works photograph of a Family model with headlights mounted on the windscreen board and without the step in the rear body panel. The car is finished in a two-colour scheme costing an extra £2 10s.

Above *The layout of the seating and controls of the 1928 Family model.*

1930 Family model.

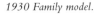

The rear body panel of the Family was modified for 1929 to remove the step at the base of the panel. This modification coincided with the restyling of the De Luxe, and the two-seater and the four-seater models were now of almost identical appearance. The most striking difference was in the location of the head-lamps. The redesign of the De Luxe had moved the headlamps back to the windscreen, whilst the Family model retained a location at the back edge of the bonnet. It would be a further year before the headlamps on the Family model were located at the windscreen. The hoods, on both the Family and De Luxe, were now attached at the back by a brass strip in place of eyelets. From the end of January 1929 the Family model used the same radiator as the De Luxe. A square door was fitted to the Family model from May 1929. The side-screens, previously an extra at £1 15s, and geared steering were by now included in the specification.

The 'M' type chassis became available, at extra charge, on all models during 1930. Vertical windscreens were by now becoming unfashionable and, from March 1930, some Family and De Luxe models on the 'B' chassis were fitted with sloping screens. The windscreen pillars were still mounted vertically,

---

1930 Morgan Family Model

Production period
1920–33 (three-speeder version: 1932–36)

Engine
Type	J.A.P air-cooled twin-cylinder side-valve
Bore and stroke	85.5 × 85.5mm
Capacity	980cc
Lubrication	Mechanical pump and sight feed
Power output	25bhp @ 2,600rpm
Ignition	ML high-tension magneto
Carburettor	Amal two-lever

Transmission
Clutch	Cone
Two-speed	5:1 and 10:1
Final drive	Enclosed propeller shaft to bevel box. Two-speed final drive with separate drive chains selected by dog clutches

Suspension
Front	Independent helical springs
Rear	Quarter-elliptic springs
Steering	Geared with 2 to 1 reduction

Brakes
	Cable operated
Front	Internal expanding, 7in diameter, operated by hand lever
Rear	External contracting, $6\frac{1}{2}$in diameter, operated by foot pedal

Dimensions
Track	4ft 2in (1,270mm)
Overall length	9ft 7in (2,920mm)
Overall width	4ft 10in (1,470m)

Weight
7cwt (355kg)

Capacities
Petrol tank	4 gallons (18ltr)
Oil tank	1 gallon (4.5ltr)

Equipment
Lucas electric three-light set, 6 volt. Electric starter optional

Seating
Two adults and three children – total weight 40 stone (254kg)

Colours
Dark blue or Panhard red with black mudguards

Performance
Maximum speed	50mph (80km/h)
Touring speed	40–45mph (64–72km/h)
Petrol consumption	40mpg (7.1ltr/100km)

Price
£87 10s; £97 10s with electric starter, speedometer and side screens; £7 10s extra for S.V. water-cooled J.A.P. or O.H.V. Anzani engine

Standard Family Model.

The Family De Luxe Model.

but bent back to incline the screen, and the headlamps relocated at the base of the windscreen.

For the 1931 season customers could purchase either a Standard Family model on the wide 'B' chassis for £85 or a Family De Luxe model on the 'M' Type chassis for £90. Other than for a few cosmetic changes, the Standard model was little changed from earlier years. The opening at the front of the coalscuttle bonnet was divided into two by a vertical bar, a feature of the De Luxe model of the previous year, and the forward-facing louvres omitted. The flat-section mudguards used on the first production Family models were retained. The De Luxe Family model was more fully redesigned in order to provide a much roomier body. The design did away with the scuttle and the longer bonnet was hinged at the windscreen. The bulkhead was inclined, allowing the windscreen to angle back without bent pillars, and the headlights located at the base of the windscreen. The dashboard was rexine covered and matched the upholstery. The opening at the front of the bonnet was divided by a vertical strip and filled by a wire mesh, suitable for keeping inquisitive fingers away from hot engines. The panel below the opening was increased in size and shaped to give enough space for a two-letter, four-digit reg-

istration number. The restyling was completed by fitment of 'close-up' cycle mudguards.

The De Luxe Family was discontinued at the end of 1931 and replaced by a three-speed model. The Standard Family was unchanged for 1932, but identified as the Two-Speed Family model. It was the last two-speeder produced by Morgans and, from July 1931, at £75 with an air-cooled JAP side-valve engine fitted, the cheapest. The model remained available, to special order only, into the early months of 1933.

Aero 1920–1932

Production of Morgan Runabouts gradually reduced as the Great War progressed and Ministry of Munitions Priority Certificates became necessary for the production of any machine not ordered under official contract. Such restrictions did not, of course, prevent HFS considering the future design of his sporting machines nor from incorporating his ideas into the few machines he was licensed to build. In April 1916 a new Grand Prix model was exhibited in the showroom of the London dealers, Messrs Elce & Co. The machine, which incorporated features of the Grand Prix and Sporting models, was simply referred to as a special sporting Morgan by the motorcycling press; it turned out to be the prototype for what would become the Aero.

The new machine was powered by a MAG water-cooled engine. The front mudguards curved straight down from the wheels and there was no gap between the mudguards and running boards. The seats were lowered, compared to the Grand Prix, and staggered to provide more elbow room for the driver and leg room for the passenger. The tail panel was domed and came to a point beyond the rear wheel. The bonnet sloped upward from the radiator and a deflector was fitted in an attempt to direct the wind over the driver's head; neither windscreen nor hood were fitted. The machine was finished in elephant grey and priced at £130.

The dashing appearance and sporting performance of the new model found favour with officers of the Royal Flying Corps. Both Lieutenant Robinson VC, who shot down a Zeppelin airship early in the war and Captain Albert Ball VC DSO MC, Britain's most famous fighter ace with forty recorded 'kills', owned machines. This association with the air aces provided valuable publicity for the firm during the war years.

The Aero was announced at the Motor Cycle Show in November 1919 but did not enter general production in 1920, although illustrated in the sales brochure. It appeared again at the 1920 show as a new model available to special order. The example on display had a V-fronted air deflector below the fuel tank forming the bonnet and behind the radiator, whilst the bonnet sides were open. Twin 'Aero' screens provided protection for the driver and passenger. The dashboard was polished with flush-fitted instruments. MAG or JAP engines were listed and an ingenious arrangement of cables allowed hand or foot control of the Binks carburettor.

A particularly striking version of the Aero was exhibited at the 1921 show. It was finished in nickel and sported such desirable extras as a snake horn and ship's-type ventilators. It had been built to special order but created a great deal of interest.

An equally striking Aero was the star exhibit at the following year's show. The bodywork was finished in polished aluminium and the flat-section mudguards were finished in black. The radiator and tank were nickel plated, as were other detailed components, and black wheel-discs were fitted. The engine was an

Captain Albert Ball VC DSO MC was widely photographed driving his disc-wheeled Morgan of 1917. The machine displays features of the post-war Aero model. The post-war owner of the machine was totally blind and employed a lady chauffeur in order to enjoy the car.

ohv 8hp water-cooled Anzani. The machine was a replica of the '200 Mile' racers and was available to special order for £200. It is referred to as either the 'flat-sided' Aero or '200-Mile' Aero.

The Aero remained in limited production, although unlisted in the sales brochures, throughout 1922 and 1923. However, during this period the Aero was to be seen increasingly taking part in competition. Opportunity

The Aero model provided the driver with an attractive, business like, dashboard in polished aluminium and an imposing view through the Aero screens of the bonnet with its filler caps, ventilators and snake's head horn.

was taken to improve the styling and the already rakish machine became yet more dashing. The aperture below the bonnet/tank was filled in by a louvred panel and the body sides swept back, with little curvature, to terminate at the small-diameter rounded tail. The top panel of the rear body was flat and parallel to the ground. The bottom of the tail panels swept up to finish at the height of the top of the rear wheel. The mudguards, of flat section, followed the general outline of the wheels and their rear section was swept back to run almost parallel to the road. The gear and brake levers were positioned outside the body, in line with the bevel box, and required the driver to reach back in order to change gear or brake. The stylish snake horn, which ran from outside the cockpit to above the front mudguard, and the ship's-type ventilators, which featured on the 1921 show car, were standardized, but the front-wheel discs were an optional extra. Twin Auster screens were retained and a small spot lamp fitted within the gap between the screens. The engine exhaust was ducted back through large-diameter flexible pipes to silencers on the underside of the body.

The *Motor Cycle* described the Aero models at the 1923 Olympia show as: 'the last word in racy appearance, although somewhat lacking in room for both occupants and the provision

1922 Aero. The Aero was available only to special order prior to the 1924 season.

Above *The Aero model displayed at the 1924 Motor Cycle show.*

Right *1924 Aero.*

for carrying luggage. For purely sports use, the Aero Morgans compare in performance with high-powered semi-racing cars of five or six times the price.'

The Aero finally became a standard catalogue model for the 1924 season. The announcement in the sales catalogue read:

> We are now listing the 'Aero' model. This machine is similar to our track racers which, when fitted

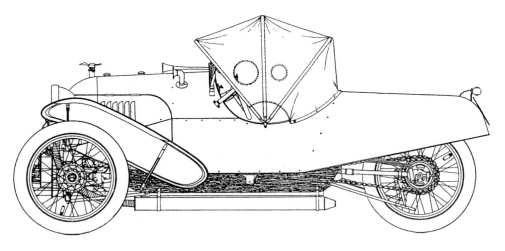

This drawing of a 1926 Aero illustrates the impracticality of the Aero hood. The Light Car and Cyclecar magazine opined that anyone buying an Aero Morgan would be of a sufficiently sporting nature to forgo a hood.

153

The Aero with flared mudguards, first introduced at the 1925 Motor Cycle Show, was arguably the most attractive of the Morgan three-wheelers and a popular prop for beach photographers in the 1920s. This Aero is seen on the sands at Margate.

George Goodall on the Brooklands banking during the 1926 International Six Day Trial.

with the latest ohv Blackburne racing engine, have lapped at Brooklands at speeds over 90mph. For track work we recommend a Hartford shock absorber fitted to the back wheel and Dunlop 26 × 3½ straight-side tyres. The tail of this machine is rounded, a single windscreen can be fitted if desired and a small hood at £3 extra. Straight-through exhaust pipes can be fitted at £1 extra, but are not recommended, as the noise is likely to cause trouble with the police. Plated fittings are standard on this model. We think we are right in saying that this is the fastest Standard passenger outfit that can be obtained at anything near its price.

The price of the Aero in 1924 was £148 when fitted with a JAP or Blackburne engine. The 10hp Anzani ohv engine, either air- or water-cooled, was available for an additional £5. Alternately a Blackburne ohv racing engine, specially ordered by Morgans for the Aero, could be fitted for £12 extra. The standard specification included an electric lighting set, but not a speedometer nor an electric starter, which were available for £4 15s and £12 respectively. Front-wheel brakes, which had been available since March 1923, cost an additional £6. The machine was supplied without weather protection, other than the aero screens. These proved popular, providing good protection without an annoying back draught. The hood, which was optional and cost £3 plus an additional £1 for the hood cover, was

less well received. It allowed no visibility to the sides or rear and hand signalling was very difficult. Its only good feature was that it could be raised or lowered from the seat without stopping the car; an essential feature as entry to the car with the hood erect was almost impossible.

In standard trim, the Aero offered 60mph performance with the ohv Anzani engine fitted and a further 10mph with the racing Blackburne.

The Aero model remained largely unchanged for the 1925 season, but prices were reduced by £13. Brochure illustrations for 1925 through to the 1927 season show the Aero with the 1924-style flat-section mudguards. However, by April 1925, cars were being fitted with the flat sideways-inclined wings, which are nowadays considered such a styling feature of the Aero model.

Three Aero models were displayed at the Olympia Show in September 1925. Two were fitted with water-cooled ohv 1100cc engines of Blackburne and Anzani manufacture, and the third was fitted with a water-cooled sv 980cc JAP engine. The flared mudguards appeared for the first time at Olympia on the JAP engined Aero.

Prices of the Aero model for 1926 were £142 if fitted with the new 10/40 Blackburne racing engine, £135 with the ohv Anzani or £130 with a water-cooled JAP. For 1927, the Aero model was fitted as standard with the ohv

Anzani engine for £127, although the 10/40hp Blackburne or JAP ohv racing engines were offered as alternatives for an additional £13. The attractive snake's head bulb horn was omitted from 1927 models, being replaced by a simpler bulb horn. Flared mudguards also became the standard fitting.

The hood fitted to the Aero, always a topic of amusement, was improved slightly from November 1928 by the use of straps, rather than springs, to retain it in the upright position.

In 1928, the Aero was replaced as the most sporting model in the Morgan range by a totally new Aero known initially as the Super Sports Aero, occasionally referred to as the Super Aero, but finally known simply as the

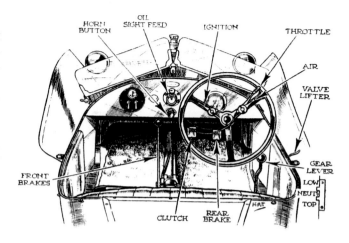

The general layout of the dash and controls of the 1928 Aero.

1927 Morgan Aero

Production period
1920–32 (Blackburne KM series engine 1922–27)

Engine
Type	10/40 Blackburne ohv
Bore and stroke	85 × 96.8mm
Capacity	1098cc
Power output	40bhp @ 4,000rpm
Ignition	High-tension magneto
Carburettor	B & B, Amac or Binks two-jet

Transmission
Clutch	Cone
Two-speed	4.6:1 and 7.9:1, optional 5:1 and 10:1
Final drive	Enclosed propeller shaft to bevel box. Two-speed final drive with separate drive chains selected by dog clutches

Suspension
Front	Independent helical springs
Rear	Quarter-elliptic springs
Steering	Direct
Brakes	Two external contracting-band brakes on back wheel, controlled by hand lever and foot pedal. Front brake optional

Dimensions
Wheelbase	6ft (1,830mm)
Track	4ft 2in (1,270mm)
Overall length	9ft 9in (2,970mm)
Overall width	4ft 8in (1,420mm)

Weight
6cwt (305kg) (varies with specification; chassis weight 3cwt (152.5kg))

Capacities
Petrol tank	3 gallons (13.64ltr)
Oil tank	½ gallon (2.27ltr)

Equipment
Lucas electric three-light set, 6 volt. Snake horn

Seating
Two persons

Colour
Grey, red, blue, purple or green

Performance
Maximum speed	72mph (115km/h)
Petrol consumption	50mpg (5.66ltr/100km)

Price
£142 (£140 with J.A.P ohv racing engine)

Super Sports. The days of the original Aero were far from over, however, as the model would remain in production, largely unchanged except for price, into 1932.

The cheapest versions of the Aero for 1928 were priced at £119 and fitted with either an ohv Anzani or a side-valve JAP engine. The 10/40 JAP ohv engine remained the sporting option and cost an additional £13, which included the cost of fitting larger exhaust pipes

Factory photograph of the 1930 Aero model fitted with JAP side-valve engine.

and silencers. The same engine options were continued through 1929 and 1930. From January 1929 the Aero was fitted with new-type wing stays and a revised hood. The basic price was reduced, first by £4 in 1929 and by a further £5 in 1930; the 10/40 JAP engine cost an additional £12. The Aero, as other models of the Morgan range, could be supplied on the 'M' chassis in 1930 for an additional £6 10s.

The Anzani engine was discontinued for 1931 and the Aero was offered with either a side-valve or overhead-valve, water-cooled JAP engine. The Aero De Luxe was fitted with the 'M' chassis and restyled with the close-fitting cycle mudguards of the Super Sports and a V-screen. A new bonnet without louvres, similar to that of the Super Sports, was introduced in June 1931 and a month later the mudguards were given a central bead. The Aero De Luxe was priced at £110 with the side-valve engine and at £124 with the 10/40hp engine. The Aero Standard model, which was fitted with the 'B' chassis and unchanged from the earlier years, was £5 cheaper.

Wider Aero bodies were introduced at the time of the 1931 Motorcycle show. The two-speed Aero on the 'B' chassis remained in production for 1932, but was significantly reduced in price to £95 with the side-valve JAP engine

The Aero De Luxe on the 'M' chassis was introduced in Sept 1930. The mudguards were of the close-fitting cycle type.

and £110 with the overhead-valve JAP engine. It was phased out during early 1933. The De Luxe model was discontinued for 1932 and replaced by a similarly styled machine fitted on the new three-speed chassis. It was priced at £115 with the side-valve engine, with an additional £10 asked for the overhead-valve engine. Production was barely underway when, in the spring of 1932, the three-speed Aero was replaced by a new Sports model.

Factory photograph of the Family Aero displayed at the 1926 Olympia show.

Sporting Four-Seaters 1927–1931

The first sporting four-seater Morgan was built in 1926 to the special order of the London Morgan agent, Arthur Maskell. It comprised a Blackburne-engined Aero fitted with the rear body section from a Family model. The machine provided accommodation for driver and three passengers or for two persons and their luggage. It was not long before it was appearing in trials with a full complement of passengers and receiving favourable comments in the press. Morgan exhibited a similar model at the Olympia show of that year. Priced at £142, it cost £5 more than the corresponding

Aero model. The Family Aero was not listed in the company's brochures, but would remain available to special order for the next four years pending the introduction of the Sports Family.

The Sports Family was a new model introduced at the Olympia show in November 1930. The machine was built to De Luxe specification on the 'C' chassis. It was fitted with the 1096cc ohv JAP engine. The four-seater body was fitted with a pointed boat-tail and V-windscreen. The front styling was based upon the Aero De Luxe, with exposed engine and cycle type mudguards. The model remained available for one year only pending the introduction of the three-speeder chassis.

Freddie James driving his Family Aero during the 1928 ISDT.

157

SPEED

Proof of the wonderful speed capacity of the Morgan is clearly established by its record.

In 1912 the " Morgan " won the Cyclecar Cup for the hour record and the Olympic Race at Brooklands. In 1913 it won the " Grand Prix " in France for Cyclecars. Since then it has won innumerable trophies for speed and hill climbing. At present it holds all 1100 c.c. records, the speeds being :—

Kilo..................104.6 m.p.h

Mile...............103.72 m.p.h.

50 miles............90.97 m.p.h.

100 miles..........91.54 m.p.h.

One hour ....91.49 miles.

The Morgan is the Fastest Three-wheeler in the World.

SPECIFICATION

The Chassis of the Morgan SUPER SPORTS AERO is the same as a standard Aero with the following modifications :—

FRAME.—Lowered 2½″, special front axles and underslung rear springs.

SHOCK ABSORBERS.—Duplex Hartford, fitted to the back forks.

ENGINE.—O.H.V. J.A.P. 10/40 h.p. high compression and specially tuned.

CARBURETTOR.—Two float B. & B. or A.M.A.C. Sports.

EXHAUSTS.—Two long plated 2″ Exhaust Pipes fitted with Ghost Silencers.

GEARS.—4 to 1 and 8 to 1 ; other gears to order.

TYRES.—26″ × 3½″, straight sided high pressure.

LAMPS.—Lucas Electric Set, 8″ headlights with dimmers.

SPEEDOMETER.—Watford.

BODY.—Special throughout. It is very well streamlined, the Tail being hinged so that it can be lifted to gain access to the Back Wheel, Oil Tank and Battery. The 4 gallon petrol tank is detachable and fitted in front. The seats are narrow and slightly staggered. A pair of small double screens are fitted and the front wheels are covered by round Cycle-type fixed Mudguards. The body and chassis can be painted any colour to choice.

Price: complete with equipment specified above - - - **£155**

The proud boast made at the time of the announcement of the Super Sport Aero.

Super Sports Aero 1928–1931

The Super Sports Aero was a late entry for the 1927 Motorcycle show and details were contained in a supplement included with the 1928 sales brochure. Morgan clearly recognized the potential of the new model and the announcement read:

> THE MORGAN SUPER SPORTS AERO is a new Morgan model specially built for speed. We can honestly claim that it is not only the fastest three-wheeler in the world but that its performance is better than that of any car costing three times the price.
>
> The MORGAN SUPER SPORTS is built on a special chassis so low that the driver's seat is only eight inches from the ground. No lower motor chassis could possibly be built. It will be readily recognized that this low gravity is the very essence of speed, while the JAP engine fitted is undoubt-

edly the best engine for high speeds. Here is a car destined to break all previous records for automobiles of its class – a very demon on wheels.

The chassis was based upon the standard Aero but lowered by $2\frac{1}{2}$ in (60mm). The rear forks were underslung and damped using duplex Hartford shock absorbers. Brakes were fitted to both front and rear wheels, as was by now standard. The body was low, streamlined and narrow, with staggered seating to afford elbow space for the driver. The tail section could be lifted to allow easy access to the rear wheel, oil tank and battery. The petrol tank was detachable and fitted at the front. The Super Sports Aero on display at Olympia was appropriately described as a new racer and was displayed without mudguards or windscreens. For sale to the public, fixed cycle mudguards and aero screens were fitted. The body and chassis were painted any colour to choice. Motive power was supplied by a specially tuned version of the 1096cc water-cooled JAP 10/40 engine fitted with a twin float B & B or A.M.A.C. carburettor. The Super Sports Aero was a true 80mph sports car at the time when most family saloons struggled to achieve 55mph.

By the time of the Olympia Show, a year after its introduction, the Super Sports Aero had been fitted with Newton–Bennet front wheel, shock absorbers and altered wing stays. It was also fitted at this time with a semi–automatic oil hand-pump. A month later the 'Ghost' silencers originally fitted were replaced by standard exhausts with plated ends. Hoods were also introduced as an optional extra. The works' records note the following modifications to the standard specification from January 1929: body increased in width from 32.5in to 34in (830mm to 860mm); low radiator bolted to the front frame and the oil tank fitted under the bonnet; battery located on a shelf behind the seat back; cycle type wings with an inner flange; wing stays cranked and attached at the bottom of the body by $\frac{5}{8}$in pipe clips; Aero pattern screens fitted; and toolbox mounted on underside of body on nearside. A new style radiator was fitted from body number 130. A one piece V–windscreen was introduced for 1930 and the front axle reduced to standard width from the end of September 1930.

When announced, the price of the Super Sports Aero was £155, but this was reduced to £150 for 1929. The price was reduced by a further £5 in 1930 for the standard model on the 'B' chassis, but by this time most machines were equipped with the new 'M' chassis, introduced from 15 October 1929, and priced at £150, inclusive of V-windscreen. The model was renamed simply as the Super Sports for 1931, its final year of manufacture as a two-

The dashboard layout and controls of the Super Sports Aero.

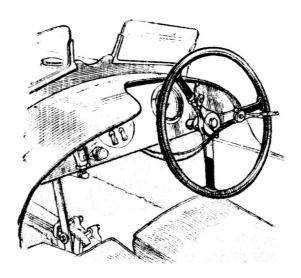

1931 Super Sport Aero.

speeder. It was priced at £145 and available only with the 'M' chassis, later changed to the 'C' variant from 4th February, and fitted with a V-screen.

Commercial Variants 1928–1931

The Commercial Carrier conversion of the Standard model introduced at the 1913 Olympia show has already been described. The model was not successful largely due to its limited capacity, but the concept was sound. A vehicle capable of carrying goods during the week, yet suitable for family excursions at the weekend, made good sense to the small businessman. By the late twenties a number of manufacturers were offering dual-purpose bodywork suitable for this purpose. Morgan reintroduced a commercial carrier at the 1927 show. It comprised a Family model fitted with

a box structure over the rear seats. The sales brochure noted that that it required only a few minutes to convert the Family model to 'a smart van, capable of carrying three hundredweight of goods in a space of 20 cubic feet'. The brochure added: 'The novel, attractive appearance of the Morgan Convertible is in itself an effective advertisement.' Unfortunately the merits of the Convertible of 1928 were no more seductive to small businessmen than had been the Commercial Carrier of 1913. The model was discontinued after one year with few machines sold.

A Delivery Van built on the short chassis of the Standard model and retaining the front mudguards and coalscuttle bonnet of the Standard was offered for 1929. It was the last model to use this chassis, as the Standard was discontinued at this time. The new body was still restricted to a load capacity of 3cwt, although bulkier items could now be carried and access was improved with double rear-doors. It was supplied finished in lead primer ready for coach painting. The Delivery Van on the two-speeder chassis was discontinued upon introduction of the three-speeder chassis for 1932.

One of the final two-speeder Super Sports. The stylish lines of the body are in marked contrast to the appearance of the car, seen in the previous photograph, with the hood fitted.

Above *'The Morgan Convertible Trade & Family Runabout – An Economical Trade Van'. This commercial convertible on a 1928 Family model was used for bakery deliveries around Kettering. The top panel was hinged to give access to the load space.*

Below *The Delivery Van, introduced for the 1929 season, offered economical delivery for the small business with £4 annual tax and an average of 50mpg. Fitted with the JAP KT engine, it was priced at £105.*

9   The Three-Speeder Models

Family 1932–1936

With the introduction of the 'R' chassis for 1932, the Family model was offered as either a two- or three-speeder. The bodywork of both versions was largely identical and based upon the two-speeder Family De Luxe model of the previous year. The only real innovation was that the new Family model could be purchased as either a four-seater or as a two-seater. The new, two-seater body provided generous space for the driver and passenger, whilst the space normally occupied by the rear seats was converted into a luggage locker with a separate hinged lid. A compartment was provided between the seat squab and the locker to house the side screens. It was priced as the Family Four-Seater. Both machines were offered with either the water- or air-cooled versions of the 60-degree JAP side-valve engine with coil ignition.

For 1933, the two-speed Family model remained in production unchanged, whilst the three-speed model was redesigned with a roomier body of more modern appearance. The coalscuttle bonnet was given a more rounded front. Both driver and passenger doors were fitted and the tail section of the body squared off to give a flat rear panel to mount the spare wheel. The Matchless MX became available during the course of the year and was offered alongside the side-valve JAP engines. Such was its popularity that it was the only engine offered with the Family model from 1934 to the close of production at the end of 1936.

A factory photograph to demonstrate that a 1932 Family model could accommodate four adults.

Above *The large-sized rear-hinged doors and forward tilting seats of this 1933 Family provided good access for both front and rear occupants.*

Above right, right *The introduction of detachable Magna wheels for 1933 resulted in the Family model being restyled with rounded front and squared-off tail.*

The seating of the 1933 Family model was as roomy as any small car of the period.

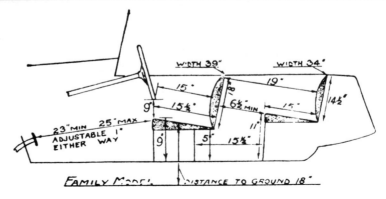

Above *1934 Family Model. The hood and side-screens offered good weather protection.*

Above right *The styling of the Family model was improved with the introduction for 1934 of the barrel-back tail conforming to the outline of the spare wheel. This machine was road tested favourably by the Light Car magazine in March 1935.*

When first introduced, the MX engine suffered overheating problems and, for 1934, alterations were made to the radiator header tank to give extra coolant capacity and to improve airflow through the radiator core. Also for 1934, the body was given a barrel-back tail, which blended more stylishly with the spare wheel.

Sports Family 1932–1936

The 1932 model was built on a special chassis, similar to that used on the Super Sports but 4in (100mm) longer. The styling, like that of the earlier two-speeder, comprised the forward section from the Aero united with the rear section of the Family. The engine options comprised water-cooled versions of the 60 degree JAP side-valve or 10/40hp ohv engines.

For 1933 the Sports Family was given a new body fitted with the stylish cutaway doors of the Sports two-seater and the square-shaped tail of the Family. The barrel-back tail, common with the Family model, was introduced for the following year. By 1934 the Sports Family was being offered with the choice of water-cooled JAP engines, either side-valve or ohv, and Matchless MX and MX2 engines. For 1936, the final year of production, Matchless MX, MX2 or MX4 engines were offered.

Catalogue illustration of the 1932 Sports Family model. The body was not fitted with doors and entry was assisted by a step on the nearside.

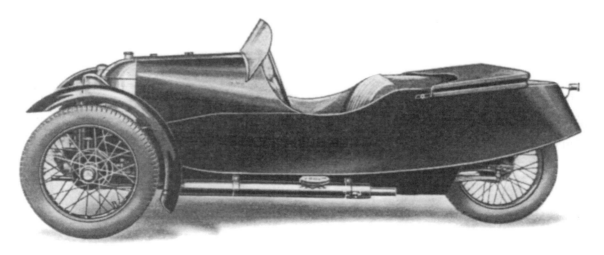

Above and right *1933 Sports Family.*

Sports 1932–1939

The Aero model on the three-speeder 'R' chassis was briefly offered for sale during early 1932, but few models were produced before it was replaced by a new Sports model. It was intended as a fast touring machine and came equipped with a luggage locker behind the seats. The body was styled with an upswept tail similar to that of the current Family model and, unlike the Super Sports, the scuttle did not project in front of the passenger. It was offered with two doors, but could be ordered with either a single near-side door or without doors. Other choices could also be made. Either a V-windscreen or a single-panel flat screen was available, although few buyers chose the latter. The exhaust system was carried along the underside of the body, although high-level exhausts similar to those of the Super Sports could be fitted if the body was supplied without doors. An exposed water-cooled JAP engine of either overhead-valve LTOWZ or side-valve LTWZ configuration was fitted.

For 1933 the Sports was built on the standardized chassis and fitted with Dunlop Magna

wheels. The tail section of the body was squared off to create a narrow barrel-back and the spare wheel, mounted on the tail panel, overlapped the body sides. The range of engine options was increased to include the Matchless MX for 1933 and the MX2 for 1934. Thereafter the only changes to the specification of the model were in respect of the exclusive use of Matchless engines. The MX and MX2 engines were fitted during 1935 and, subsequently, the MX4 engine was also offered. Only the MX2 engine was being fitted for 1938 and the model ceased production during the early part of 1939.

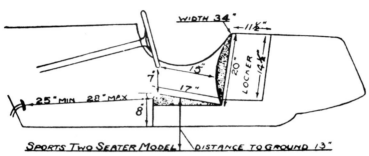

WIDTH 34"
11½"
LOCKER
20"
14½"
7"
25" MIN 28" MAX
17"
8"

SPORTS TWO SEATER MODEL DISTANCE TO GROUND 13"

Above *The Sports model had a higher bonnet than the Super Sports, and the oil and petrol filler caps were fitted closer together. In addition the beading around the edge of the body was turned up rather than under. The illustration is of a 1936 Sports.*

The drawing details the seating and storage dimensions of the Sports model.
The layout was derived from the Family two-seater of 1932.

Super Sports 1932–1939

There was little change in the appearance of the Super Sports model announced in October 1931 to denote that it was now fitted with the three-speed chassis rather than the earlier two-speed 'C' chassis. Perhaps most noticeable was the D-shaped cut-out replacing the louvres at the side of the bonnet, the introduction of an oil filler cap on the bonnet, and a body slightly wider than before. The mudguards were of the close-fitting cycle type with an inner valence. These were initially of plain section but later modified to have a central rib. The headlamps were mounted on vertical pillars attached to the top chassis cross-tubes. Machines were fitted with a specially tuned LTOWZ 60 degree JAP engine and twin-float Amal sports carburettor. The compression ratio was raised from the standard 6.9 to 1 ratio to

7.5 to 1. Coil ignition was fitted with a round Lucas distributor driven from the camshaft.

For 1933 the Super Sports used the chassis common across the Morgan range. The consequence of reducing the bends in the front cross tubes and of fitting 18in Dunlop Magna wheels was to raise the height by approximately 1in. The beetle-back body styling was retained, but the exhaust pipes were raised to a higher level and ran back along the side of the body. In this position they greatly enhanced the sporting appearance of the car, but at significant risk to the elbows of driver and passenger. Stainless-steel radiator panels were announced but appear not to have been used. The introduction of detachable wheels created a problem of where to locate the spare. Initially the wheel was carried at an angle of 45 degrees right at the point of the beetle-back top panel, but after three months, in December 1932, it was repositioned to lie flat on top of the beetle-back.

The problem of where to mount the spare wheel on the Super Sports was solved with the introduction of the barrel-backed body at the 1933 Olympia show. The rear section of the body was circular and the spare wheel was inset with its hub and spokes covered by a polished aluminium disk. The disk carried the rear number plate and lights. A simple luggage grid, comprising three chromed-steel strips sup-

ported by two wooden cross-bearers, was a practical replacement for the spare wheel on the top of the tail panel. The beetle-back Super Sports continued to be produced; indeed it was the only model listed in the early catalogues for 1934, but was gradually phased out during the course of the year. On both models, the D-shaped cut-outs on the sides of the bonnet were replaced by a double 'D' design. A new winged 'M' mascot replaced the stork on the radiator cap of the barrel-back. The

---

1939 Morgan Super Sports MX4

Production period 1934–39

Engine	
Type	Matchless MX4
	Twin cylinder, 50-degree, water cooled. Push rod overhead-valve
Bore and stroke	85.5 × 85.5mm
Capacity	990cc
Power output	42bhp @ 4,800rpm
Ignition	Battery and coil
Carburettor	Amal
Transmission	
Clutch	Single dry plate
Gearbox	Three-speed and reverse
Ratios	4.58, 7.5, and 12.4 to 1; reverse, 16.5 to 1
Final drive	Enclosed propeller shaft with centre bearing, worm and counter shaft to final drive chain
Suspension	
Front	Independent helical springs
Rear	Quarter-elliptic springs
Brakes	Girling mechanical
Front	Internal expanding. Cable operated by hand lever
Rear	Internal expanding. Cable operated by foot pedal
Efficiency	88 per cent by Ferodo-Tapley meter
Dimensions	
Wheelbase	7ft 3in (2,210mm)
Track	4ft 2in (1,270mm)
Overall length	10ft 4in (3,120mm)

Overall width	4ft 11in (1,500mm)
Weight	8cwt 58lb★ (433kg)
Capacities	
Petrol tank	4 gallons (18.2ltr)
Oil tank	1 gallon (4.5ltr)
Equipment	Lucas
Seating	Two-seater
Colours	Choice of three: black body and chassis with wheels in red, green or aluminium; red body, chassis and wings with cream wheels; British Racing Green through-out
Performance	
Maximum speed	73 mph (117km/h)
Standing $\frac{1}{2}$ mile	21.0sec
Touring speed	55mph (88km/h)
Petrol consumption	40mpg (7.08ltr/100km)
Price	£136 10s (£128 for model fitted with Matchless MX2 ohv air-cooled engine

★This figure, which was taken from a road test published by *Light Car* in June 1939, places the MX4 Super Sports outside the weight limit for the concessionary Road Tax. The later, more fully equipped, cars struggled to remain within the 8cwt limit. Stories abound of cars being stripped of seating and spare wheels before being driven onto weighbridges.

stork mascot was initially retained for the beetle-back and offered as an extra on all models.

The beetle-back Super Sports was offered with the new water-cooled MX4 engine for £150. The beetle-back model cost £125 with the air-cooled MX2 engine or £135 with the 60 degree ohv JAP. The JAP engine was only available with the beetle-back model and was dropped when the beetle-back was discontinued.

The Super Sports was available with either an air-cooled MX2 or water-cooled MX4 engine in 1935. Both engines were now fitted with the double-ended coil ignition system. The height of the exhaust pipes was lowered to lessen risk of injury and the luggage grid was chromium plated. The company was by now concentrating on the four-wheeler models and further changes to the specification of the Super Sports were few. Girling brakes were introduced in September 1937 and the MX2 engine was phased out in June 1939. Production was discontinued at the start of the war, although a few machines were produced to special order after the war.

Above *A special-bodied 1933 Super Sports photographed outside the factory. The car has been fitted with a folding windscreen and modified scuttle. The exhaust pipes have also been lowered to reduce the risk of burned elbows.*

Above *1936 Super Sports with two tone colour scheme. The barrel-back styling with recessed spare wheel was introduced at the 1933 Olympia show. The wheel hub and spokes were covered by polished aluminium disks.*

1934 MX4 Super Sports. The suction windscreen wiper motor has been replaced by a more reliable electric motor. Whatever the position chosen, mounting of the spare wheel on a beetle-back looks to be an afterthought.

MX2 Super Sports displayed at the 1937 Olympia show.

Delivery Van 1932–1935

The 1932 Delivery Van was offered either with doors, as shown, or with cut-away sides that the driver stepped over.

A reverse gear, if not three speeds, was of considerable advantage for a light commercial and the Delivery Van was supplied on the new 'R' chassis immediately it became available. The machine was fitted with the coalscuttle bonnet hinged at the windscreen, cycle mudguards and the forward-mounted headlights of the Family model. During the first year of its production bodies were offered with either a simple cut-away to create an aperture for the driver to step through to gain entry, or a door. Later models were available only with doors.

For 1933 the van was redesigned with a flat top and back. It was 6in (150mm) longer and 3in (75mm) wider than previously. The overall dimensions were length 10ft 3in (3.12m), height 5ft (1.52m) and width 4ft 10in (1.47m). The internal dimensions were length 4ft 4ins (1.32m) from rear of seat to doors, height 3ft 3in (990mm) and width 3ft 5in (1.04m), giving an internal volume of 48.5cu. ft (1.37cu. m). Load capacity was stated to be 4cwt (203kg). The van body was mounted on the standardized chassis and fitted with Dunlop Magna wheels. The spare wheel was mounted on the side of the body adjacent to the driver,

who was required to enter the vehicle via a door on the near-side. The bodywork was stated to offer full protection for driver and passenger. Side screens and windscreen wipers were not fitted but could be supplied as extras. The machines were finished in lead primer.

The first versions of the Delivery Van were fitted with the 60-degree LTZ air-cooled JAP engine. Later machines were offered with a 60-degree water-cooled JAP engine and finally a water-cooled Matchless MX engine.

Despite the factory offering to build bodies to customers' own specifications, the Delivery Van was never a popular model. The combined output of vans on both the two- and three-speeder chassis during the eight years of production was no more than about forty. The production must have been disappointing for Morgan, but was perhaps to be expected, as the Morgan chassis layout, with a single rear wheel, was not well suited for fitment of a commercial body. The Raleigh three-wheeler, with its single front-wheel, was to prove the more popular choice.

Introducing A NEW FOUR CYL. MODEL

Morgan

PRICE:

FULLY EQUIPPED WITH ELECTRIC LIGHTING & STARTING SET, WIPER, AND ALL-WEATHER EQUIPMENT TOOLS, & FITMENTS:

£120

TAX - - - - £4

OTHER MODELS:

FAMILY TWIN, S.V. WATER-COOLED	£105
SPORTS FAMILY TWIN, S.V. WATER-COOLED	£115
SPORTS FAMILY TWIN, O.H.V. AIR-COOLED	£120
SPORTS FAMILY TWIN, O.H.V. WATER-COOLED	£125
SPORTS 2-SEATER TWIN, S.V. WATER-COOLED	£110
SPORTS 2-SEATER TWIN, O.H.V. AIR-COOLED	£115
SPORTS 2-SEATER TWIN, O.H.V. WATER-COOLED	£120
SUPER SPORTS TWIN, O.H.V. WATER-COOLED	£135

ALL MODELS ARE SOLD WITH FULL EQUIPMENT!

After several years of experimental work The Morgan Motor Co., Ltd., are able to introduce to the public an entirely new departure in Three-wheelers, the "MORGAN" THREE-WHEELER MODEL F., fitted with a powerful four-cylinder water-cooled engine. This new model will still enjoy the advantages of low taxation as the weight is less than the 8 cwt. limit.

The engine has four-cylinders, giving a total capacity of 933 c.c. and R.A.C. Rating of 7.95 h.p. The chassis is of a special patented design, particularly suitable for a Three-wheeler. Brakes are operated by a simple system giving efficient braking on all wheels from the foot pedal.

We would stress the fact that the new and extra model in no way replaces the twin-cylinder model on which the reputation of the name "Morgan" has been built.

Don't forget to see all the "Morgans" at Olympia—or send for complete catalogue.

**MORGAN MOTOR CO., LTD.,
MALVERN LINK - - - WORC.**

OUR STAND AT
OLYMPIA
IS OPPOSITE
ADDISON RD. ENTRANCE
NUMBER

54

EACH MORGAN IS A MODEL OF MECHANICAL PERFECTION

OFFERING CAR COMFORT & PERFORMANCE AT MUCH LESS COST

10 The Ford-Powered Models

F4 1933–1952

The F4, introduced at the end of 1933, was equipped with the Ford 8hp 933cc engine fitted with a 'Silver Top' aluminium-alloy cylinder head that permitted the use of increased compression with greater power output. A Zenith downdraught carburettor was fitted and controlled both by an accelerator pedal, fitted to the right of the brake pedal, and a hand lever on the steering wheel.

The body, described as an occasional four, had a low sporting appearance. The forward radiator and a car-type engine behind the front axle resulted in the front of the body being similarly styled to many small cars of the day. The back of the body, however, was typically Morgan and based upon the barrel-back style of the previous year. The construction was based upon a wooden framework with steel panels. A pair of wide doors, with elbow cutaways in the sporting style of the day, provided easy access to the front seats. The

seats could be folded forward for access to the rear and, when in the tilted position, could be adjusted for position by a single bolt. The rear-mounted spare wheel stood proud of the body panels. Removal of the spare wheel and back panel provided easy access to the rear wheel. The steel bonnet was of conventional butterfly design with hinges at the centre and sides of the top panel. Louvres were cut into the side panels of the bonnet. The radiator, positioned in front of the front axle tubes, was enclosed in a chromium-plated shell and was fitted with a stone guard and a screw filler-cap. The rear tilt of the radiator was followed through in the angle of the bonnet louvres and the bulkhead. The brackets of the single fixed-pane windscreen attached directly to the bulkhead.

The Model F had the same track of 4ft 2in (1.27m) as the other models in the Morgan range, but it was much longer overall. The wheelbase of 8ft 3in (2.51m) was about 8in (200mm) greater than that of the Sports

Opposite Advertisement issued at the time of the launch of the Model F in November 1933.

Interior photograph of the 1934 Model F. The oval Lucas dash-panel incorporated the ignition/lighting switch on the left and an ammeter on the right. The central speedometer incorporated a trip and a 30mph marker easily seen from the driving seat. The controls followed conventional car practice. Foot pedals operated clutch, brake and accelerator. The latter was coupled to a hand throttle operated by Bowden lever from an arm on the steering column. The brake pedal was connected to all three wheels. The left-hand lever operated the rear brake for parking. The right-hand lever was the gear change and operated in an 'H' opposite to normal convention.

Family and 12in (300mm) greater than the remaining models. The ground clearance of 6½ins (170mm) was also fractionally greater. The weight remained comfortably within the 8cwt (407kg) limit for the £4 annual tax bracket. The Model F was no slouch, possessing a top speed of approximately 70mph (112km/h), while petrol consumption was between 36 and 45mpg (7.86 and 6.29ltr/100km). The price, complete with electric lighting and starter, windscreen wiper and full weather equipment, plus tools and fitments, was a very competitive £120.

The first production Model F was given chassis number F1 and left the factory on 25 April 1934.

The first models were fitted with cycle-type mudguards of similar style to those fitted to the twin-cylinder models. By the time of the 1934 Olympia Show, these had been changed to the long flowing type more commonly associated with the model. The rear of the body was modified to slope away less, given a more circular section and recessed to take the spare wheel. Louvres were also included within the top panels of the bonnet. The show models were finished in duo blue and in blue and cream.

By the time of the 1935 Olympia Show, the body had been restyled to enclose the spare wheel. The following year the bonnet was changed to a two-piece design with a single,

---

1934 Morgan Model F Four-Seater

Production period 1933–1952

Engine		**Brakes**	Cable operated, internal expanding
Type	Ford 8hp water-cooled, with 'Silver Top' aluminium head (Ford 10hp engine fitted from 1947)	Foot brake	Coupled operation of front and rear brakes
		Hand brake	Operates rear brake only and fitted with ratchet
Bore and stroke	56.6 × 92.5mm		
Capacity	933cc	**Dimensions**	
Lubrication	Automatic	Wheelbase	8ft 3in (2,510mm)
Power output	23.4bhp at 4,000rpm	Track	4ft 2in (1,270mm)
Ignition	Lucas coil ignition	Overall length	11ft 6in (3,510mm)
Carburettor	Zenith down-draught type	Overall width	4ft 11in (1,500mm)
Transmission		**Capacities**	
Clutch	Plate	Petrol tank	5 gallons (22.7ltr)
Drive	Enclosed propeller shaft to rear worm-drive and gearbox	**Equipment**	Lucas electric
Gears	Three-speed and reverse. Ratios, 4.85, 8 and 13.1 to 1. Reverse 17.5 to 1	**Seating**	Occasional four-seater.
Final drive	¾in chain	**Colours**	Saxe blue with black mudguards and cream wheels
Suspension		**Performance**	
Front	Independent helical springs	Maximum speed	65mph (104km/h)
Rear	Quarter-elliptic springs	Petrol consumption	36–45 mpg (7.86–6.29ltr/100km)
Steering	Geared with 2 to 1 reduction	**Price**	£120

---

central hinge. A de-luxe version was also made available. Detailed improvements included: fully chromium-plated headlamps, external door handles (now omitted from the basic model), coach lining, flying 'M' radiator mascot, pockets in the doors and glove boxes incorporated into the dash.

Originally the four-seater model was catalogued as the 4-cylinder Model 'F'. For the 1936 season the name was changed to the Model 'F' 4-Seater to avoid confusion with the newly introduced two-seater version, which was identified as the Model 'F' 2-Seater. This nomenclature was to survive until the two-seater model was replaced by the 'F' Super for the 1938 season, when the four-seater model became simply the 'F-4'; the name now used to refer to all the 4-cylinder four-seater models.

A number of improvements were made to the F4 model for the 1938 season. The radiator filler-cap was changed to the push down and twist, clip type, and the wire stone-guard replaced by vertical slats. The height and width of the radiator remained unchanged at $23\frac{3}{4}$in and 19in (600mm and 480mm) respectively. The radiator surround was restyled, necessitating changes to the bonnet. The number plate covered the lower section of the radiator and was hinged upwards to allow use of the starting handle. The windscreen, previously squared off with vertical anchorage points for

The radiators on the early model cars were fitted with a wire stone-guard with a cut-away at the base for the starting handle. The filler cap was of the screw-in type.

the hood clamps, was now rounded and the hood attached by 'lift-a-dots'. The cast-iron bell housing attached to the rear of the engine was replaced by one of aluminium and the scuttle support for the bonnet was changed from being a wooden hoop to steel. Girling brakes were fitted. The external bonnet catches were retained until 1946, before being replaced by the internal type used on the F Super Sports. The F4 was fitted with the Ford 10hp engine in 1947 and went out of production in 1952.

F2 1936–1938

The first F-type two-seater Morgan was introduced in 1935 for the 1936 season. It was identified by the factory as the Model 'F' 2-Seater, but referred to by most of the magazines as the

1946 F4. The curved top windscreen was introduced on 1937 models.

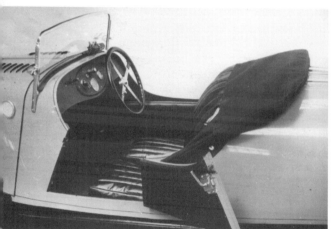

Interior of 1937 Morgan F2. Each seat consisted of a padded cushion resting on thin three-ply, which, in the view of the Light Car, gave a 'resilient effect'. A one-piece squab hinged forward to disclose a luggage space and small objects could also be stored under each seat.

new Super Sports. It is now identified simply as the F2. It comprised a two-seater body built onto the chassis of the four-seater model. The manufacturers claimed 'the lines of the body closely followed those of the well known and popular Super Sports Morgan with the added advantage of extra leg room and a door to the off side'. In the event, the purchaser would be offered the choice of two doors, a single door on the passenger side or no doors. A fold-flat windscreen was fitted. The model was available either with the 933cc Ford 8 engine for 115 guineas, or with the 1172cc 10hp engine from the De Luxe Ford for an extra seven guineas. The larger engine provided a top speed of 74mph (118km/h), and performance on a par

with the Matchless MX4 Super Sports. Most purchasers considered it represented good value. The F2 was offered concurrently with the new F Super Sports during 1938, before being deleted from the catalogue.

F Super Sports and F Super 1937–1952

The F Super Sports, which was announced in September 1937, was a fairly major redesign of the 4-cylinder model. A new chassis was used; the track remained 4ft 2in (1.27m) but the wheelbase was reduced 4in (100mm) to 7ft 11in (2,410mm). The engine was the Ford 10hp and an aluminium bell-housing was used. Girling brakes with Bowden cable operation were fitted, allowing improved adjustment and efficiency. The body, both shorter and wider than before, was also lowered by 2in (50mm). It was fitted as standard with a single door on the passenger side, although a second door could be fitted if required. The rear panels followed the barrel-back styling of the twin-cylinder Super Sports, with the spare wheel set within the body. The radiator was reduced in height by $2\frac{1}{4}$in (60mm) to correspond with the lowered body and fitted with a clip-type filler cap and a stone guard. The bonnet was centrally hinged and fitted with louvres along its entire length. The windscreen was of the fold-flat type with a curved top and was equipped with twin wiper arms. Cycle mudguards were originally fitted, but the flowing type were optional. The headlights were mounted low down between the mudguards and radiator. The width of the car was unchanged at 4ft 11in (1.5m) but the overall length was reduced by 6in (150mm) to 11ft (3,350mm). A top speed of over 70mph (112km/h) was available with the ability to cruise indefinitely at 65mph (104km/h).

At its announcement the Model F Super Sports was the most expensive model in the Morgan range, costing £136 10s compared with the ohv Matchless Super Sports at £126. The corresponding price of the F2 with the 10hp engine was £128 2s.

Both the F Super Sports and the F2 two-seaters were produced during for the 1938 season. For 1939 the F2 was dropped from the catalogue and only the sporting model, now referred to as the F Super, was listed.

Post-war only the 'F' models were produced. The F Super was initially little changed from the pre-war model, but very soon the valanced mudguards replaced the cycle type and the radiator stone-guard was replaced by vertical slats. The model survived in limited production until 1952.

1949 F Super.

1950 F Super.

11 The Continental Models

Darmont 1919–1939

Morgans were extremely popular in France following the success achieved by McMinnies in the Cyclecar Grand Prix in 1913. One hundred and fifty machines were sold in 1914 and a further 500 machines were on order for 1915 before war intervened. After the war the French agents, Darmont et Badelogue, were granted a license by Morgan in 1919 for the manufacture of the Darmont Morgan. This agreement had two benefits for HFS. Firstly, the Morgan factory in Malvern lacked the capacity to satisfy demand. Secondly, and perhaps more importantly, cars built in France avoided the prohibitive French duties on imported vehicles. By October 1920 production at the factory at 27 Rue Jules Ferry, Courbevoie, Paris had reached fourteen cars per week.

The Darmont concern had been founded by Roger Darmont and was run by Roger together with his brother, André. Both were engineers and Roger had gained early experience working at the Douglas motorcycle factory in Bristol. Roger had driven a Morgan in the Paris–Nice–Monte Carlo endurance test in 1914, but André would do most of the postwar competition driving.

The Darmont Morgans were similar to the Malvern versions and were built almost entirely within the French factory. The first machines were based upon the Morgan De Luxe of 1919 and fitted with a side-valve air-cooled JAP engine concealed within the coalscuttle bonnet. The second model, which was to prove more popular, was based upon the

Grand Prix. It was fitted with a much narrower radiator than the English cars, which gave a leaner, more upright, stance that was to become a Darmont feature. The machine could be supplied with a side-valve JAP engine, either air- or water-cooled, or a water-cooled MAG ioe engine. The French cars were strengthened using stronger shafts and frames, and used pressings where possible to make them better able to cope with the French road conditions.

Darmont Morgans were soon competing with considerable success in continental hillclimbs, races and long-distance reliability trials. Both single-seater and two-seater bodies were used in competition. Engines varied from 8-valve MAG to 750cc Blackburne twin and a 500cc water-cooled single built up using a KMA Blackburne cylinder. André Darmont won the flying kilometre event at Nimes in 1922 with a time of 27.4s (81mph, 130km/h), beating all cars up to 3 litres.

In 1923 the two original models, the De Luxe and the Grand Prix, known respectively as the 'Sporting' and the 'Sport' models, were joined by the 'Camionnette', a machine with a boxed-in tail suitable for light commercial duties. The guaranteed top speed of the Sporting model was 50mph (80km/h) and that of the Sport model was 63mph (100km/h). All models were guaranteed to exceed 55mpg (5.15ltr/100km). Darmont also introduced certain improvements over the basic Morgan specification. These comprised front shock absorbers and an ingenious design of rear axle allowing the rear wheel to be removed from the forks without disturbing the transmission

The single-seater Darmont of Dhôme competing in the Coeur Volant Hill Climb, near Paris in March 1923.

CAMIONNETTE

The Camionnette bodywork offered by Darmont during the early 1920s was styled to appeal to the French farmer.

Above *1924 Darmont.
Darmonts, like most
French cars of the period,
were right-hand drive. The
driver is dressed
appropriately in sporting
style with goggles and a
cloth 'flying helmet'.*

*Front view of the
Darmont shown in the
previous photograph. The
engine is an air-cooled
side-valve Darmont, based
closely on the JAP KT.
The script on the dummy
radiator reads 'Morgan'
'CONSTRUIT PAR
R. DARMONT'.*

chains or band brakes. Other extras comprised an automatic oil-pump replacing the dashboard-mounted plunger pump, a revised exhaust-system and an 'Aero' windscreen similar to that of the later Morgan Super Sports. By 1924 Darmont was also offering his own engine, which was based closely on the air-cooled side-valve JAP. It was readily distinguished from the Prestwich product by having 'Morgan' cast into the crankcase and a differently shaped timing-chest. Subsequently a Darmont version of the ohv Blackburne engine was produced, with 'Darmont' cast into the various components.

In 1925 Darmont announced a new model for the sporting driver, the Morgan-type 'Darmont Special', capable of a speed of 93mph (150km/h). In appearance the machine was similar to the early Super Aero, with a straight tube chassis and low streamlined body. Originally it was devoid of mudguards, windscreen and silencers. It was equipped with front-wheel brakes and Hartford-type friction

dampers were fitted to the front springs. The engine was an ohv water-cooled Blackburne equipped with two magnetos supplying two plugs per cylinder.

Without benefit of the road-tax concessions afforded three-wheelers in the United

Darmont		
	Modèle Tourisme	'Special'
Bore × stroke	84.5 × 97mm	85 × 96mm
Capacity	1087cc	1089cc
Carburettor	Solex 35mm	Solex 35mm
Ignition	Coil	Twin magnetos
Tyres	27 × 400	27 × 400
Maximum speed	75mph (120km/h)	94mph (150km/h)
Weight	771lb (350kg)	717lb (325kg)

By the late 1920s, the Darmont Special was fitted with a Blackburne engine, of Darmont manufacture, and a three-speed and reverse gearbox. The front bumper is a feature unique to the French-built cars.

R. DARMONT, Constructeur du MORGAN

USINE : Rue Jules-Ferry
COURBEVOIE (Seine)
Téléphone : COURBEVOIE 525

VENTE EXCLUSIVE A PARIS
178, Rue de Courcelles

A la demande d'un grand nombre de Sportsmen désireux de participer à des épreuves publiques, nous avons décidé de créer un nouveau modèle

MORGAN Type DARMONT SPÉCIAL

susceptible d'une vitesse de
150 km. à l'heure

Carrosserie très basse, établie suivant les tout derniers principes. Châssis renforcé. Moteur à culbuteurs 1.100 cmc. Deux magnétos à allumage jumelés. Freinage très puissant sur roues avant. Pneus de 27×4 sur jante à base creuse.

ses récents Succès...

1er

Course de Côte des 17 Tournants	catég. 750 cmc.
	catég. 1.100 —
Coupe de l'Armistice (180 km)....	catég. 1.100 —
Course de Côte de Gometz-le-Châtel	catég. 500
	catég. 750
	catég. 1.100

Des Conditions très avantageuses sont faites aux Sportsmen qui feront l'acquisition de ce Modèle, dans le but de prendre part à des compétitions de vitesse.

Roger Darmont, like HFS, appreciated the role of competition success for promoting the product.

Kingdom, the market for three-wheeled cyclecars in France had all but ceased to exist by the late 1920s. The Darmont company survived through to 1939, but for the last four years produced a conventional four-wheeled light car powered by a French Ruby engine.

Sandford 1923–1938

The Sandford is an interloper within this chapter, as it is not a true Morgan. Rather it is a Morgan-inspired interpretation by an Englishman of the ideal three-wheeler for the French market. Its constructor, Malcolm Stewart Sandford, was born in Birmingham in 1889 but moved to France, with his widowed mother at the age of two, where he was brought up and educated. At the age of fourteen his mother sent him back to England for

two years to perfect his English and it was during this time that he gained a love of motorcycling. He first became aware of the new sporting cyclecars, typified by the Morgan, when he visited the Motor Cycle Show at Olympia in 1911. During the war he worked in a factory making components for aircraft and military vehicles. With the end of hostilities he set up his own business in Paris buying and selling surplus military machines. He soon acquired an agency for Metro Tyler, the British manufacturer of a 269cc two-stroke motorcycle. He had hoped to obtain the agency for Morgans. However, this was already held by Darmont and he was restricted to act as the agent for Darmont in the Paris district. Stewart Sandford soon became a successful competitor in French races driving Darmont-built Morgans.

Whilst the English machine proved to be very popular with the French, the motorcycle-derived V-twin power unit was not universally liked and customers would often express a preference for the machine to be equipped with a 4-cylinder engine. Sandford agreed and he approached Morgans with his ideas to improve the Runabout. HFS was not at that time ready to entertain the idea of a 4-cylinder Morgan, that would need to wait for a further twelve years, and as a result Sandford decided to build a 4-cylinder three-wheeler along Morgan lines but incorporating his own ideas. He introduced innovations in the design of the three-wheeler many years before similar features were incorporated in the Malvern product. Sandford's thoughts were influenced to some extent by the French legal system, which, between 1921 and 1925, formally defined a cyclecar and afforded it the benefit of considerable savings in annual tax. The classification was for a vehicle with capacity and weight limits of 1100cc and 350kg, respectively, to carry no more than two persons; it did not specify the number of wheels. The intention was to create an environment for the manufacture of cheap

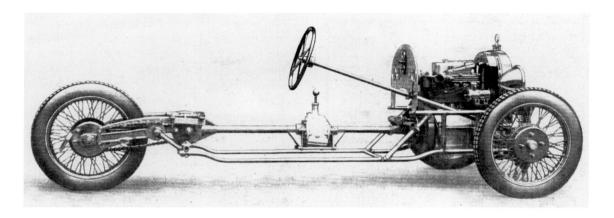

General layout of the Sandford Model P (Tourisme). The engine is a 4-cylinder Ruby side-valve of 985cc.

vehicles for the masses but the outcome was the production of exciting small sports cars such as Salmson, Amilcar and Sandford.

The Sandford chassis and suspension were of substantial construction and well able to cope with the pot-holed roads and pavé of France. The chassis was constructed of heavy-gauge steel tubing and assembled using split-lugs without brazing, a considerable advantage when dealing with accident damage. The engine was mounted on four support lugs attached to vertical tubes linking the upper and lower longitudinal tubes. The front suspension was similar to the Morgan sliding pillar design but employed square-section helical springs and was more robust. The rear forks

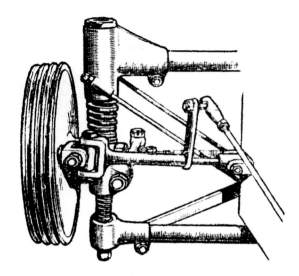

Above *The Morgan-inspired front suspension. The brakes were operated by rods via a telescopic sleeve and universal joint.*

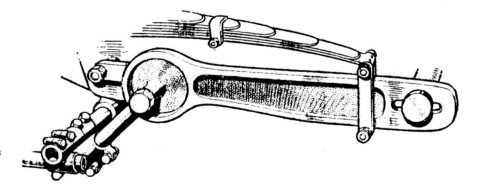

The drop-forged rear forks incorporated friction disks for suspension damping.

comprised heavy-section steel stampings for the swinging arm and long semi-cantilever springs. The pivot point for the forks incorporated friction discs, which formed adjustable double-acting shock absorbers of the 'Hartford' type. Nineteen inch, spoked or pressed steel wheels were fitted and were readily detachable and interchangeable.

The engine was directly attached to the flywheel and multiple-plate clutch. A short Cardan shaft enclosed within a thick walled tube transmitted the power to a three-speed and reverse gearbox, which was constructed by the Ruby Engine Co. to Sandford's design. From the gearbox a further short Cardan shaft carried the drive back to a bevel box and countershaft, on which was mounted the sprocket for the final drive chain. The chain, like the rest of the machine, was greatly over designed and virtually unbreakable, no matter how roughly the machine was driven.

Stewart Sandford powered his machines by the most readily available French propriety engine, the famous 'Ruby', used by many successful French sports car manufacturers such as BNC, D'Yrsan and Senechal. This was a 4-cylinder water-cooled unit and was fitted with a special camshaft with high-lift cams. Alternative versions of the engine were used. The Model P touring machines used the 985cc, 57mm × 95mm, engine, which produced 24bhp at 3,500rpm and gave a top speed of about 65mph (105km/h). The Model S sports model used the larger 60mm × 97mm, 1097cc ohv engine, which gave a top speed approaching 85mph (135km/h). A Sandford fitted with the supercharged version of the larger engine exceeded 115mph (184km/h).

Sandfords were expensive machines and, if reproached for producing a costly car rather than a cheap three-wheeled runabout for the enthusiast, Stewart Sandford simply stated 'I give speed for money'. The statement was irrefutable, as Sandfords, like Morgans, out-performed any four-wheeled car of comparable price. Nevertheless, Sandford introduced both a four-wheeler in 1930 and a cut-price three-wheeler in 1934. The four-wheeler used the larger Ruby engine and is interesting in its adaptation of the front suspension to provide independent suspension at the rear. The three-wheeled 'Popular' model of 1934 sold at about half the price of the other models in the range. The engine was an air-cooled side-valve flat-twin constructed in-unit with the clutch and three-speed gearbox. It had been designed by Sandford in collaboration with Ruby and was built by Ruby. The bore and stroke were 84mm × 86mm respectively, giving a capacity of 950cc. The output was 26bhp at 3,800rpm, enabling Sandford to guarantee a top speed of 74mph (118km/h).

Stewart Sandford was forced to end production towards the end of 1936, as the entire output of the Ruby company was acquired by Georges Irat and no alternative proprietary engine unit was available. He took the agency for Morgan parts when Darmont ended the exclusive agreement with Morgans and he also imported four wheelers until the war started.

Sandford Grand Sport

Engine	6CV Ruby 4-cylinder water-cooled ohv	**Brakes**	
Bore and stroke	60 × 97mm	Front	Internal expanding, 255mm diameter, hand operated by rod and Cardan shaft.
Capacity	1097cc		
Power output	30CV @ 3300rpm (Type E), 35CV (Type ES with special high-lift cams), 50CV with Cozette supercharger	Rear	Internal expanding, 255mm diameter, operated by foot pedal
Ignition	Magneto	**Wheels**	19in wire or disc, detachable and interchangeable
Transmission		**Dimensions**	
Clutch	Dry multi-plate with short rigid shaft to gearbox.	Wheel base	8ft (2,440mm)
		Track	4ft 6in (1,370mm)
Gearbox	Three-speed and reverse, with ball change gear lever.	Overall length	11ft 8in (3,550mm)
		Chassis weight	5.7cwt (290kg)
Gear ratios	4.6, 6.8 and 11.0 to 1; reverse 16.5 to 1	**Bodywork**	Standard doorless two-seater.
Final drive	Enclosed propeller shaft, bevels and heavy duty roller chain.	**Colour**	Polished alloy.
Suspension		**Performance**	
Front	Independent helical springs	Maximum speed	85mph (135kph) without supercharger, 100mph (160kph) with Cozette supercharger
Rear	Quarter-elliptic springs		
		Petrol consumption	40mpg (7ltr/100km)

12 An Enduring Legacy

The Morgan Motor Company

The Morgan factory no longer produces three-wheelers, indeed has not done so for over fifty years, to the disappointment of many. The cars produced by the factory, however, still embrace the design philosophy and ideals of the company's founder. With the exception of the ultra-modern Aero 8, launched at the Geneva Salon in February 2000, all Morgans retain sliding-pillar front suspension and hand-crafted bodywork constructed on an ash frame. Even the chassis frame derives from the Z-section frame of the Model 'F'. The policy, adopted by HFS, of buying-in engines has continued and continues to allow Morgan to use the best and most advanced engines without financial risk. Just as JAP, Blackburne, Anzani and other firms would develop engines to meet Morgan requirements, so today manufacturers such as BMW and Ford allow Morgan to use engines at the forefront of technology.

Whilst HFS would find the Aero 8 unfamiliar, he would well appreciate the design philosophy behind the car. The benefits of combining a light, yet strong, chassis with an engine of more than adequate power and a light functional body are as much a recipe for a sporting performance now as then. HFS would readily recognize the other cars in the range, the 4/4, +4 and +8, as the descendants of his 4-4 of 1936.

HFS would have no difficulty recognizing the present day Morgan factory, which until only a few years ago had remained largely unchanged. In recent years a new building has been constructed at the bottom of the yard for the assembly of the Aero 8, and a new reception and office block has been constructed on the right of the entrance. Morgans continue to be constructed by hand without the benefit of moving production lines, which are not considered appropriate for the level of throughput. Changes have, however, been made to traditional working practices in order to improve efficiency and more components are bought-in now than previously, but the Morgan remains an essentially hand-built car for the sporting motorist.

Morgan has never employed a research department or a styling company. The first cars were designed by HFS and modified and improved according to experience gained in competition. The styling was functional and dictated as much by the mechanism of the car and the benefits of a low centre of gravity as by the sporting styles of the day. The tradition is continued to this day. The bodywork of the Aero 8 was designed in-house to create a modern flowing style reminiscent of pre-war sporting cars.

The Aero 8 demonstrates continuity with the past, yet a willingness to move forward to the future. The company has never made changes for changes' sake, but has always been willing to make changes and introduce new models according to market demands. In detail respects the cars are continually evolving. Step changes in design have been few: three-speeds and reverse replaced the twin chain two-speeder drive, 4-cylinders replaced the V-twins, four wheels replaced three, and now the Aero 8 has introduced a new chassis and suspension.

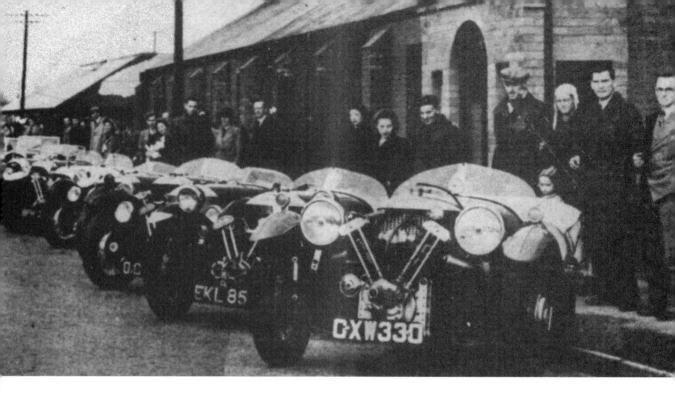

Morgans lined up outside the factory on the occasion of the Inaugural General Meeting of the Morgan Three-Wheeler Club held at the Morgan works on 25 September 1945.

The Morgan Motor Company has always been an independent company. In the early days of the three-wheeler, HFS had considered and rejected external manufacturers and partnerships to produce his cars in the numbers required. Again in 1950 he rejected a bid from Sir John Black, chairman of the Standard Motor Company. The Morgan family recognized at that time that the long-term future of the company and of the cars that bore the family name could only be ensured through independence. In a world of global rationalization the importance of remaining independent is appreciated more than ever. The company is now under the management of the third generation of the Morgan family. Charles Morgan, Peter Morgan's son and HFS's grandson, was born in 1951 and joined the company in 1985 after a career in television. He brought to the company skills and training in business management. Most importantly, he recognizes the need to improve production methods and efficiency without compromising the traditional character of the cars.

The Morgan Three-Wheeler Club

The first club exclusively for Morgan owners was in existence from the early twenties. It boasted HFS as president and was concerned more with social than sporting activities. It was reconstituted in August 1927 as the New Cyclecar Club, in order to admit any cyclecar as defined by the Auto Cycle Union. The objective was to create an organizing body to hold races between three- and four-wheeled cyclecars at Brooklands, thus circumventing the ban imposed by the Junior Car Club following Ware's accident in 1924. The club later became the Light Car Club. Morgan owners dominated the membership and the club declined with declining popularity of the cyclecar.

Several Morgan owners still hankered for a club offering social gatherings and runs rather than sporting activities. To satisfy these needs, a general club, named The Three Wheeler

185

"THIS LOOKS LIKE THE RIGHT PLACE."

Club and open to owners of three-wheelers of any make, was duly formed in April 1934. The President was the editor of *Motor Cycling* and Vice-Presidents represented the three-wheeler manufacturers JMB, Raleigh, BSA and Morgan. Despite initial enthusiasm, popularity for three-wheelers was in decline and the club folded upon the outbreak of war.

The present Morgan Three Wheeler Club dates back to the final years of the war. The proposal to set up the club was made by Lt. W.D. Griffin in a letter to *Motor Cycling* magazine in May 1944. Walter Seaman, who wrote for *Motor Cycling* under the pseudonym of 'Trepenpol', welcomed the idea but considered formation of a club would be difficult during wartime. He suggested a start could be made by forming a register of Morgan owners and agreed that he would do this. The idea was popular and letters of interest poured in. Amongst the first to enrol were Eric Fenton and Alan Ashford. Eric, who wrote on Morgans using the pseudonym 'Triang', produced the first newssheet in September. Alan started the Mutual Aid and Spares Service.

The first MTWC meeting was held at the Greyhound Hotel at Carshalton, Surrey in February 1945. By this time the club's register listed 150 three-wheelers and membership

The original club spares scheme was known as Mutual Aid and comprised a central base for buying and selling second hand parts.

was approaching fifty. Motor clubs, the MTWC amongst them, were lobbying the government at this time for restoration of a basic petrol ration. This was conceded on 1 June 1945 and it again became legal to drive for pleasure, albeit within a five gallons a month allowance. The club lost no time in organizing its first club run, to watch a scramble held at Bagshot. The inaugural general meeting to constitute the club formally was held at the Morgan works on 23 September 1945, under the chairmanship of George Goodall. A committee was elected under the chairmanship of Walter Seaman and HFS was elected President. At this time the club had 102 members, plus a few associate members, and circulation of the Bulletin had reached 200. The club subscription was set at 7s 6d and the Bulletin priced at 4s for twelve issues.

Despite this promising start, the club experienced some difficulty in maintaining enthusiasm during its early years. This was to be expected, as during the early years the Morgan three-wheeler was merely transport for those who could not afford better! There remained several, however, who appreciated the intrinsic worth and unique character of the Morgan; before long there would be many more. From an initial membership of 102 the Club has grown and can now boast a membership of more than 1,100 members in the United Kingdom and 200 overseas.

The MTWC comprises a central organization to look after the general running of the club, together with regional groups, in the United Kingdom and overseas, to look after local interests and hold monthly social gatherings. The Club publishes a monthly magazine, the *Bulletin*, which includes a wealth of technical and historical articles as well as keeping members informed about the membership, social events and sporting activities. The *Bulletin* now represents a vast reference source of Morgan data and an answer to most problems can be found in its pages. Club members are fortunate that past issues have been transferred to compact disc for ready access. Alternatively, recourse can be made to the Club's extensive library of manuals, photographs and so on, or to technical advisers.

Morgan three-wheelers are still active in competition. The MTWC is affiliated to the Auto Cycle Union, the controlling body for motorcycle/three-wheeler sport in the United Kingdom. The Club's competition secretary organizes entries to race meetings, sprints and hill-climbs, as well as closed-to-club events. Morgans can be seen most weekends competing against other three-wheelers or motorcycle combinations both at home and overseas. Morgans also compete on occasion against vintage four-wheelers. The Club's sporting activities receive the support of the Morgan Motor Company, which sponsors a challenge series.

The Company also supports the MTWC in other ways. Peter Morgan was the Hon. Life President until his death in October 2003, a position now held by his son, Charles. The Company has also given the Club access to existing records and technical information.

It is no surprise that the Company no longer supplies parts for three-wheelers, given their age. However, the maintenance or restoration of a three-wheeler can never have been easier than at present. There are several specialist companies offering parts and services. The MTWC has also established its own spares organization, known as 'Mogspares', whose team of volunteers prepares engineering drawings and commissions new patterns and tooling for the manufacture of spares. This is a mammoth task made manageable by coordination with existing suppliers to manufacture only those parts not otherwise available.

The registry of surviving cars maintained by the MTWC contains two and a half thousand entries. However, many of the cars listed from the early days of the registry may not have survived. Some will have been broken for spares. Others will have metamorphosed from a humble touring model into a more glamorous sporting machine and could well appear twice with different identities. Evidence from current membership suggests perhaps no more than two thousand cars survive.

The survival rate of the two-speeder 'B' types represents about 2 per cent of the approximately 17,000 machines built. Production was dominated by Standard, De Luxe and Family models, but barely a handful of De Luxe and Standard Runabouts now exist, whilst the figures for the Family models are little better. Approximately 10 per cent of the 'M' chassis two-speeders survive. The survival rate of about 50 per cent for the three-speeder is a very good figure, but inspection suggests that more Super Sports models now exist than the factory manufactured! The survival rates of the F-type models are somewhat less than those of the V-twin three-speeders.

The survival rates may appear disappointing, especially for the early cars, but are really very good for a lightly constructed economy car. They are a measure of the affection the cars engendered in the past and the appeal that Morgans retain to this day.

Bibliography

In compiling this book on the Morgan Three-Wheeler I have referred extensively to articles and reviews in the contemporary motoring press. Magazines referred to include:

Motor Cycling
The Motor Cycle
The Cyclecar, later renamed *The Light Car and Cyclecar*
The Autocar

The *Bulletin* of the Morgan Three-Wheeler Club contains a wealth of technical and historic information. It comprises a distillation of the combined knowledge of the club members and is available on two cds.

The annual sales brochures issued by the Morgan Motor Company Limited provide model production histories, specifications and prices. However, it was appreciated that the data are not always reliable in the case of a small company with sporting interests and a depressed market.

I have also made reference to handbooks issued by the Morgan Company and the engine suppliers, and to the following books.

Alderson, Dr J. D. & Rushton, D. M. *Morgan Sweeps the Board* (Gentry Books, London, 1978)

An Anzani Anthology (The Morgan Three-Wheeler Club Ltd, 2000)

Boddy, Bill *The Vintage Years of the Morgan Three-Wheeler* (Grenville Publishing, London, 1970)

Bowden, Gregory Houston *More Morgan* (Gentry Books, London, 1976)

Bowden, Gregory Houston *Morgan – First and Last of the Real Sports Cars* (Gentry Books London, 1972. Revised second edition 1986)

Clarke, R. M. *Morgan Three-Wheeler Gold Portfolio* (Brooklands Book Distribution Ltd, 1989)

Clarke, R. M. *Morgan Three-Wheelers 1930–1952* (Brooklands Books, Surrey)

Clew, Jeff *J.A.P. The Vintage Years* (Haynes Publishing Group, 1985)

Coombes, Clarrie *Best of Clarrie* (The Morgan Three-Wheeler Club Ltd, 1994)

Coombes, Clarrie *No More Twins* (Morgan Three-Wheeler Club, c1965)

Davidson, Barry, ed. *The Best of the Bulletin* (The Morgan Three-Wheeler Club, 1973)

Hill, Ken *Completely Morgan, Three-Wheelers 1910 to 1952* (Veloce Publishing plc, 1995)

Hill, Ken *The Best of British in Old Photographs, Morgan* (Sutton Publishing Ltd, 1997)

Hutton, Egan *Fifty Years of Experience* (Morgan Motor Company, 1960)

Jelley, Harold *The Book of the Morgan* (Pitman & Sons, London, 1935, third edition)

Laban, Brian *Morgan. First and Last of the Real Sports Cars* (Virgin, 2000)

The History of a Famous Car (Morgan Motor Company Ltd., c1970)

Thirlby, David *Minimal Motoring, from Cyclecar to Microcar* (Tempus Publishing Inc., 2002)

Walton, G. T. *The Book of the Morgan* (Pitman & Sons, London, 1930)

Watts, Brian *The Three-Wheeler* (Morgan Three-Wheeler Club, 1970, revised 1999)

Worthington-Williams, Michael *From Cyclecar to Microcar* (Dalton Watson Ltd, 1981)

Appendix: Morgan Three-Wheeler Production Models

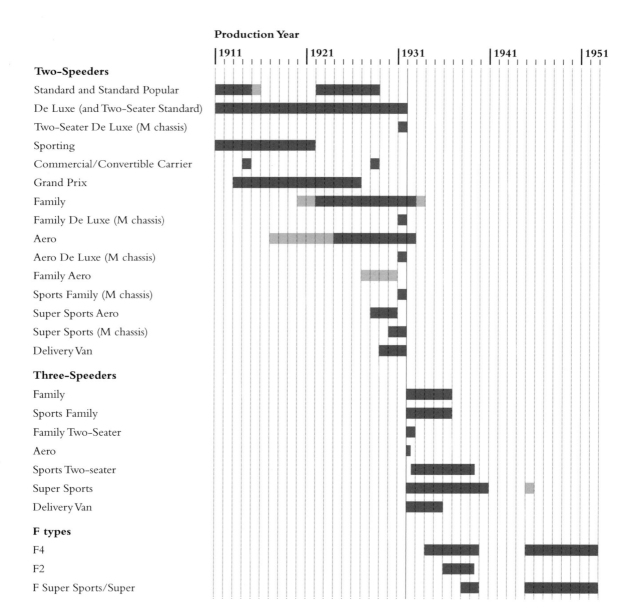

Production Year

| | 1911 | 1921 | 1931 | 1941 | 1951 |

Two-Speeders

Standard and Standard Popular

De Luxe (and Two-Seater Standard)

Two-Seater De Luxe (M chassis)

Sporting

Commercial/Convertible Carrier

Grand Prix

Family

Family De Luxe (M chassis)

Aero

Aero De Luxe (M chassis)

Family Aero

Sports Family (M chassis)

Super Sports Aero

Super Sports (M chassis)

Delivery Van

Three-Speeders

Family

Sports Family

Family Two-Seater

Aero

Sports Two-seater

Super Sports

Delivery Van

F types

F4

F2

F Super Sports/Super

Index